Country
HOME PLANS

Publisher James D. McNair III

Cover Photography by John Ehrenclou • Cover Design by Anthony Lavorgna

Library of Congress No.: 94-073697

ISBN 0-938708-62-7

GARLINGHOUSE

Submit all *Canadian* plan orders to:
The Garlinghouse Company
20 Cedar Street North
Kitchener, Ontario N2H 2WB

Canadian Orders Only: 1-800-561-4169
Fax #: 1-519-743-1282
Customer Service #: 1-519-743-4169

PHOTOGRAPHY BY JOHN EHRENCLOU

Country Comforts

DESIGN 10550

★ First floor	1,027 sq. ft.
★ Second floor	974 sq. ft.
★ Basement	978 sq. ft.
★ Garage	476 sq. ft.
★ Bedrooms	Three
★ Baths	2(Full), 1(Half)
★ Foundation	Basement

REFER TO PRICE CODE C

Here's a compact Country charmer that unites tradition with today in a perfect combination. Imagine waking up in the roomy master suite with its romantic bay and full bath with double sinks. Two additional bedrooms, which feature huge closets, share the hall bath. The romance continues in the sunny breakfast room off the island kitchen, in the recessed ceilings of the formal dining room, and in the living room's cozy fireplace. Sun lovers will appreciate the sloping, skylit ceilings in the living room, and the rear deck accessible from both the kitchen and living room.

An EXCLUSIVE DESIGN
By Karl Kreeger

BEDROOM
10'-6"x11'-4"

BEDROOM
10'-8"x11'-6"

LIN.
HALL

DN

MASTER BEDROOM
11'-0" x 21'-2"

B.

BATH 1/2 WALL UP

C.

TO ATTIC

SECOND FLOOR

Total Living Area:
2,001 sq. ft.

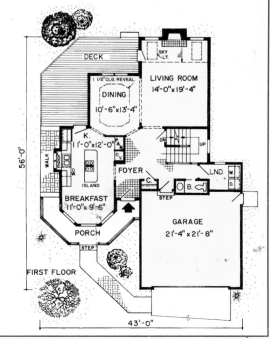

DECK

SKY LT.

1 1/2 CLG. REVEAL

DINING
10'-6"x13'-4"

LIVING ROOM
14'-0"x19'-4"

K.
11'-0"x12'-0"

DN

UP

WALK

FOYER

LND. W. D.

ISLAND

STEP

B.

56'-0"

BREAKFAST
11'-0"x 9'-6"

GARAGE
21'-4" x 21'-8"

PORCH

STEP

FIRST FLOOR

43'-0"

Detailing Enhances Facade

A charming porch shelters the entrance of this four bedroom home, with a delightful Country kitchen. In colder climates, the closed vestibule cuts heat loss. Off the central foyer, the cozy living room shares a fireplace with the family room, which contains a bar and access to both the patio and screened porch for easy entertaining. The bay-windowed breakfast room is handy for quick meals. Use the dining room, with an octagonal recessed ceiling, for formal meals. All the bedrooms, located on the second floor for bedtime quiet, have walk-in closets. Two linen closets are conveniently placed and complete the second floor. This home's good looks as well as it's practical layout make it a great home for anyone.

PHOTOGRAPHY BY JOHN EHRENCLOU

COUNTRY KITCHEN TREASURES

This large kitchen, with it's stove top center island, contains handy features such as a pantry and a planning desk and conveniently adjoins the breakfast area with a sunny bay window.

SUNNY WINDOW TREATMENTS

Plants will flourish is this skylit sun room located directly off the family room. It's a great spot for informal gatherings as well private reading time. Relax & enjoy!!

Total Living Area: 2,791 sq. ft.

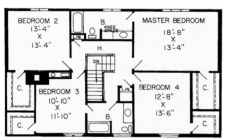

BEDROOM 2
13'-4"
X
13'-4"

B.

KNEE SPACE

H.

MASTER BEDROOM
18'-8"
X
13'-4"

DN.

LIN.

C.

LIN.

BEDROOM 3
10'-10"
X
11'-10"

BEDROOM 4
12'-8"
X
13'-6"

C.

B.

C.

SECOND FLOOR

DESIGN 10593

★ First floor	1,450 sq. ft.
★ Second floor	1,341 sq. ft.
★ Basement	1,450 sq. ft.
★ Garage	629 sq. ft.
★ Bedrooms	Four
★ Baths	2(Full),1(Half)
★ Foundation	Basement

REFER TO PRICE CODE E

BRICK PATIO

SCREENED PORCH
11'-8"
X
11'-8"

FAMILY ROOM
19'-4"
X
13'-4"

BAR

BRKFST.
12'-0"
X
9'-8"

DW

COUNTRY KICHEN
14'-4" X 15'-6"

BKS.

WOOD STORAGE

DN.

BKS.

DESK

PANT.

H.

2-CAR GARAGE
22'-0"
X
27'-4"

DRIVE

LIVING ROOM
12'-10"
X
19'-4"

FOYER

DINING ROOM
14'-0"
X
13'-6"

C.

LAUND.

D. W.

34'-0"

PORCH

69'-8"   FIRST FLOOR

An
EXCLUSIVE DESIGN
By Karl Kreeger

Gingerbread Charm

Victorian elegance combines with a modern floor plan to make this a dream house without equal. A wrap-around porch and rear deck add lots of extra living space to the roomy first floor, which features a formal parlor and dining room just off the central entry. Informal areas at the rear of the house are wide-open for family interaction. Gather the crew around the fireplace in the family room, or make supper in the kitchen while you supervise the kids' homework in the sunwashed breakfast room. Three bedrooms, tucked upstairs for a quiet atmosphere, feature skylit baths. And, you'll love the five-sided sitting nook in your master suite, a perfect spot to relax after a luxurious bath in the sunken tub.

OPEN LIVING SPACES

Open living spaces include the fireplaced family room, a cozy breakfast area and the U-shaped kitchen conveniently located next to the laundry center.

COZY FIVE-SIDED NOOK

Enjoy your unique bedroom suite with a cozy sitting area, large walk-in closet, step-up tub and a handy shower stall.

DESIGN 10690

★ First floor	1,260 sq. ft.
★ Second floor	1,021 sq. ft.
★ Basement	1,186 sq. ft.
★ Garage	840 sq. ft.
★ Bedrooms	Three
★ Baths	2(Full),1(Half)
★ Foundation	B, S, C

REFER TO PRICE CODE D

Total Living Area: 2,281 sq. ft.

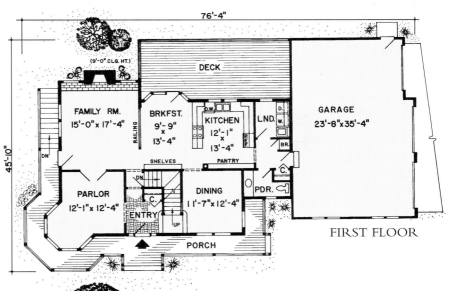

FIRST FLOOR

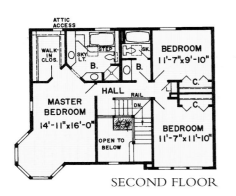

SECOND FLOOR

Packed With Amenities

Here's a compact beauty with a wide-open feeling. Step past the inviting front porch and savor a breathtaking view of active areas: the columned entry with its open staircase and windows high overhead; the soaring living room, divided from the kitchen and dining room by the towering fireplace chimney; the screened porch beyond the triple living room windows. Tucked behind the stairs, you'll find a cozy parlor. And, across the hall, a bedroom, with an adjoining full bath, features access to the screened porch. Upstairs, the master suite, with its romantic dormer window seat, private balcony, and double-vanitied bath, is an elegant retreat you'll want to come home to.

STACKED WINDOWS, COZY LIVING SPACES

Treasure this cozy spot in your new home! This plan is packed with interesting living spaces and has endless decorating possibilities!

SOARING CEILING HEIGHTS

When entering into this home, the soaring ceilings and the abundance of windows will simply take your breath away. This home has been a long time "Garlinghouse Favorite".

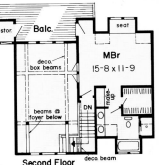

Total Living Area:
1,695 sq. ft.

Second Floor

stor. | Balc. | seat

deco. box beams

MBr
15-8 x 11-9

make-up

beams @ foyer below

DN

deco. beam

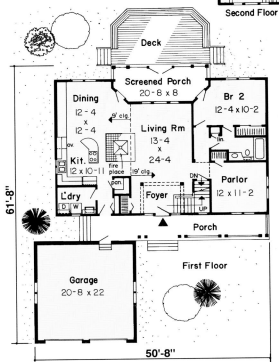

Deck

Screened Porch
20-8 x 8

Dining
12-4
x
12-4

9' clg.

Living Rm
13-4
x
24-4

Br 2
12-4 x 10-2

lin.

Kit.
12 x 10-11

fire place

ov.

pan.

19' clg.

Parlor
12 x 11-2

L'dry

DN

Foyer

D W

UP

Porch

61'-8"

Garage
20-8 x 22

First Floor

50'-8"

DESIGN 19422

★ First floor	1,290 sq. ft.
★ Second floor	405 sq. ft.
★ Screened porch	152 sq. ft.
★ Garage	513 sq. ft.
★ Bedrooms	Two
★ Baths	2(Full)
★ Foundation	B, C

REFER TO PRICE CODE B

Traditional Sun Catcher

*W*indows and skylights in all shapes and sizes give this airy home a cozy feeling. From the two story foyer to the skylit breakfast nook off the island kitchen, active areas are arranged in an open plan just perfect for entertaining with ease. In warm weather, you'll enjoy the huge rear deck, accessible from both the living and breakfast rooms. Overnight guests will feel right at home with the convenience of the full bath adjoining the downstairs den. Upstairs, three bedrooms open to a balcony overlooking the floor below. Look at the master suite and all it's amenities; a walk-in closet, shower, double vanities, and a raised, skylit tub, make this spacious area a luxurious retreat.

PHOTOGRAPHY BY JOHN EHRENCLOU

FORMAL LIVING SPACES

Entertain with ease in your attractive formal dining room, with views to the rear yard and conveniently located next to the kitchen for ease in serving.

COMFORTABLE LIVING

This attractive stone fireplace is surrounded by floor to ceiling windows. Warmed by the sun or the cozy fireplace, you'll enjoy this relaxing room.

DESIGN 20096

★ First floor	1,286 sq. ft.
★ Second floor	957 sq. ft.
★ Bedrooms	Four
★ Baths	3(Full),1(Half)
★ Foundation	Basement

REFER TO PRICE CODE D

Total Living Area: 2,243 sq. ft.

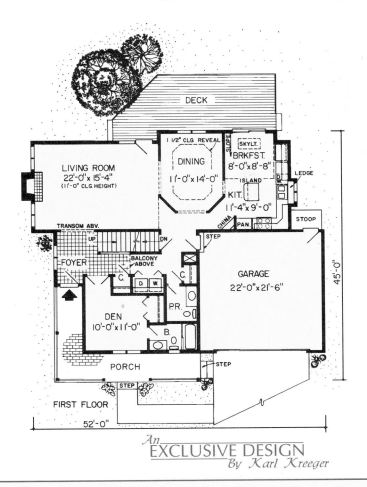

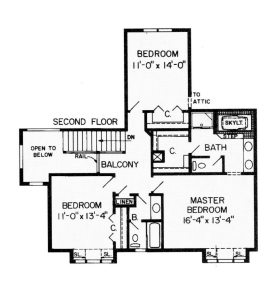

An EXCLUSIVE DESIGN *By Karl Kreeger*

Popular Country Design

*T*his pleasant Country design has a farmhouse flavor exterior that incorporates a covered porch and features a circle wood louver on its garage, giving this design a feeling of sturdiness. Inside, on the first level to the right of the foyer, is a formal dining room complete with a bay window and an elevated ceiling. To the left of the foyer is the living room with a wood-burning fireplace. The kitchen is connected to the breakfast room and there is also a room for the laundry facilities. A half-bath is also featured on the first floor. The master bedroom, on the second floor, has its own private bath and walk-in closet. The other two bedrooms share a full bath. A two-car garage is also added into this design.

PHOTOGRAPHY BY LAURIE SOLOMAN

SIMPLE EXTERIOR LINES

The rear of this Country home is as attractive as the front facade. The deck is handy for outdoor entertaining or carefree relaxing!

TRENDY KITCHEN ELEMENTS

This U-shaped kitchen is conveniently located next to both the breakfast room and the living room. Quick meals are easy — just pull up a seat!

DESIGN 34901

★ First floor	909 sq. ft.
★ Second floor	854 sq. ft.
★ Basement	899 sq. ft.
★ Garage	491 sq. ft.
★ Bedrooms	Three
★ Baths	2(Full), 1(Half)
★ Foundation	B, S, C

REFER TO PRICE CODE B

Total Living Area: 1,763 sq. ft.

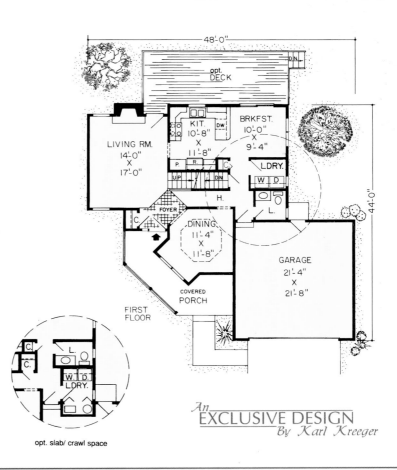

FIRST FLOOR

An EXCLUSIVE DESIGN *By Karl Kreeger*

opt. slab/ crawl space

Beautiful Country Detailing

*Y*ou'll never get bored with the rooms in this charming, three-bedroom Country design. The angular plan gives every room an interesting shape. From the wrap-around veranda, the entry foyer leads through the living room and parlor, breaking them up without confining them, and giving each room an airy atmosphere. In the dining room, with its hexagonal recessed ceiling, you can enjoy your after-dinner coffee and watch the kids playing on the deck. Or, eat in the sunny breakfast room off the island kitchen, where every wall has a window, and every window has a different view. You'll love the master suite's bump-out windows, walk-in closets, and double sinks. This plan has everything you need and more!

PHOTOGRAPHY BY JOHN EHRENCLOU

RELAXED FAMILY LIVING

This fireplace is guaranteed to warm you up on the coldest nights and makes a great room where the whole family can relax and unwind.

INTERESTING LINES & SPACES

A center island, a charming breakfast area just steps away from your deck, and a kitchen loaded with amenities — just a few reasons why this design is simply perfect!

THE PHOTOGRAPHED HOME HAS BEEN MODIFIED TO SUIT INDIVIDUAL TASTES

DESIGN 34926

- ★ First floor — 1,409 sq. ft.
- ★ Second floor — 1,116 sq. ft.
- ★ Basement — 1,409 sq. ft.
- ★ Garage — 483 sq. ft.
- ★ Bedrooms — Three
- ★ Baths — 2(Full), 1(Half)
- ★ Foundation — B, S, C

REFER TO PRICE CODE D

Total Living Area:
2,525 sq. ft.

opt. slab/ crawl space

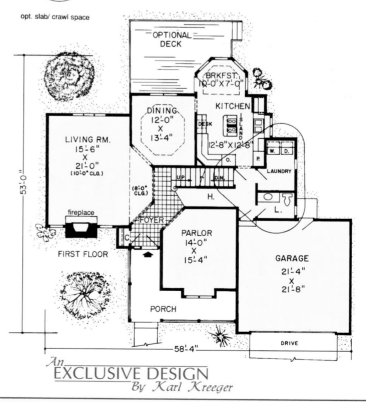

SECOND FLOOR

FIRST FLOOR

An EXCLUSIVE DESIGN
By Karl Kreeger

Traditional With A Country Flair

E*njoy the beauty and tradition of a two-story home. From the spacious, tiled entry, with it's handy coat closet, to the seclusion of second floor bedrooms, you'll appreciate the classic features that distinguish a two-story home. And, you'll delight in the modern touches that make this plan sparkle: the handsome window treatment in the living room; the oversized master bedroom with a walk-in closet and deluxe, skylit bath; the efficient kitchen and charming breakfast nook; and the sweeping deck for outdoor entertaining.*

DESIGN 20070

★ First floor	877 sq. ft.
★ Second floor	910 sq. ft.
★ Basement	877 sq. ft.
★ Garage	458 sq. ft.
★ Bedrooms	Three
★ Baths	2(Full),1(Half)
★ Foundation	Basement

REFER TO PRICE CODE B

An
EXCLUSIVE DESIGN
By Karl Kreeger

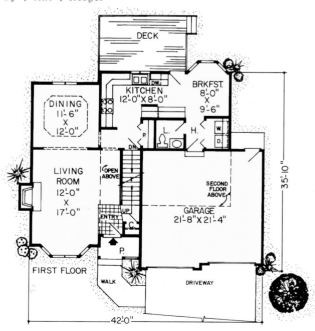

SECOND FLOOR

Total Living Area: 1,787 sq. ft.

Dramatic Ranch Design

DESIGN 20198

★ Main living area	1,792 sq. ft.
★ Basement	864 sq. ft.
★ Garage	928 sq. ft.
★ Bedrooms	Three
★ Baths	2(Full)
★ Foundation	Basement

REFER TO PRICE CODE B

Total Living Area:
1,792 sq. ft.

The exterior of this Ranch home is all wood with interesting lines. More than an ordinary Ranch home, it has an expansive feeling to drive up to. The large living area has a stone fireplace and decorative beams. The kitchen and dining room lead to an outside deck. The laundry room has a large pantry, and is located off the eating area. The master bedroom has a wonderful bathroom with a huge walk-in closet. In the front of the house, there are two additional bedrooms with a shared bathroom. This house offers one floor living and has nice big rooms.

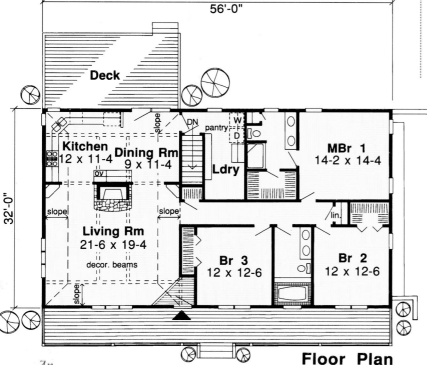

56'-0"

32'-0"

Deck

Kitchen
12 x 11-4

Dining Rm
9 x 11-4

slope

DN

pantry

W
D

Ldry

MBr 1
14-2 x 14-4

slope

slope

Living Rm
21-6 x 19-4

decor. beams

lin.

Br 3
12 x 12-6

Br 2
12 x 12-6

slope

Floor Plan

An EXCLUSIVE DESIGN *By Karl Kreeger*

Detailed Charmer

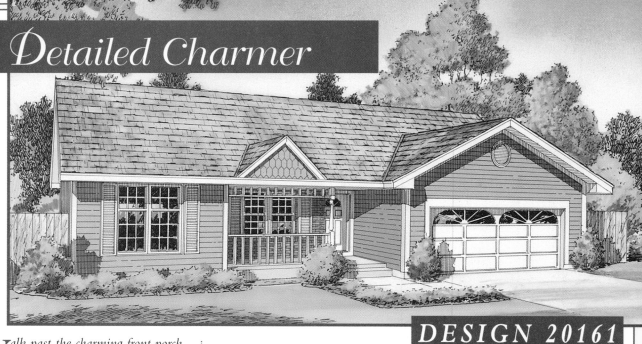

alk past the charming front porch, in through the foyer and you'll be struck by the exciting, spacious living room. Complete with high sloping ceilings and a beautiful fireplace flanked by large windows. The large master bedroom shows off a full wall of closet space, its own private bath, and an extraordinary decorative ceiling. Just down the hall are two more bedrooms and another full bath. Take advantage of the accessibility off the foyer and turn one of these rooms into a private den or office space. The dining room provides a feast for your eyes with its decorative ceiling details, and a full slider out to the deck. Along with great counter space, the kitchen includes a double sink and an attractive bump-out window.

DESIGN 20161

★ Main living area	1,307 sq. ft.
★ Basement	1,298 sq. ft.
★ Garage	462 sq. ft.
★ Bedrooms	Three
★ Baths	2(Full)
★ Foundation	B, S, C

REFER TO PRICE CODE A

Total Living Area: 1,307 sq. ft.

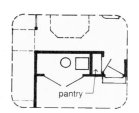

Slab/Crawl Space Option

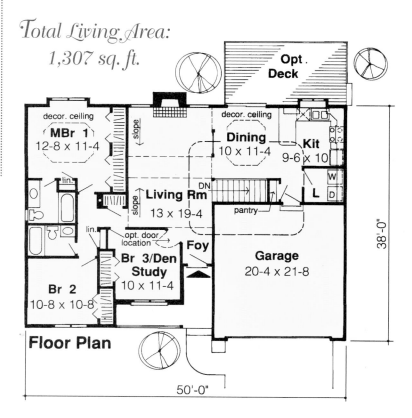

Floor Plan

- MBr 1 12-8 x 11-4
- Dining 10 x 11-4
- Kit 9-6 x 10
- Living Rm 13 x 19-4
- Br 3/Den Study 10 x 11-4
- Br 2 10-8 x 10-8
- Foy
- Garage 20-4 x 21-8
- Opt. Deck
- pantry
- decor. ceiling
- slope
- 38'-0"
- 50'-0"

An
EXCLUSIVE DESIGN
By Karl Kreeger

Farmhouse Flavor

DESIGN 10785

★ First floor	1,269 sq. ft.
★ Second floor	638 sq. ft.
★ Basement	1,269 sq. ft.
★ Bedrooms	Three
★ Baths	2(Full),1(Half)
★ Foundation	B, S, C

REFER TO PRICE CODE C

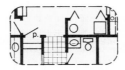

Slab/Crawl Space Option

An
EXCLUSIVE DESIGN
By Karl Kreeger

The charm of an old-fashioned Farmhouse combines with sizzling contemporary excitement in this three-bedroom home. Classic touches abound, from the clapboard exterior with its inviting, wrap-around porch to the wood stove that warms the entire house. Inside, the two-story foyer, crowned by a plant ledge high overhead, affords a view of the soaring, skylit living room and rear deck beyond sliding glass doors. To the right, there's a formal dining room with a bay window, just steps away from the kitchen. The well-appointed master suite completes the first floor. Upstairs, you'll find a full bath and two more bedrooms, each with a walk-in closet and cozy gable sitting nook.

FIRST FLOOR

Total Living Area: 1,907 sq. ft.

SECOND FLOOR

A Warm Welcome

DESIGN 24245

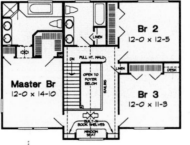

Total Living Area: 2,047 sq. ft.

Master Br 12-0 x 14-10

Br 2 12-0 x 12-5

LINEN

FULL HT. HALL

DN

OPEN TO FOYER BELOW

LINEN

DESK

RAILING

Br 3 12-0 x 11-3

BUILT-IN BOOK SHELVES

WINDOW SEAT

Second Floor

★ First floor	1,095 sq. ft.
★ Second floor	952 sq. ft.
★ Basement	1,095 sq. ft.
★ Garage	480 sq. ft.
★ Bedrooms	Three
★ Baths	2(Full),1(Half)
★ Foundation	B, S, C

REFER TO PRICE CODE C

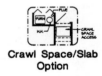

Crawl Space/Slab Option

P*icture a porch swing, cozy rocking chairs and a pitcher of lemonade on this country porch. What an inviting picture. The cozy feeling continues throughout this house. The formal areas are located in the traditional places, flanking the entry hall. The living room includes a wonderful fireplace and the dining room has direct access to the kitchen. The U-shaped kitchen includes a breakfast bar, built-in pantry, planning desk and a double sink. A mudroom entry will help keep the dirt from muddy shoes away from the rest of the house. A convenient laundry area is close at hand in the half-bath off the mudroom. The sunny breakfast nook is a cheerful place to start your day, and the expansive family room has direct access to the rear wood deck. Sleeping quarters are located on the second floor. The master suite is highlighted by a walk-in closet and private master bath. The two additional bedrooms, one with a built-in desk, share a full hall bath with a double vanity. A window seat in the hallway provides a cozy place to curl up with a book. In fact, bookshelves have been built-in on either side of the seat.*

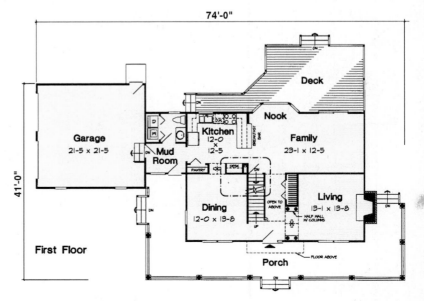

74'-0"

41'-0"

Deck

Garage 21-5 x 21-5

Mud Room

Kitchen 12-0 x 12-5

Nook

BREAKFAST BAR

Family 23-1 x 12-5

PANTRY

DESK

DN

OPEN TO ABOVE

Dining 12-0 x 13-8

HALF HALL W/ COLUMNS

UP

Living 13-1 x 13-8

FLOOR ABOVE

First Floor

Porch

DN

Attractive Stone Detailing

DESIGN 10550

★ First floor	2,069 sq. ft.
★ Second floor	821 sq. ft.
★ Basement	2,045 sq. ft.
★ Garage	562 sq. ft.
★ Bedrooms	Four
★ Baths	3(Full), 2(Half)
★ Foundation	Basement

REFER TO PRICE CODE E

*T*here's lots of room for your growing family in this four bedroom Country beauty. Recessed ceilings in the dining room and master bedroom suite, a vaulted front office, and a beamed great room give first floor living areas distinctive angles. And, the sunporch off the breakfast nook is a warm place to curl up even on the coldest days. You'll never have to worry about traffic jams on busy weekday mornings. With two full baths upstairs and two convenient lavatories on the first floor, everyone can get out on time.

An
EXCLUSIVE DESIGN
By Karl Kreeger

78'-0"

PATIO

SUNPORCH
SKYLIGHT
10'-0" X 10'-0"

GREAT ROOM
15'-2" X 23'-4"

BRKFST.
10'-0" X 12'-8"

48'-4"

LAV.

KITCHEN
15'-4" X 11'-6"

LAUN.

STUDY
8'-6" X 11'-4"

DESK

P.   O.   R.

M. BEDROOM
15'-10" X 15'-4"

DINING
13'-10" X 13'-4"

GARAGE
23'-4" X 23'-4"

UP

LAV.

H.

FOYER

BOOKS

OFFICE
11'-4" X 12'-0"

P.

BEDROOM 3
11'-8" X 13'-10"

BEDROOM 4
11'-10" X 11'-2"

BEDROOM 2
12'-10" X 11'-4"

C.

B.

H.

C.

DN.

FOYER BELOW

B.

Total Living Area: 2,890 sq. ft.

*D*oes your family enjoy entertaining? Here's your home! This handsome, rambling beauty can handle a crowd of any size. Greet your guests in a beautiful foyer that opens to the cozy, bayed living room and elegant dining room with floor-to-ceiling windows. Show them the impressive two-story gallery and book-lined study, flooded with sunlight from atrium doors and clerestory windows. Or, gather around the fire in the vaulted family room on chilly nights. The bar connects to the efficient kitchen, just steps away from both the nook and formal dining room. And, when the guests go home, you'll appreciate your luxurious first-floor master suite and the cozy upstairs bedroom suites with an adjoining sitting room.

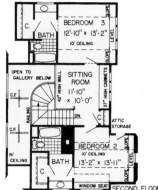

DESIGN 10663

★ First floor	2,310 sq. ft.
★ Second floor	866 sq. ft.
★ Garage	679 sq. ft.
★ Bedrooms	Three
★ Baths	3(Full),1(Half)
★ Foundation	Slab

REFER TO PRICE CODE E

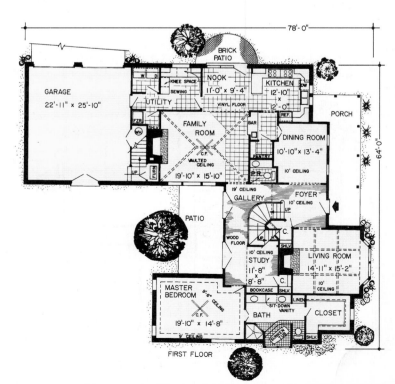

Total Living Area: 3,176 sq. ft.

Country Comforts Abound

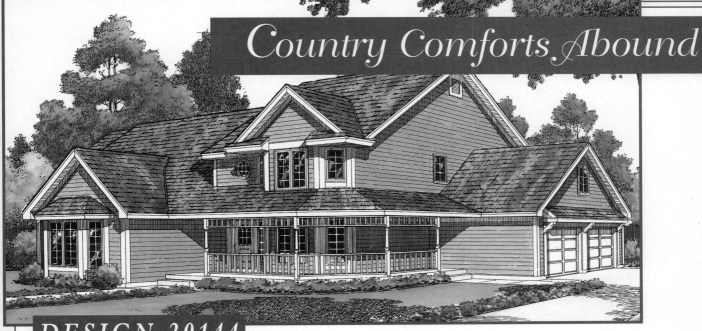

DESIGN 20144

★ First floor	1,737 sq. ft.
★ Second floor	826 sq. ft.
★ Basement	1,728 sq. ft.
★ Bedrooms	Four
★ Baths	3(Full),1(Half)
★ Foundation	Basement

REFER TO PRICE CODE D

An
EXCLUSIVE DESIGN
By Karl Kreeger

First Floor

*F*rom the sprawling front porch to the two-way fireplace that warms the hearth room and living room, this house says "Welcome" to all who enter. Even your houseplants will love the cozy, sunny atmosphere of this country classic. A central hallway links the formal, bayed dining room with the spacious kitchen at the rear of the house. Relax over an informal meal in the adjoining hearth room, or out on the deck when the weather's warm. It's accessible from both the hearth room and soaring, wide-open living room. Enjoy the privacy of your first-floor master suite, which features a bath with every amenity, and a huge, walk-in closet. Step upstairs for a great view of active areas, where you'll find three more bedrooms, each adjoining a full bath.

Second Floor

Total Living Area: 2,563 sq. ft.

Single Level Charmer

An expansive entrance plus a cathedral ceiling in the living room provides a view of the entire house. The washer and dryer are located in the bedroom area. Even with a modest square footage, this home still has a large master bedroom area and a separate dining room and breakfast area. The deck is partially under the roof. The roof framing on this plan is simple, but the exterior is very interesting with its large window and a terrific farmhouse porch.

DESIGN 20054

★ First floor	1,461 sq. ft.
★ Basement	1,458 sq. ft.
★ Garage	528 sq. ft.
★ Bedrooms	Three
★ Baths	2(Full)
★ Foundation	Basement

REFER TO PRICE CODE A

An
EXCLUSIVE DESIGN
By Karl Kreeger

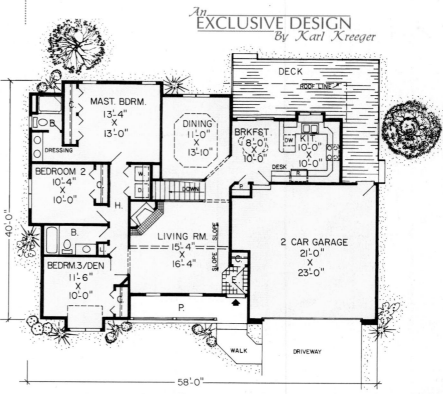

Total Living Area:
1,461 sq. ft.

DESIGN 34029

★ Main living area	1,698 sq. ft.
★ Garage	484 sq. ft.
★ Bedrooms	Three
★ Baths	2(Full)
★ Foundation	B, S, C

REFER TO PRICE CODE B

Slab/Crawlspace
Option

An
EXCLUSIVE DESIGN
By Karl Kreeger

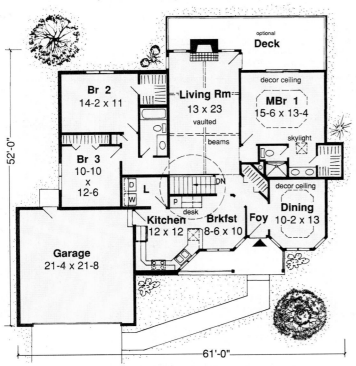

*K*eep dry during the rainy season under the covered porch entryway of this gorgeous home. A foyer separates the dining room, with a decorative ceiling, from the breakfast area and kitchen. Off the kitchen, conveniently located, is the laundry room. The living room features a vaulted beamed ceiling and fireplace. Located between the living room and two bedrooms, both with large closets, is a full bath. On the other side of the living room is the master bedroom. The master bedroom not only has a decorative ceiling, but also a skylight above the entrance of its private bath. The double-vanitied bathroom features a large walk-in closet. For those who enjoy outdoor living, an optional deck is offered, accessible through sliding glass doors off of the wonderful master bedroom.

Total Living Area: 1,698 sq. ft.

PRICE CODE F

DESIGN 10534

Total Living Area: 3,440 sq. ft.

The luxurious master suite is secluded on the first floor. Elegant touches include a library, morning room with built-ins, a bar with wine storage, and a sun porch with French doors leading into the dining room. The living room and foyer rise to the second floor which is comprised of three large bedrooms and two well-placed baths.

First floor — 2,486 sq. ft.
Second floor — 954 sq. ft.
Basement — 2,486 sq. ft.
Garage — 576 sq. ft.
Bedrooms — Four
Bathrooms — 3(Full), 1(Half)
Foundation — Basement

An
EXCLUSIVE DESIGN
By Karl Kreeger

DESIGN 10574

Total Living Area: 3,240 sq. ft.

Bedrooms — Three
Bathrooms — 2(Full), 1(Half)
Foundation — Basement

Every inch of space is put to good use in this home. The well-designed floor plan revolves around a two-story central foyer. You'll find utility and dining areas grouped together. The screened porch off the breakfast room is a lovely mealtime spot on a summer day. Right down the hall, family and living rooms insure a cozy atmosphere day and night with expansive windows and fireplaces. You'll find the master suite, with its double vanities and room-size closet, tucked away at the end of the hall.

First floor — 2,215 sq. ft.
Second floor — 1,025 sq. ft.
Basement — 1,634 sq. ft.
Garage & storage — 618 sq. ft.
Crawl Space — 581 sq. ft.

PRICE CODE E

DESIGN 10501

*M*ake a wonderful first impression or return home to the massive, welcoming foyer of this tastefully appointed design. The Great room is enlarged by a wrap-around deck and highlighted by a fireplace, built-in bookcases and wetbar. The first floor master suite is equally inviting with its spacious dressing area and separate bath. Adjacent to the central Great room, the kitchen area has its own built-in desk, octagonal morning room and central island. The second floor includes three bedrooms linked by a balcony which overlooks the open foyer.

First floor — 2,419 sq. ft.
Second floor — 926 sq. ft.
Garage — 615 sq. ft.
Basement — 2,419 sq. ft.
Bedrooms — Four
Bathrooms — 3(Full), 1(Half)
Foundation — Basement

Total Living Area: 3,345 sq. ft.

An
EXCLUSIVE DESIGN
By Karl Kreeger

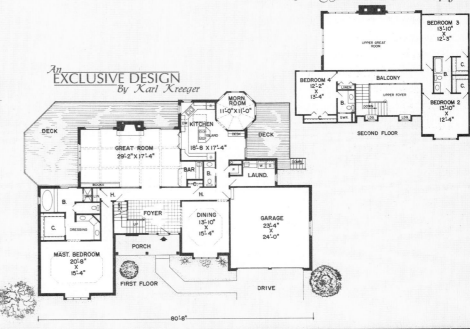

PRICE CODE E

Two Story Charmer

PRICE CODE C

DESIGN 34027

*T*his beautiful home accommodates the needs of a growing family and looks stunning in any neighborhood. The porch serves as a wonderful relaxing area to enjoy the outdoors. At the rear of the home is a patio, handy for a barbeque or for more private time away from the kids. Inside is just as delightful. The dining room features a decorative ceiling and has an easy entry to the kitchen. The kitchen/utility area has a side exit into the garage. The living room has double doors into the fireplaced family room which features a back entrance to the patio. Upstairs is the sleeping area with three bedrooms plus a vaulted-ceiling master bedroom. The master bedroom has two enormous walk-in closets, as well as a dressing area and private bath.

First floor — 925 sq. ft.
Second floor — 975 sq. ft.
Garage — 484 sq. ft.
Bedrooms — Four
Bathrooms — 2(Full), 1(Half)
Foundation — Basement, Slab, Crawl Space

Total Living Area: 1,900 sq. ft.

Slab/Crawlspace Option

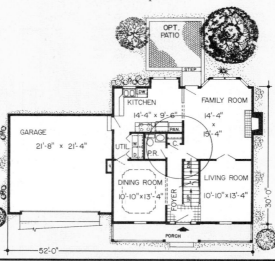

An EXCLUSIVE DESIGN
By Karl Kreeger

DESIGN 20366

*T*he eaves of this splendid Victorian classic are perfect spots for covered porches: one to shelter the entry, and one for relaxing on a warm summer night. The central foyer separates the gathering room and formal dining room. To the rear, you'll find an island kitchen that opens to a sunny breakfast room overlooking a rear deck. A handy powder room and laundry room complete the main living area. The second floor possesses a character all its own, with a cozy window seat flanked by planters at the top of the stairs, a hall bath, built-in bookcases, and a walk-in closet for extra storage. Look at the luxurious master suite, with its private, oversized shower and garden spa, double vanities, and room-size closet.

First floor — 1,244 sq. ft.
Second floor — 1,100 sq. ft.
Bedrooms — Three
Bathrooms — 2(Full), 1(Half)
Foundation — Basement

Total Living Area: 2,344 sq. ft.

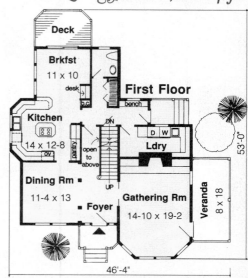

DESIGN 20158

*F*rom the welcoming porch to the balcony overlooking the skylit living room, this three bedroom beauty is loaded with sunny appeal. An elegant, bayed dining room adjoins the centrally-located island kitchen, which features easy access to a screened porch. A short hall leads past the laundry and handy powder room to a huge, fireplaced living room that opens to a rear deck. Walk under the balcony to the first floor master suite with its walk-in closet and luxury bath. The second floor balcony, overlooking the living room and two-story foyer, links two more bedrooms, each with a huge closet, and a large divided bath.

First floor — 1,293 sq. ft.
Second floor — 526 sq. ft.
Basement — 1,286 sq. ft.
Garage — 484 sq. ft.
Bedrooms — Three
Bathrooms — 2(Full), 1(Half)
Foundation — Basement

Total Living Area: 1,819 sq. ft.

An **EXCLUSIVE DESIGN** *By* **Karl Kreeger**

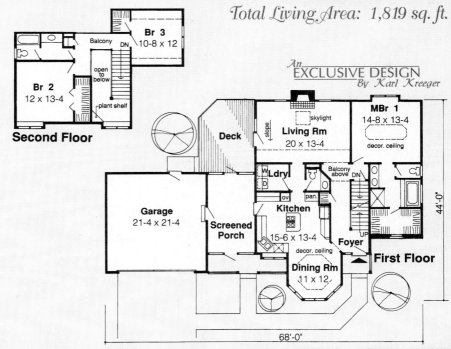

Second Floor

Br 2
12 x 13-4

Br 3
10-8 x 12

Balcony

DN

open to below

plant shelf

First Floor

Garage
21-4 x 21-4

Screened Porch

Deck

Living Rm
20 x 13-4

skylight

slope

decor. ceiling

MBr 1
14-8 x 13-4

Ldry

W D

ov

pan.

Kitchen
15-6 x 13-4

decor. ceiling

Balcony above

DN

UP

Foyer

Dining Rm
11 x 12

44'-0"

68'-0"

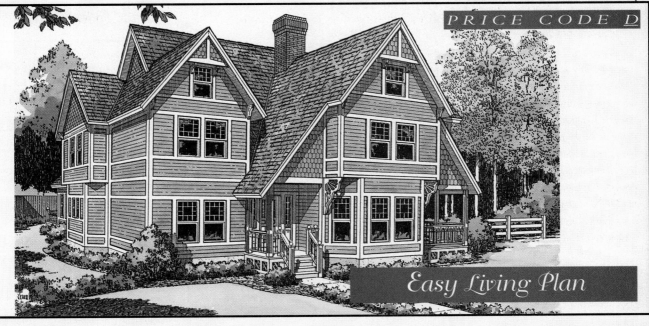

Easy Living Plan

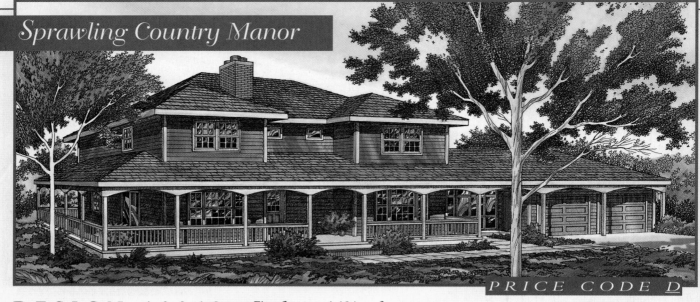

PRICE CODE D

DESIGN 10362

*T*his house says "home" to everyone who remembers the bygone era but thinks ahead for comfort and values. The big wrapped porch follows tradition. Imagine the cool summer evenings spent there. A split landing stairway leads to the four bedrooms on the upper level, complete with two bathrooms and lots of closets, perfect for the growing family. On the main level a wood-burning, built-in fireplace in the living room adds to the nostalgic charm of this home. Sliding glass doors open onto the porch. The main level also boasts a den, lavatory, utility room, kitchen and separate dining room overlooking the porch. An enclosed breezeway connects the double garage to the house.

First floor — 1,104 sq. ft.
Second floor — 1,124 sq. ft.
Basement — 1,080 sq. ft.
Garage — 528 sq. ft.
Bedrooms — Four
Bathrooms — 2(Full), 1(Half)
Foundation — Basement

Total Living Area: 2,228 sq. ft.

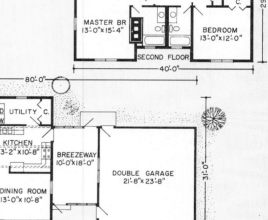

DESIGN 26001

A varied gabled roof, a large railed front porch and wood combine to create a picturesque rural farmhouse profile. On the lower level a central hallway channels traffic easily to all rooms — a spacious formal living room and family/dining area with a bay window and fireplace in the front, a bedroom suite, utility area, and the kitchen at the back. A mudroom is suitably located adjacent to the utility area. A sheltered outside entrance to the utility room and the double garage is provided by a breezeway-porch. On the second level three bedrooms nearly encircle a center bath.

First floor — 1,184 sq. ft.
Second floor — 821 sq. ft.
Basement — 821 sq. ft.
Garage — 576 sq. ft.
Bedrooms — Four
Bathrooms — 3(Full)
Foundation — Basement

Total Living Area: 2,005 sq. ft.

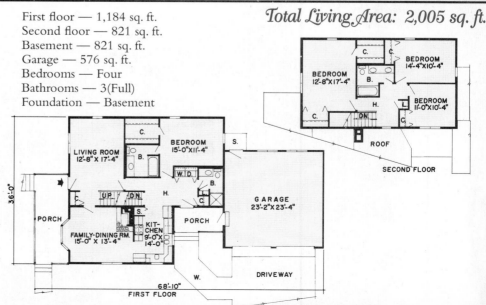

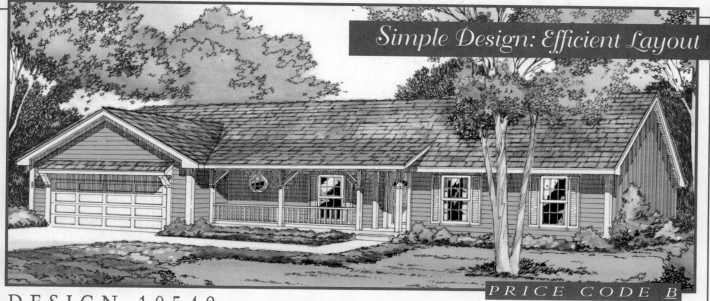

PRICE CODE **B**

DESIGN 10548

*T*he fireplace and sloped-ceiling in the family room offer something a bit out of the ordinary in a small home. The master bedroom is complete with a full bath and a dressing area. Bedrooms two and three share a full bath across the hall, and a half-bath is conveniently located adjacent to the kitchen. A bump-out bay window is shown in the spacious breakfast room, and a bay window with a window seat has been designed in the master bedroom. The screened porch off of the breakfast room is an inviting feature for meals outside.

Main living area — 1,688 sq. ft.
Basement — 1,688 sq. ft.
Screened porch — 120 sq. ft.
Garage — 489 sq. ft.
Bedrooms — Three
Bathrooms — 2(Full), 1(Half)
Foundation — Basement

An
EXCLUSIVE DESIGN
By Karl Kreeger

Total Living Area: 1,688 sq. ft.

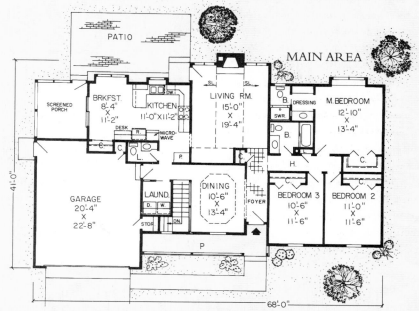

MAIN AREA

PRICE CODE **C**

DESIGN 20100

Stacked windows fill the wall in the front bedroom of this one-level home, creating an attractive facade and a sunny atmosphere inside. Around the corner, two more bedrooms and two full baths complete the bedroom wing, set apart for bedtime quiet. Notice the elegant vaulted ceiling in the master bedroom, the master tub and shower illuminated by a skylight, and the double vanities in both baths. Active areas enjoy a spacious feeling. Look at the high, sloping ceilings in the fireplaced living room, the sliders that unite the breakfast room and kitchen with an adjoining deck, and the vaulted-ceilings in the formal dining room.

Main living area — 1,727 sq. ft.
Basement — 1,727 sq. ft.
Garage — 484 sq. ft.
Bedrooms — Three
Bathrooms — 2 (Full)
Foundation — Basement

PRICE CODE B

Total Living Area: 1,727 sq. ft.

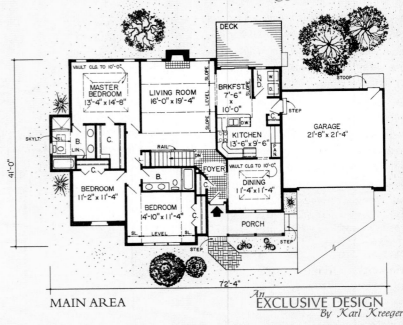

MAIN AREA

An EXCLUSIVE DESIGN *By Karl Kreeger*

DESIGN 20364

Thanks to vaulted ceilings and an absence of unnecessary walls, this compact gem feels larger than it really is. Step into the foyer and look up to a ceiling two stories high, an open staircase, and a spacious living/dining room arrangement with vaulted ceilings. At the core of the house, an efficient island kitchen opens to a sunny breakfast room with sliders to the rear patio. Whether you're serving a formal dinner, or a snack in the fireplaced family room, you're never more than a few steps away. Walk up the U-shaped stairs to a loft overlooking the scene below, which serves as a link to the three bedrooms and hall bath. The master suite features its own private bath with a garden tub and double vanities.

First floor — 1,060 sq. ft.
Second floor — 990 sq. ft.
Basement — 1,060 sq. ft.
Garage — 462 sq. ft.
Bedrooms — Three
Bathrooms — 2 (Full), 1 (Half)
Foundation — Basement

Total Living Area: 2,050 sq. ft.

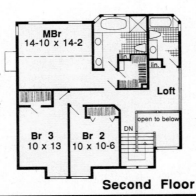

Second Floor

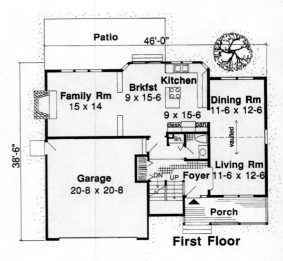

First Floor

DESIGN 34005

*T*he covered entrance of this classy home adds a touch of charm and elegance. The living room features a cozy fireplace set between two windows and a sloped ceiling. Off the living room is the kitchen, equipped with a plant shelf and perfect for growing a herb garden. A patio is accessible through sliding glass doors. The dining room features a beautifully designed ceiling enhancing formal occasions. Up a few stairs, past an octagonal window, is the sleeping wing. The master bedroom, also featuring a decorative ceiling, has a private bath and linen closet. A second bath is equipped with washer and dryer, located across the hall from the other two bedrooms.

Main living area — 1,441 sq. ft.
Garage — 2-car
Bedrooms — Three
Bathrooms — 2(Full)
Foundation — Basement, Crawl Space

Total Living Area: 1,441 sq. ft.

52'-0"

Patio

slope   slope

plant shelf →

Kitchen
11-8 x 11-4

Living Rm
15-4 x 18

decor. ceiling

MBr 1
13-4 x 13-11

lin.

W
D

DN

UP

Dining
11-8 x 13

decor. ceiling

lin.

Br 3
10-6 x 11-8

Br 2
11-7 x 11-8

38'-0"

An
EXCLUSIVE DESIGN
By Karl Kreeger

Floor Plan

Lofty Views

Inviting Country Porch

DESIGN 24400

★ First floor	1,034 sq. ft.
★ Second floor	944 sq. ft.
★ Basement	944 sq. ft.
★ Garage	684 sq. ft.
★ Bedrooms	Four
★ Baths	2(Full),1(Half)
★ Foundation	B, S, C

REFER TO PRICE CODE C

Total Living Area: 1,978 sq. ft.

*T*his delightful home's wrap-around covered porch recalls the warmth and charm of days past — lounging in the porch swing and savoring life. Inside, a spacious foyer welcomes guests and provides easy access to the formal dining room, secluded den/guest room (which might serve as your home office), and the large living room. Ceilings downstairs are all 9' high, with decorative vaults in the living and dining rooms. The kitchen, with its island/breakfast bar, is large enough for two people to work in comfortably. The adjacent laundry room also serves as a mudroom for boots and clothes, and leads directly to the garage, which features an ample storage/shop area at the rear. Upstairs, three bedrooms, each with cathedral ceilings, share a cheery, sunlit sitting area that also features a cathedral ceiling. For privacy, the master bedroom is separated from the other bedrooms, and boasts a palatial bathroom, complete with a whirlpool tub. If room to relax is what you're after, this home is loaded with irresistible features.

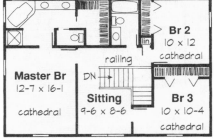

SECOND FLOOR

- **Master Br** 12-7 × 16-1 cathedral
- **Sitting** 9-6 × 8-6
- **Br 2** 10 × 12 cathedral
- **Br 3** 10 × 10-4 cathedral
- railing
- DN

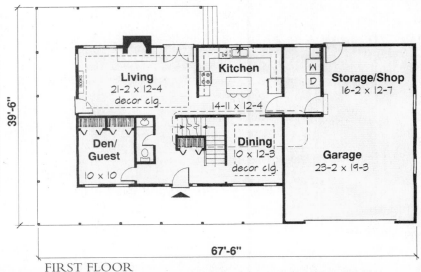

FIRST FLOOR

- **Living** 21-2 × 12-4 decor clg.
- **Kitchen** 14-11 × 12-4
- **Storage/Shop** 16-2 × 12-7
- **Den/Guest** 10 × 10
- **Dining** 10 × 12-3 decor clg.
- **Garage** 23-2 × 19-3
- crawl access
- **Dining**
- furn. w/h
- 39'-6"
- 67'-6"

An EXCLUSIVE DESIGN By Upright Design

PRICE CODE E

Master Suite Dominates Second Floor

No. 10533

■ This plan features:

— Three bedrooms

— Two and one half baths

■ A Master Suite including a sitting room plus individual walk-in closets and baths

■ A formal Parlor and Dining Room

■ A Great Room with a massive fireplace and a bar

■ A convenient laundry area accessing the three-car Garage

FIRST FLOOR — 1,669 SQ. FT.
SECOND FLOOR — 1,450 SQ. FT.
BASEMENT — 1,653 SQ. FT.
GARAGE — 823 SQ. FT.

TOTAL LIVING AREA:
3,119 SQ. FT.

An
EXCLUSIVE DESIGN
By Karl Kreeger

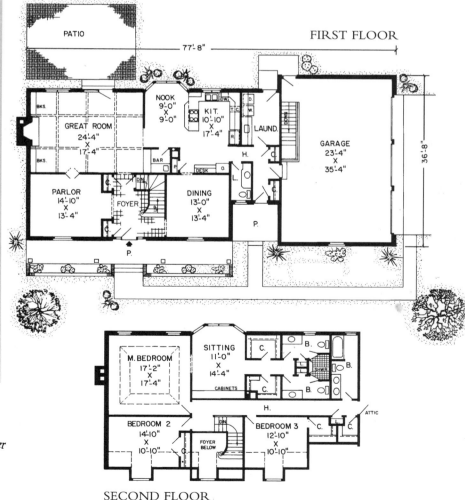

PRICE CODE B

No. 24324

■ This plan features:

— Three bedrooms

— Two full and one half baths

■ A fireplaced Family Room only divided from the Kitchen by an eating bar

■ A U-shaped Kitchen with a pantry and ample cabinet space

■ A pan-vaulted ceiling in the formal Dining Room

■ A spacious Living Room, flowing easily into the Dining Room and viewing the front porch

■ A Master Suite enhanced with a walk-in closet, a double vanity, a whirlpool tub, a step-in shower and a compartmentalized toilet

■ Two additional bedrooms, one with a walk-in closet, share the second full bath

FIRST FLOOR — 916 SQ. FT.
SECOND FLOOR — 884 SQ. FT.
GARAGE — 480 SQ. FT.

TOTAL LIVING AREA: 1,800 SQ. FT.

FOCUS ON THE FAMILY

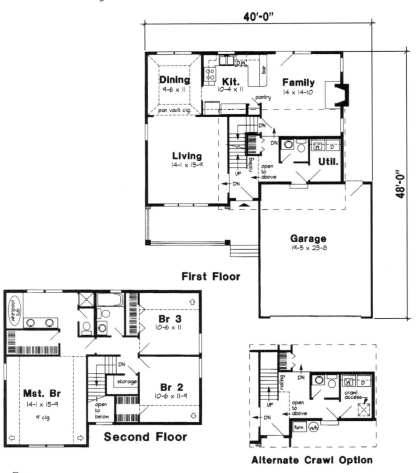

An
EXCLUSIVE DESIGN
By Marshall Associates

No materials list available

PRICE CODE E

TODAY'S AMENITIES, YESTERDAY'S OLD-FASHIONED CHARM

No. 10805

■ This plan features:

— Three bedrooms

— Two and one half baths

■ Wide corner boards, clapboard siding, and a full-length covered porch lending a friendly air to this classic home

■ A central entry opening to a cozy Den on the right, a sunken Living Room with adjoining Dining Room on the left

■ An informal Dining Nook accented by bay windows

■ A Master Suite spanning the rear of the home including a huge, walk-in closet, a private bath with double vanities, and a whirlpool tub

FIRST FLOOR — 1,622 SQ. FT.
SECOND FLOOR — 1,156 SQ. FT.

TOTAL LIVING AREA:
2,778 SQ. FT.

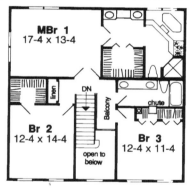

Second Floor

MBr 1
17-4 x 13-4

Br 2
12-4 x 14-4

Br 3
12-4 x 11-4

linen

DN

Balcony

chute

open to below

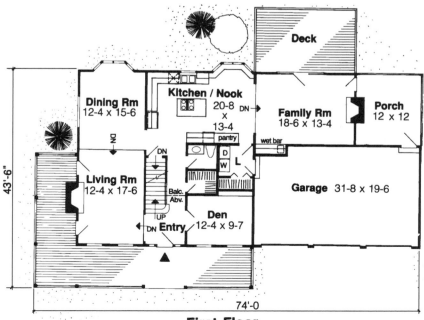

First Floor

Deck

Dining Rm
12-4 x 15-6

Kitchen / Nook
20-8 x 13-4

Family Rm
18-6 x 13-4

Porch
12 x 12

pantry

wet bar

Living Rm
12-4 x 17-6

Garage 31-8 x 19-6

Balc. Abv.

UP
DN

Entry

Den
12-4 x 9-7

43'-6"

74'-0"

PRICE CODE E

SPRAWLING COUNTRY STYLE

No. 98724

■ This plan features:

— Three bedrooms

— Three full baths

■ A country porch wrapping around one entire side of the home, two wooden decks and a patio further expanding the living space

■ A formal Living Room highlighted by a fireplace

■ An elegant Dining Room with a built-in china hutch

■ A Family Room with a two-way fireplace and built-in shelves

■ A large walk-in pantry, double sink, and a window that views the rear yard in the Kitchen

■ A first floor Master Suite served by a full bath with an elevated spa tub and a walk-in closet

■ Two additional second floor bedrooms and a full hall bath

FIRST FLOOR — 2,039 SQ. FT.
SECOND FLOOR — 640 SQ. FT.
GARAGE — 843 SQ. FT.

TOTAL LIVING AREA:
2,679 SQ. FT.

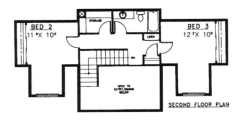

SECOND FLOOR PLAN

An
EXCLUSIVE DESIGN
By Landmark Designs, Inc.

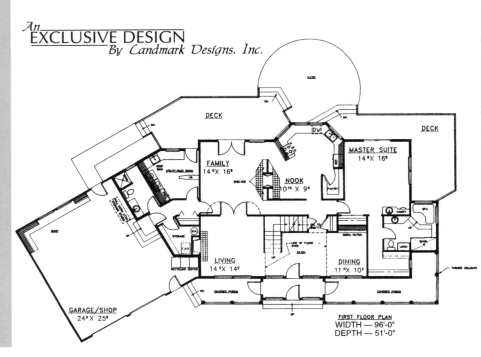

FIRST FLOOR PLAN
WIDTH — 96'-0"
DEPTH — 51'-0"

PRICE CODE D

GENTEEL COUNTRY HOME

No. 99796

- ■ This plan features:
- — Three bedrooms
- — Two full and one half bath
- ■ A wrap-around porch
- ■ A formal Living Room with a fireplace, built-in shelves and double doors for privacy
- ■ A large first floor Master Suite with a bath and a walk-in closet
- ■ A corner wood stove adding a cozy touch to the Family Room
- ■ A built-in wetbar dividing the Family Room from the Nook area
- ■ An efficient U-shaped Kitchen with a built-in planning desk and an easy garage entry
- ■ Two second floor bedrooms and a compartmented bath
- ■ Utility and Powder Rooms near the garage and the Kitchen

FIRST FLOOR — 1,923 SQ. FT.
SECOND FLOOR — 675 SQ. FT.
GARAGE — 858 SQ. FT.
WIDTH — 62'-0"
DEPTH — 67'-0"

TOTAL LIVING AREA:
2,598 SQ. FT.

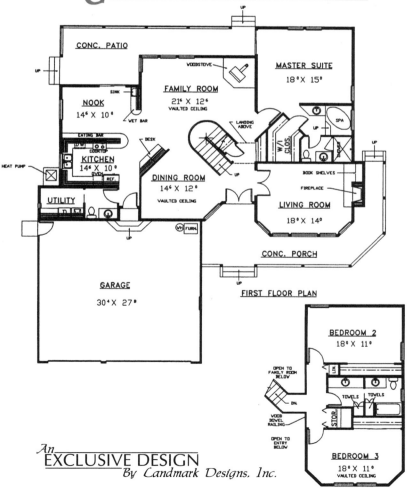

An
EXCLUSIVE DESIGN
By Landmark Designs, Inc.

SECOND FLOOR PLAN

PRICE CODE E

No. 90405

■ This plan features:

— Four bedrooms

— Two full and one half baths

■ Three large bay windows bringing natural illumination to both the interior and the exterior

■ A Kitchen with direct access to the Dining Room and the Breakfast Area

■ A fireplaced Family Room with a built-in bar

■ A Screened Porch for expanded three-season living

■ A luxurious Master Bedroom Suite with two walk-in closets, a garden tub, a separate shower and twin vanities

■ Three additional bedrooms with walk-in closets

■ A second floor Sitting Area

■ A basement or crawl space foundation — please specify when ordering

FIRST FLOOR — 2,005 SQ. FT.
SECOND FLOOR — 1,063 SQ. FT.

**TOTAL LIVING AREA:
3,068 SQ. FT.**

BAY WINDOWS ENHANCE THS HOME

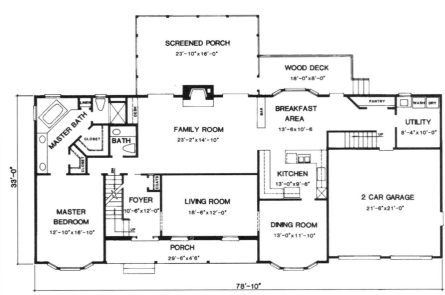

MAIN FLOOR PLAN

UPPER FLOOR PLAN

PRICE CODE C

RUSTIC L-SHAPED DESIGN

No. 90416

■ This plan features:

— Three bedrooms

— Two full baths

■ An L-shaped layout, ideal for a corner lot, provides rear yard privacy

■ A fireplaced Living Room

■ Screened Porch located off the Dining Room

■ The Kitchen, easily located between the Dining Room and the Breakfast area, equipped with a center work island

■ A bayed Breakfast area with access to the pantry and a laundry area

■ A Master Bedroom Suite with a Master Bath that includes a garden tub, a step-in shower, a cathedral ceiling, a double vanity and a large walk-in closet

■ An optional basement, slab or crawl space foundation — please specify when ordering

MAIN AREA — 1,909 SQ. FT.

TOTAL LIVING AREA: 1,909 SQ. FT.

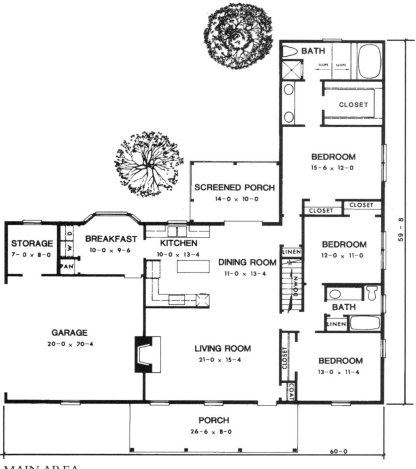

MAIN AREA

PRICE CODE D

CHARMING AND COZY

No. 90126

■ This plan features:

— Three bedrooms

— Two full and one half baths

■ A large Family Room with a cozy fireplace and sliding doors to the patio

■ An efficiently organized Kitchen easily serving either the formal Dining Room or the informal Nook

■ A Master Bedroom with a large walk-in closet and private Master Bath

■ Two additional bedrooms sharing a full hall bath with double vanity

■ An optional basement or crawl space foundation — please specify when ordering

FIRST FLOOR — 1,260 SQ. FT.
SECOND FLOOR — 952 SQ. FT.

TOTAL LIVING AREA: 2,212 SQ. FT.

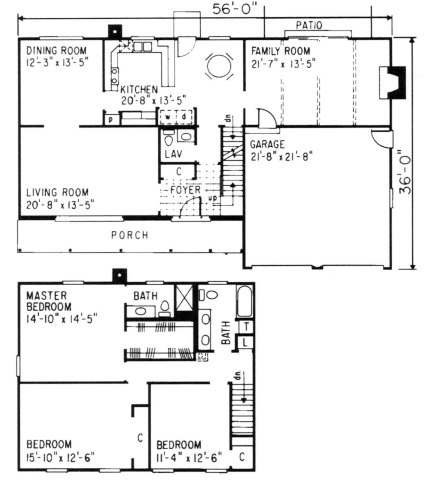

SECOND FLOOR

PRICE CODE A

No. 90163

■ This plan features:

— Three bedrooms

— One full bath

■ A country porch to enjoy the outdoors and enhance curb appeal

■ Convenient one level, energy efficient home

■ A Foyer area with a convenient coat closet

■ An open layout between the Great Room, Kitchen and Dining Area

■ An L-shaped Kitchen equipped with a double sink and a built-in broom closet

■ A Master Suite to the rear of the home with private access to the full bath

■ Two additional bedrooms share the full hall bath

■ An optional basement, slab or crawl space foundation — please specify when ordering

MAIN AREA — 1,232 SQ. FT.
BASEMENT — 1,232 SQ. FT.

TOTAL LIVING AREA:
1,232 SQ. FT.

OPTIONS ABOUND

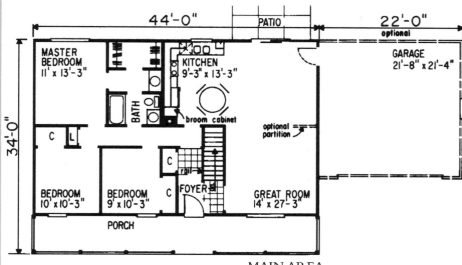

MAIN AREA

PRICE CODE F

No. 93328

- ■ This plan features:
- — Four bedrooms
- — Three full and one half baths
- ■ A Foyer with a balcony above
- ■ A coffered ceiling in the Family Room which includes sliding glass doors, a fireplace and a built-in entertainment area
- ■ A formal Living Room with a fireplace and a private porch area
- ■ A gourmet Kitchen with a cook-top island, built-in pantry and an abundance of work space
- ■ A Library with a spiral staircase to a loft, as well as a fireplace and built-in bookcases
- ■ Lavish Master Suite with a cozy fireplace, a private deck, a large walk-in closet, access to the Library's loft and Master Bath
- ■ Three additional bedrooms with private access to a full bath

FIRST FLOOR — 2,277 SQ. FT.
SECOND FLOOR — 1,838 SQ. FT.
BASEMENT — 2,277 SQ. FT.
GARAGE — 1,196 SQ. FT.

**TOTAL LIVING AREA:
4,115 SQ. FT.**

OUTSTANDING LUXURY

No materials list available

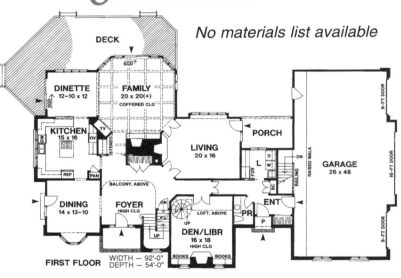

An EXCLUSIVE DESIGN
By Patrick Morabito, A.I.A. Architect

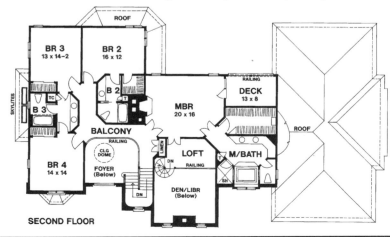

PRICE CODE E

SPACIOUS, OPEN LAYOUT

No. 93251

- This plan features:
  — Three bedrooms
  — Two full and one half baths
- An open layout between the Living Area, Dining Room, Breakfast Room and the Kitchen
- A Master Suite with a bay window, compartmented Master Bath and a walk-in closet
- A large deck
- A lower level Family Room with a fireplace
- Two additional bedrooms that share use of a full bath
- A balcony and Loft overlooking the Living Area

FIRST FLOOR — 1,536 SQ. FT.
SECOND FLOOR — 194 SQ. FT.
LOWER LEVEL — 958 SQ. FT.
BASEMENT — 514 SQ. FT.

**TOTAL LIVING AREA:
2,688 SQ. FT.**

No materials list available

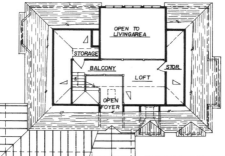

SECOND FLOOR

FIRST FLOOR

LOWER LEVEL

An
EXCLUSIVE DESIGN
By Jannis Vann & Associates, Inc.

PRICE CODE D

ROOM FOR FAMILY ACTIVITIES

No. 10649

■ This plan features:

— Three bedrooms

— Two and one half baths

■ A Family Room warmed by a fireplace, contains lots of windows, French doors, a wetbar and access to the covered porch

■ A Kitchen centered between a bay window breakfast nook and a formal Dining Room

■ Window seats adorning the front bedrooms

FIRST FLOOR — 1,285 SQ. FT.
SECOND FLOOR — 930 SQ. FT.
GARAGE — 492 SQ. FT.

TOTAL LIVING AREA:
2,215 SQ. FT.

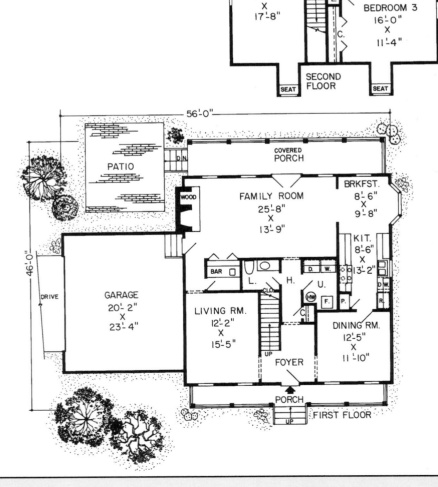

PRICE CODE B

MODERN HOME WITH COUNTRY FLAIR

No. 90399

- This plan features:
— Three bedrooms
— Two full and one half baths

- A covered porch giving a country slant to this up-to-date home

- A central staircase descending into the Foyer area

- A formal Living Room/Dining Room combination located next to the Kitchen and off the Foyer

- A space efficient Kitchen with a double sink and a peninsula counter/eating bar separating it from the Breakfast Room

- A cozy fireplaced Family Room with a vaulted ceiling open to the Breakfast Room for a spacious feeling

- A second floor Master Suite includes a private bath and half-round, vaulted front window

FIRST FLOOR — 984 SQ. FT.
SECOND FLOOR — 744 SQ. FT.

TOTAL LIVING AREA:
1,728 SQ. FT.

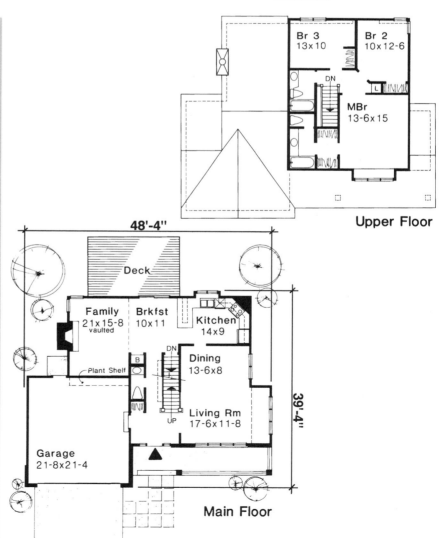

Br 3
13 x 10

Br 2
10 x 12-6

DN

MBr
13-6 x 15

Upper Floor

48'-4"

Deck

Family
21 x 15-8
vaulted

Brkfst
10 x 11

Kitchen
14 x 9

Plant Shelf

B

DN

Dining
13-6 x 8

UP

Living Rm
17-6 x 11-8

39'-4"

Garage
21-8 x 21-4

Main Floor

PRICE CODE D

EMBRACING WRAP-AROUND PORCH

No. 24255

■ This plan features:

— Three bedrooms

— Two full and one half bath

■ A skylit, vaulted ceiling in the Family Room with a fireplace

■ A modern, well-equipped Kitchen with cooktop island, double sink and ample storage and counter space

■ A vaulted ceiling in the Living Room which flows easily into the Dining Room

■ A Master Bedroom with a vaulted ceiling and skylit, private Master Bath

■ Additional bedrooms share a full hall bath

FIRST FLOOR — 1,370 SQ. FT.
SECOND FLOOR — 1,000 SQ. FT.
BONUS ROOM — 194 SQ. FT.
GARAGE — 667 SQ. FT.

**TOTAL LIVING AREA:
2,370 SQ. FT.**

SECOND FLOOR

An EXCLUSIVE DESIGN
By Energetic Enterprises

FIRST FLOOR

PRICE CODE A

COMPACT RANCH LOADED WITH LIVING SPACE

No. 34328

■ This plan features:

— Three bedrooms

— One full bath

■ A central entrance, opening to the Living Room with ample windows

■ A Kitchen, featuring a Breakfast area with sliding doors to the backyard and an optional deck

MAIN AREA — 1,092 SQ. FT.
BASEMENT — 1,092 SQ. FT.

**TOTAL LIVING AREA:
1,092 SQ. FT.**

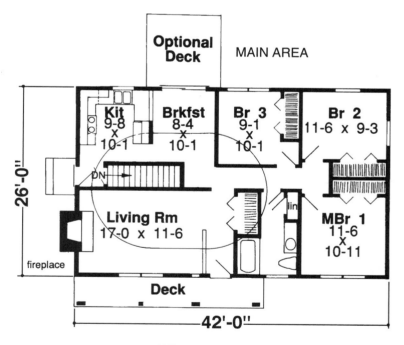

MAIN AREA

Optional Deck

Kit
9-8
x
10-1

Brkfst
8-4
x
10-1

Br 3
9-1
x
10-1

Br 2
11-6 x 9-3

DN

Living Rm
17-0 x 11-6

lin

MBr 1
11-6
x
10-11

fireplace

Deck

26'-0"

42'-0"

**ALTERNATE FLOOR PLAN
for Crawl Space**

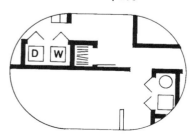

D W

PRICE CODE B

SAVOR THE SUMMER

No. 24242

■ This plan features:

— Four bedrooms

— Two and a half baths

■ A efficient home with a friendly front Porch and a practical back porch

■ A cozy fireplace and a boxed window with a built-in seat in the Living Room

■ A formal Dining Room opening to front entrance and Kitchen

■ A well-equipped Kitchen with an old-fashion booth and ample cabinet and counter space adjoining Laundry area and back porch

■ A convenient, first floor Master Suite with two closet and a private Bath

■ Three additional bedrooms, on second floor, sharing a full hall bath

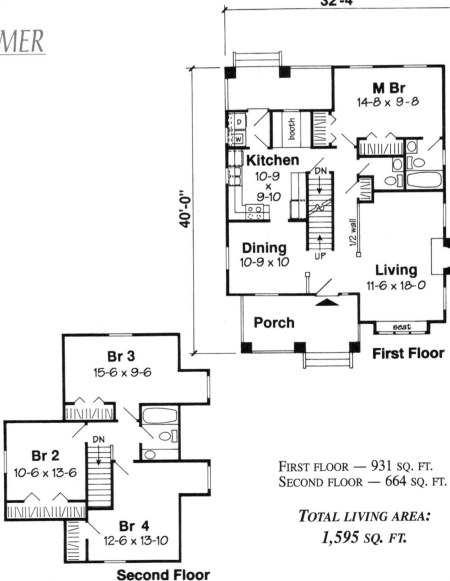

FIRST FLOOR — 931 SQ. FT.
SECOND FLOOR — 664 SQ. FT.

TOTAL LIVING AREA:
1,595 SQ. FT.

PRICE CODE B

ABUNDANCE OF CLOSET SPACE

No. 20204

◼ This plan features:

— Three bedrooms

— Two full baths

◼ Roomy walk-in closets in all the bedrooms

◼ A Master Bedroom with decorative ceiling and a private full bath

◼ A fireplaced Living Room with sloped ceilings and sliders to the deck

◼ An efficient Kitchen with plenty of cupboard space and a pantry

MAIN AREA —1,532 SQ. FT.
GARAGE — 484 SQ. FT.

TOTAL LIVING AREA:
1,532 SQ. FT.

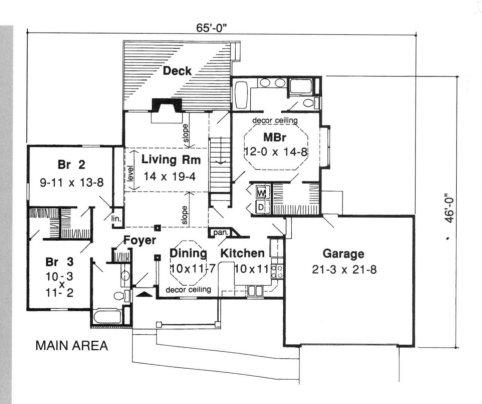

65'-0"

Deck

decor ceiling

MBr
12-0 x 14-8

Br 2
9-11 x 13-8

Living Rm
14 x 19-4

slope

level

slope

W.
D.

lin.

Foyer

pan.

Br 3
10-3
x
11-2

Dining
10x11-7

Kitchen
10 x 11

Garage
21-3 x 21-8

decor ceiling

46'-0"

MAIN AREA

An
EXCLUSIVE DESIGN
By Karl Kreeger

PRICE CODE A

MASTER SUITE OFFERS PRIVACY

No. 24318

■ This plan features:

— Four bedrooms

— Two full baths

■ A large covered porch and dormer windows creating a friendly invitation to enter

■ A Living Room with a beamed ceiling and atrium door accessible to the Patio

■ A Dining Room, adjoining the Living Room and Kitchen, making entertaining easy

■ A efficient, U-shaped Kitchen with a curved counter that serves as a pass-through and a snack bar

■ A exclusive Master Suite, with a double vanity Bath, on the second floor offering a quiet place

■ Three bedrooms on the first floor sharing a full hall bath

FIRST FLOOR — 1,044 SQ. FT.
SECOND FLOOR — 354 SQ. FT.

TOTAL LIVING AREA:
1,398 SQ. FT

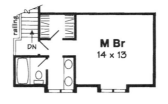

Second Floor

An
EXCLUSIVE DESIGN
By Marshall Associates

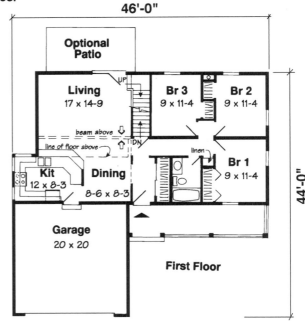

First Floor

PRICE CODE F

No. 20155

- This plan features:
- — Four bedrooms
- — Four and one half bath
- An L-shaped Living and Dining Room arrangement with a fireplace flanked by bookcases and a decorative ceiling in the Dining area
- A gourmet Kitchen with range-top island/snack bar, built-in pantry and double sinks
- A massive fireplace, with wood storage, that separates the Hearth/Breakfast Room from the sky-lit Sun Room
- A Master Suite with a decorative ceiling, walk-in closet, elegant bath and private access to the screened porch
- Three additional bedrooms that share use of a full hall bath

FIRST FLOOR — 2,800 SQ. FT.
SECOND FLOOR — 1,113 SQ. FT.
BASEMENT — 2,800 SQ. FT.
SCREEN PORCH — 216 SQ. FT.
GARAGE — 598 SQ. FT.

TOTAL LIVING AREA:
3,913 SQ. FT.

BUILT-IN BEAUTY

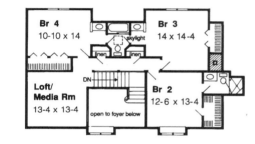

Second Floor

An EXCLUSIVE DESIGN *By Karl Kreeger*

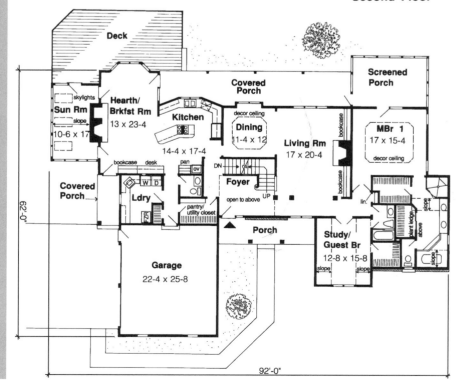

PRICE CODE B

ANGULAR FIREPLACE ADDS INTEREST

No. 20125

- This plan features:
- — Three bedrooms
- — Two and a half baths
- A cozy fireplaced Living Room and an elegant formal Dining Room
- A Master Suite with walk-in closet and private Master Bath
- Two additional bedrooms sharing a full hall bath

FIRST FLOOR — 1,340 SQ. FT.
SECOND FLOOR — 455 SQ. FT.
BASEMENT — 347 SQ. FT.
GARAGE — 979 SQ. FT.

TOTAL LIVING AREA:
1,795 SQ. FT.

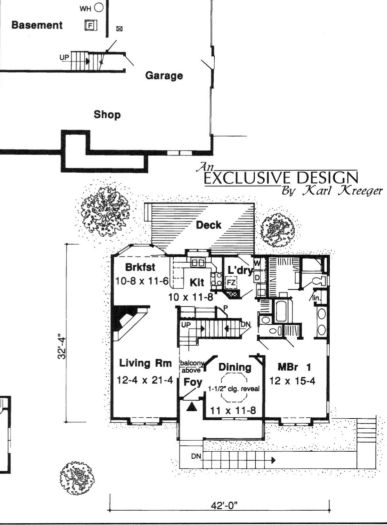

An
EXCLUSIVE DESIGN
By Karl Kreeger

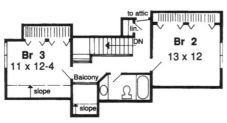

PRICE CODE E

UPDATED SALTBOX DESIGN

No. 20404

■ This plan features:

— Five bedrooms

— Three full baths

■ Flower boxes and a friendly front porch introducing an updated saltbox

■ A formal Dining Room and Parlor adjoining the open Foyer offers a classic arrangement with a contemporary approach

■ A wonderful gathering place, where the Kitchen, Breakfast area, and Family Room join together, enhanced by a cozy fireplace and a wall of windows overlooking the Deck

■ A Guest Suite including a full Bath with handicap access

■ A private Deck and luxurious Bath highlighting the Master Suite

■ A Balcony that links two, optional three, bedrooms and a full bath together on the second floor

FIRST FLOOR — 2,285 SQ. FT.
SECOND FLOOR — 660 SQ. FT.
GARAGE — 565 SQ. FT.

TOTAL LIVING AREA:
2,945 SQ. FT.

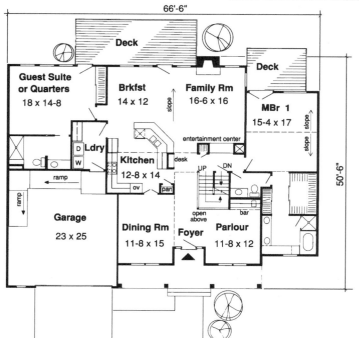

PRICE CODE D

RANCH STYLE WITH COUNTRY FLAIR

No. 99723

■ This plan features:

— Three bedrooms

— Three full and one half baths

■ A covered porch stretching across the front

■ A formal Living Room accented by a bay window and a fireplace

■ A Kitchen layout with access to the Utility Room, Lavatory, Garage and Front Porch, and a pantry, desk and appliances

■ Two direct entrances from the front porch

■ A Master Suite with a walk-in closet, spa tub, shower stall, double vanity and a deck

■ A Family Room with an entertainment center, vaulted ceiling and a fireplace

■ Two additional bedrooms, one with a private bath

MAIN AREA — 2,371 SQ. FT.
BASEMENT — 2,170 SQ. FT.
GARAGE — 686 SQ. FT.
WIDTH — 90'-0"
DEPTH — 47'-0"

TOTAL LIVING AREA:
2,371 SQ. FT.

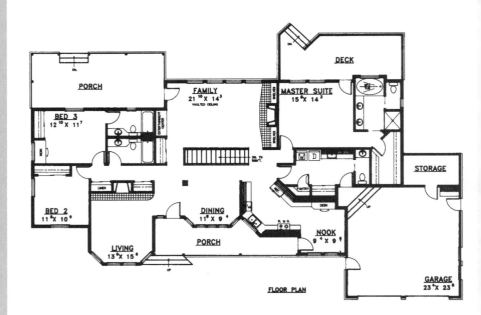

An
EXCLUSIVE DESIGN
By Landmark Designs, Inc.

PRICE CODE D

GABLED GRACE

An
EXCLUSIVE DESIGN
By Karl Kreeger

No. 20176

■ This plan features:

— Four bedrooms

— Three full and one half bath

■ An angular Kitchen with built-in pantry, double sinks, peninsula counter that opens to the sunny Breakfast bay and the Hearth Room

■ A cozy fireplace that warms the Hearth Room, Breakfast bay and Kitchen

■ A sloped ceiling with skylights in the Living Room

■ A Master Suite with private Master Bath and a walk-in closet

■ Three additional bedrooms, two with walk-in closets, one with a private bath

FIRST FLOOR — 1,625 SQ. FT.
SECOND FLOOR — 916 SQ. FT.
BASEMENT — 1,618 SQ. FT.
GARAGE — 521 SQ. FT.

TOTAL LIVING AREA:
2,541 SQ. FT.

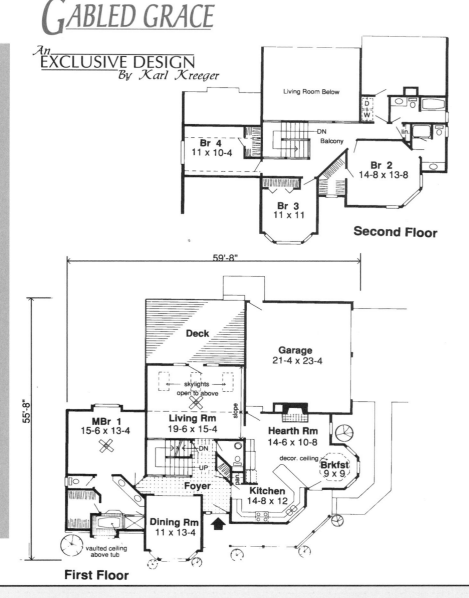

Second Floor

Br 4
11 x 10-4

Living Room Below

Br 2
14-8 x 13-8

Br 3
11 x 11

First Floor

59'-8"

55'-8"

Deck

Garage
21-4 x 23-4

MBr 1
15-6 x 13-4

Living Rm
19-6 x 15-4

skylights
open to above

Hearth Rm
14-6 x 10-8

decor. ceiling

Brkfst
9 x 9

Foyer

Kitchen
14-8 x 12

Dining Rm
11 x 13-4

vaulted ceiling above tub

PRICE CODE C

FRIENDLY FACADE GRACES GREAT PLAN

No. 90850

■ This plan features:

— Three bedrooms

— Two full baths and one half bath

■ A covered country porch that welcomes guests and family

■ A spacious Living Room with a stone fireplace and an elegant bay window

■ A formal Dining Room that views the front porch

■ An efficient Kitchen situated conveniently between the Dining Room and the Family area

■ A main floor Master Suite

■ Two big bedrooms on the second floor that share a full hall bath

■ Lots of closet space

FIRST FLOOR — 1,190 SQ. FT.
SECOND FLOOR — 702 SQ. FT.
BASEMENT — 1,178 SQ. FT.
WIDTH — 37'-0"
DEPTH — 29'-0"

TOTAL LIVING AREA:
1,892 SQ. FT.

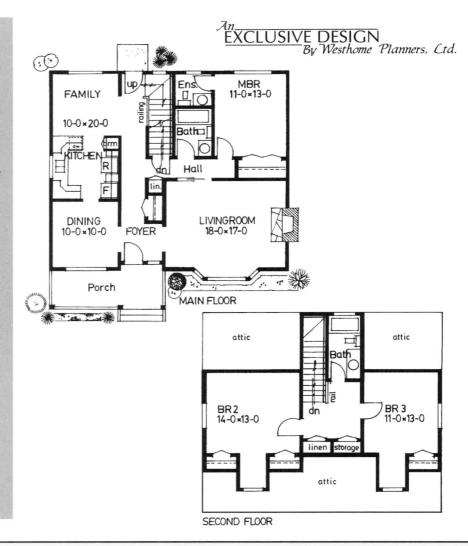

An
EXCLUSIVE DESIGN
By Westhome Planners, Ltd.

PRICE CODE C

REMINISCENT OF AMERICA'S FARM HOUSE

No. 93029

■ This plan features:

— Three bedrooms

— Two full baths

■ A covered front Porch

■ Ten foot ceilings

■ A matching pair of double French doors in the Great Room that flank the fireplace

■ A formal Dining Room with square columns connected by arched openings

■ An angled bar design in the Kitchen, providing a convenient pass-through for entertaining and family gatherings

■ A Master Suite with a coffered ceiling and an enormous walk-in closet

■ A double vanity, corner whirlpool tub and a shower in the Master Bath

MAIN AREA — 1,834 SQ. FT.
GARAGE — 547 SQ. FT.

TOTAL LIVING AREA:
1,834 SQ. FT.

An
EXCLUSIVE DESIGN
By Belk Home Designs

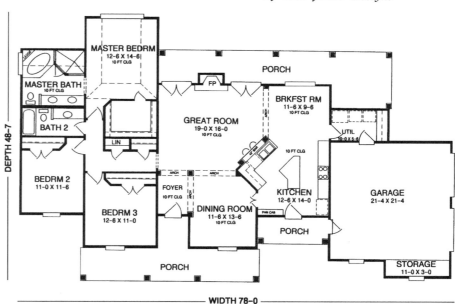

No materials list available

PRICE CODE B

ECONOMY AT IT'S BEST

No. 91746

■ This plan features:

— Three bedrooms

— Three full baths

■ An attractive front porch

■ A vaulted ceiling topping the Entry, Living and Dining Rooms

■ A lovely bay window in the Living Room, with direct access to a side deck

■ A Master Suite with a walk-in closet, and a compartmented bath with an over-sized shower

■ Two additional bedrooms share a full hall bath topped by a skylight

■ A walk-in pantry adds to the storage space of the cooktop island Kitchen, which is equipped with a windowed double sink

■ Garage offers direct entrance to the house

MAIN AREA — 1,717 SQ. FT.
GARAGE — 782 SQ. FT.
WIDTH — 80'-0"
DEPTH — 42'-0"

TOTAL LIVING AREA:
1,717 SQ. FT.

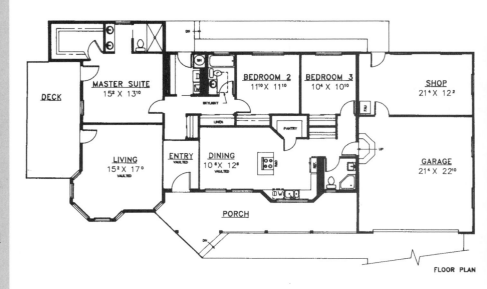

An EXCLUSIVE DESIGN
By Landmark Designs, Inc.

PRICE CODE C

LOTS OF ROOM FOR ENTERTAINING

No. 91761

■ This plan features:

— Three bedrooms

— Two full baths

■ An open floor plan that is spacious and easy to adapt for wheelchair accessibility

■ A Kitchen, with an eating bar, that flows into the Family Room; allowing for continued conversation between the two rooms

■ Direct access to the wood deck from the Family Room that features a vaulted ceiling with skylights

■ A Master Suite enhanced by a private bath with a skylight and direct access to the wood deck

■ A combination Living Room/Dining Room making entertaining easy

■ Two additional bedrooms that share a full hall bath

MAIN AREA — 2,072 SQ. FT.
GARAGE — 585 SQ. FT.
WIDTH — 60'-0"
DEPTH — 70'-0"

TOTAL LIVING AREA:
2,072 SQ. FT.

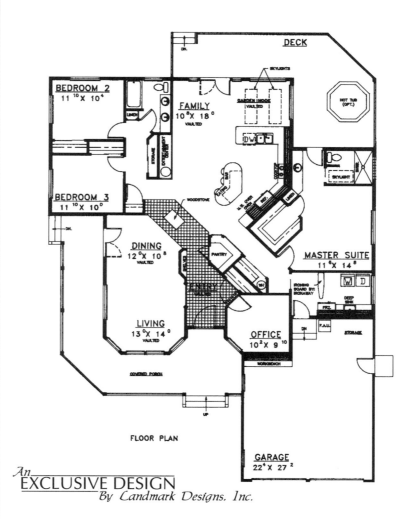

FLOOR PLAN

An EXCLUSIVE DESIGN
By Landmark Designs, Inc.

PRICE CODE F

VERANDA MIRRORS TWO-STORY BAY

No. 10780

■ This plan features:

— Four bedrooms

— Two and one half baths

■ A huge foyer flanked by the formal Parlor and Dining Room

■ An island Kitchen with an adjoining pantry

■ A Breakfast bay and sunken Gathering Room located at the rear of the home

■ Double doors opening to the Master Suite and the book-lined Master Retreat

■ An elegant Master Bath including a raised tub and adjoining cedar closet

FIRST FLOOR — 2,108 SQ. FT.
SECOND FLOOR — 2,109 SQ. FT.
BASEMENT — 1,946 SQ. FT.
GARAGE — 764 SQ. FT.

**TOTAL LIVING AREA:
4,217 SQ. FT.**

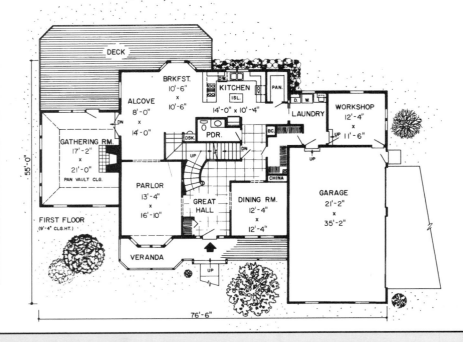

PRICE CODE B

CONTEMPORARY WITH A COUNTRY FLAIR

No. 20203

■ This plan features:

— Three bedrooms

— Two and a half baths

■ A fireplaced Living Room flowing easily into the Dining Room with decorative ceiling

■ A Master Suite with a walk-in closet and private Master Bath

■ Two additional bedrooms sharing a sky-lit full bath

FIRST FLOOR — 1,229 SQ. FT.
SECOND FLOOR — 515 SQ. FT.
GARAGE — 452 SQ. FT.

TOTAL LIVING AREA:
1,744 SQ. FT.

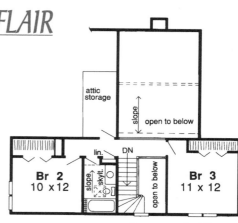

Second Floor

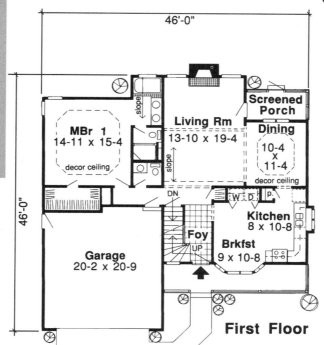

First Floor

An
EXCLUSIVE DESIGN
By Karl Kreeger

PRICE CODE F

COMPLETE WITH SERVANT'S QUARTERS

No. 93327

■ This plan features:

— Four bedrooms

— Two full and one half baths

■ Decorative tray ceilings in the Dining Room, Living Room, Library, Master Suite, Sitting Area and Bath

■ A Foyer with a balcony above

■ A gourmet Kitchen with a cooktop work island and an abundance of work space

■ Sliding glass doors in the Family Room, which add natural lighting and give access to the rear yard

■ A lavish Master Suite with a whirlpool tub, his-n-her walk-in closets, his-n-her vanities, and a step-in shower

■ Three additional bedrooms that share a full hall bath

■ A servant's quarters

FIRST FLOOR — 2,730 SQ. FT.
SECOND FLOOR — 2,054 SQ. FT.
SERVANT'S QUARTER — 688 SQ. FT.
BASEMENT — 2,730 SQ. FT.
GARAGE — 1,008 SQ. FT.

TOTAL LIVING AREA:
5,472 SQ. FT.

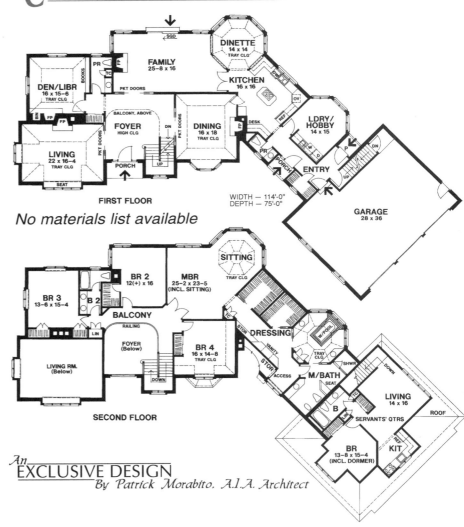

No materials list available

WIDTH — 114'-0"
DEPTH — 75'-0"

FIRST FLOOR

SECOND FLOOR

An
EXCLUSIVE DESIGN
By Patrick Morabito, A.I.A. Architect

PRICE CODE C

STYLISH, CONTEMPORARY COUNTRY HOME

No. 93282

■ This plan features:

— Three bedrooms

— Two full and one half baths

■ A covered country front porch and bay windows enhancing the front elevation of the home

■ A elegant two-story Foyer

■ A Traditional front room position for the formal Living and Dining Rooms

■ An efficiently-located Kitchen

■ A Master Bedroom with a private bath that includes an oval tub, a double vanity, a separate shower and a compartmented toilet

■ Two additional bedrooms, one with a bay window, that share a full hall bath

FIRST FLOOR — 1,062 SQ. FT.
SECOND FLOOR — 976 SQ. FT.
BONUS ROOM — 410 SQ. FT.
BASEMENT — 1,012 SQ. FT.
GARAGE — 536 SQ. FT.

TOTAL LIVING ARE:
2,038 SQ. FT.

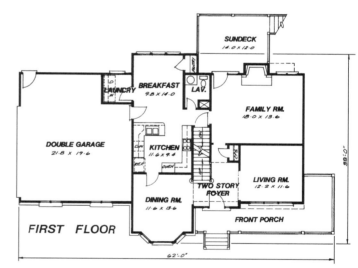

An
EXCLUSIVE DESIGN
By Jannis Vann & Associates. Inc.

No materials list available

PRICE CODE E

FARMHOUSE FLAVOR, FAMILY STYLE DESIGN

No. 99205

■ This plan features:

— Four bedrooms

— Two full and two half baths

■ A sunny Breakfast bay with easy access to the efficient Kitchen

■ A large and spacious Family Room with a fireplace and a pass-through to the Kitchen

■ Sliders that link the Family and Dining Rooms with the rear terrace

■ A private Master Suite with his-and-her walk-in closets, a dressing room with built-in vanity and a convenient step-in shower

FIRST FLOOR — 1,590 SQ. FT.
SECOND FLOOR — 1,344 SQ. FT.

TOTAL LIVING AREA: 2,934 SQ. FT.

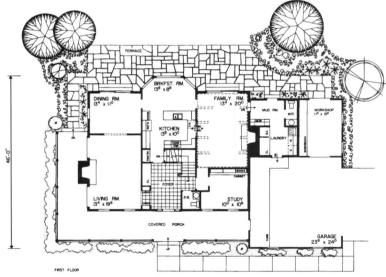

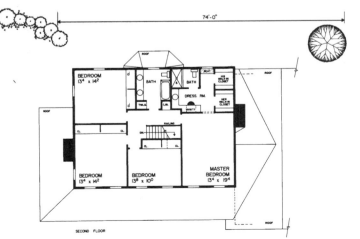

PRICE CODE E

No. 90860

■ This plan features:

— Three bedrooms

— Three full baths

■ A formal sunken Living Room and a Dining Room which are sheltered by the railed porch

■ A large, well-appointed island Kitchen that includes a built-in pantry, double sinks and ample cabinet and counter space

■ A large Nook area with a built-in desk, a two-sided fireplace and direct access to the Sun Deck

■ A sunken Family Room which includes the other side of the Nook's two-sided fireplace

■ A Master Suite equipped with a walk-in closet and a private Master Bath

■ Two additional bedrooms share a full hall bath

FIRST FLOOR — 1,389 SQ. FT.
SECOND FLOOR — 1,245 SQ. FT.
BASEMENT — 1,389 SQ. FT.
WIDTH — 57'-0"
DEPTH — 39'-0"

**TOTAL LIVING AREA:
2,634 SQ. FT.**

A PRACTICAL PORCH ENHANCES CHARM

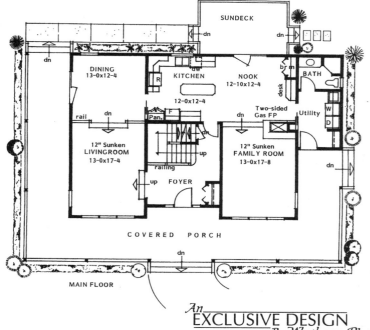

MAIN FLOOR

An
EXCLUSIVE DESIGN
By Westhome Planners, Ltd.

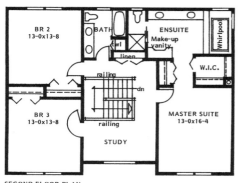

SECOND FLOOR PLAN

PRICE CODE C

*T*WO-SINK BATHS EASE RUSH

No. 90622

■ This plan features:

— Four bedrooms

— Two full and one half baths

■ A wood beam ceiling in the spacious Family Room

■ An efficient, island Kitchen with a sunny bay window dinette

■ A formal Living Room with a heat-circulating fireplace

■ A large Master Suite with a walk-in closet and a private Master Bath

■ Three additional bedrooms sharing a full hall bath

FIRST FLOOR — 983 SQ. FT.
SECOND FLOOR — 1,013 SQ. FT.
MUDROOM — 99 SQ. FT.
GARAGE — 481 SQ. FT.

TOTAL LIVING AREA:
2,095 SQ. FT.

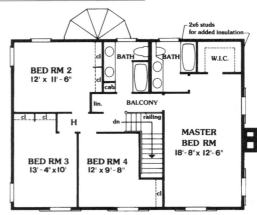

SECOND FLOOR PLAN

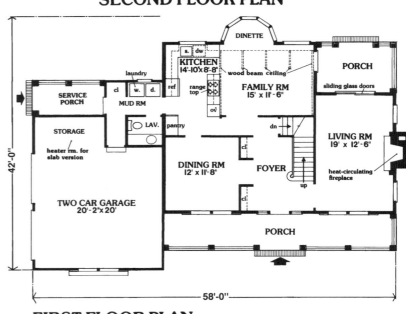

FIRST FLOOR PLAN

PRICE CODE B

INSPIRED BY COUNTRY PORCHES OF OLD

No. 20211

- This plan features:
- — Three bedrooms
- — Two full baths
- Decorative and sloped ceilings
- A large country Kitchen with a central island, double sink, pantry, ample cabinet and counter space and access to deck
- A Master Suite with a decorative ceiling, walk-in closet and a private Master Bath
- A decorative Dining Room ceiling
- A central fireplace in the sloped ceilinged Living Room, providing a focal point and adding warmth to the room
- Two additional bedrooms that share use of a full hall bath

MAIN AREA — 1,609 SQ. FT.
GARAGE — 707 SQ. FT.
BASEMENT — 902 SQ. FT.

TOTAL LIVING AREA:
1,609 SQ. FT.

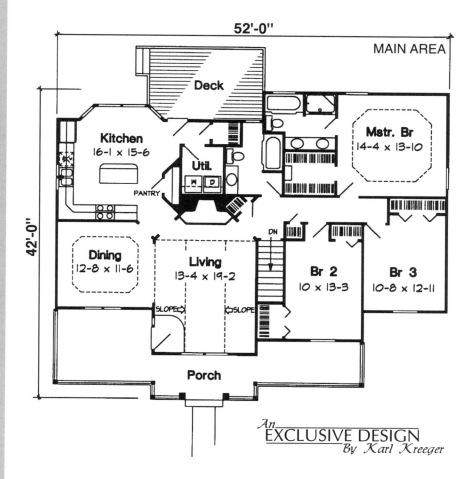

52'-0"

MAIN AREA

Deck

Kitchen
16-1 x 15-6

Util.

PANTRY

Mstr. Br
14-4 x 13-10

42'-0"

Dining
12-8 x 11-6

Living
13-4 x 19-2

DN

Br 2
10 x 13-3

Br 3
10-8 x 12-11

SLOPE   SLOPE

Porch

An
EXCLUSIVE DESIGN
By Karl Kreeger

PRICE CODE E

A SOUTHERN ACCENT

No. 93252

■ This plan features:

— Four bedrooms

— Two full and one half baths

■ A large columned porch

■ A sprawling Family Room with a large fireplace

■ A screened-in porch for mild weather

■ A cooktop island and double sinks in the Kitchen

■ A formal Dining Room and Living Room that flow into each other for ease in entertaining

■ A Master Suite that includes a tray ceiling and a private Master Bath

■ Three additional bedrooms that share a full hall bath

MAIN AREA — 2,644 SQ. FT.
BASEMENT — 2,644 SQ. FT.

TOTAL LIVING AREA: 2,644 SQ. FT.

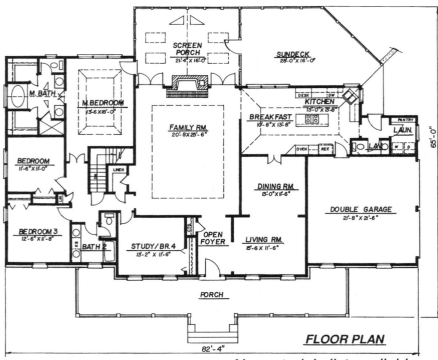

FLOOR PLAN

No materials list available

An
EXCLUSIVE DESIGN
By Jannis Vann & Associates, Inc.

PRICE CODE D

SUBSTANCE AND GRACE

No. 99782

■ This plan features:

— Four bedrooms

— Three full and one half baths

■ Brick detailing, a step-pitched roof, rounded bay windows and a wrap-around porch

■ A large two-story Foyer

■ A Living Room, rich with glass, with a tile hearth fireplace

■ A Kitchen with a raised dishwasher, peninsula counter and a walk-in pantry

■ An informal Nook area naturally illuminated by skylights

■ A Family Room with a built-in entertainment center

■ An Master Suite with walk-in closets, a security system, dual basins, a separate water closet and an over-sized shower

■ Three bedrooms, one a Guest Suite, with access to a full bath

FIRST FLOOR — 1,680 SQ. FT.
SECOND FLOOR — 919 SQ. FT.
BASEMENT — 1,580 SQ. FT.
GARAGE — 794 SQ. FT.

TOTAL LIVING AREA: 2,599 SQ. FT.

An EXCLUSIVE DESIGN
By Landmark Designs, Inc.

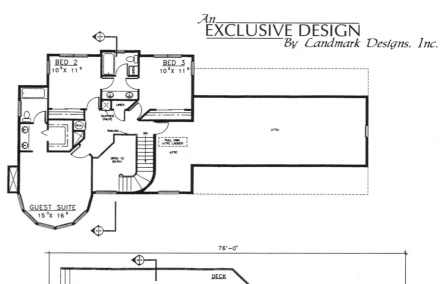

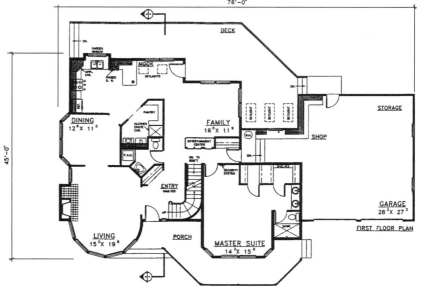

PRICE CODE C

COUNTRY LIVING IN ANY NEIGHBORHOOD

No. 90436

■ This plan features:

— Three bedrooms

— Two full and two half baths

■ An expansive Family Room with fireplace

■ A Dining Room and Breakfast Nook lit by flowing natural light from bay windows

■ A first floor Master Suite with a double vanitied bath that wraps around his-n-her closets

■ An optional basement, slab or crawl space foundation — please specify when ordering

FIRST FLOOR — 1,477 SQ. FT.
SECOND FLOOR — 704 SQ. FT.
BASEMENT — 1,374 SQ. FT.

**TOTAL LIVING AREA:
2,181 SQ. FT.**

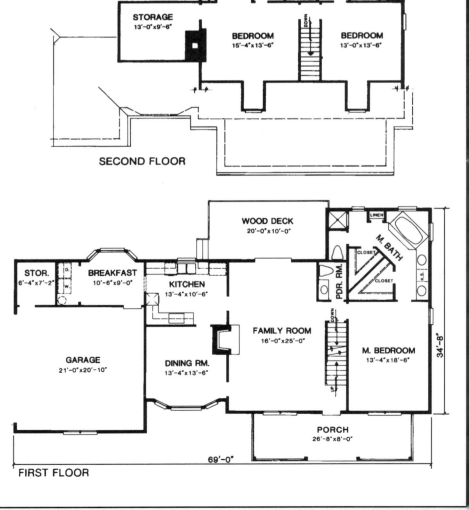

SECOND FLOOR

FIRST FLOOR

P·R·I·C·E C·O·D·E C

No. 93106

■ This plan features:

— Four bedrooms

— Two full and one half baths

■ A classic country front porch leading to the Foyer and second entrance into Mud/Utility Room

■ A formal Dining Room located next to the Kitchen

■ A large country Kitchen with an angled island/eating bar and a Breakfast Area

■ A Screened Porch expanding living space in the warmer months

■ An expansive Great Room enhanced by a cozy fireplace

■ A Master Suite highlighted by a Jacuzzi, surrounded by a wall of glass

■ Three additional bedrooms sharing a full bath

FIRST FLOOR — 1,570 SQ. FT.
SECOND FLOOR — 592 SQ. FT.
BASEMENT — 1,570 SQ. FT.
GARAGE — 548 SQ. FT.

TOTAL LIVING AREA:
2,162 SQ. FT.

CONTEMPORARY WITH A COUNTRY LOOK

An
EXCLUSIVE DESIGN
By Ahmann Design Inc.

No materials list available

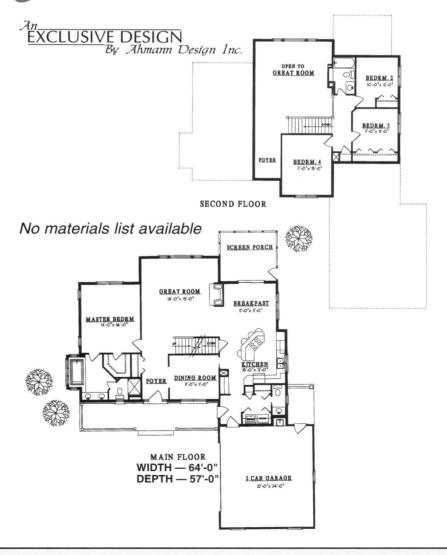

SECOND FLOOR

MAIN FLOOR
WIDTH — 64'-0"
DEPTH — 57'-0"

PRICE CODE B

MODIFIED CAPE WITH PASSIVE SOLAR FEATURES

No. 10386

■ This plan features:

— Three bedrooms

— Two baths

■ A solar greenhouse on the south side of the home employing energy storage rods and water to capture the sun's warmth

■ Triple glazed windows for energy efficiency

■ A Living Room accentuated by a heat-circulating fireplace

■ Sliding doors leading from the sitting area of the Master Bedroom to a private patio

■ A Garage with a large storage area

FIRST FLOOR — 1,164 SQ. FT.
SECOND FLOOR — 574 SQ. FT.
BASEMENT — 1,164 SQ. FT.
GARAGE & STORAGE AREA — 574 SQ. FT.
GREENHOUSE — 238 SQ. FT.

TOTAL LIVING AREA: 1,738 SQ. FT.

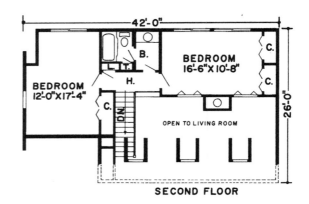

SECOND FLOOR

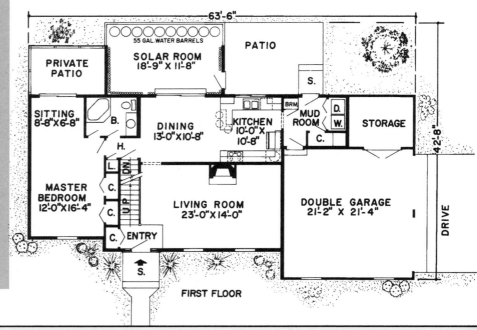

FIRST FLOOR

PRICE CODE A

THREE BEDROOM TRADITIONAL COUNTRY CAPE

No. 99022

- This plan features:
— Three bedrooms
— Two full and one half baths
- Entry area with a coat closet
- An ample Living Room with a fireplace
- A Dining Room with a view of the rear yard and located conveniently close to the Kitchen and Living Room
- A U-shaped Kitchen with a double sink, ample cabinet and counter space and a side door to the outside
- A first floor Master Suite with a private Master Bath
- Two additional, second floor bedrooms that share a full, double vanitied bath with a separate shower

FIRST FLOOR — 913 SQ. FT.
SECOND FLOOR — 581 SQ. FT.

TOTAL LIVING AREA:
1,494 SQ. FT.

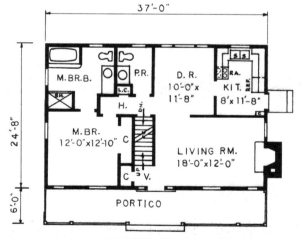

FIRST FLOOR PLAN

No materials list available

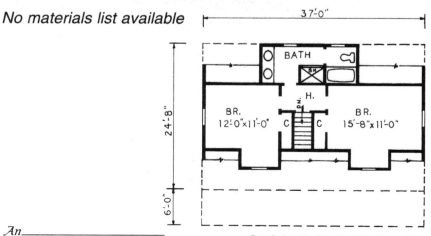

SECOND FLOOR PLAN

An
EXCLUSIVE DESIGN
By Westhome Planners, Ltd.

PRICE CODE C

TRADITIONAL ELEMENTS COMBINE IN FRIENDLY COLONIAL

No. 90606

■ This plan features:

— Four bedrooms

— Two and one half baths

■ A beautiful circular stair ascending from the central foyer and flanked by the formal Living Room and Dining Room

■ Exposed beams, wood paneling, and a brick fireplace wall in the Family Room

■ A separate dinette opening to an efficient Kitchen

FIRST FLOOR — 1,099 SQ. FT.
SECOND FLOOR — 932 SQ. FT.

TOTAL LIVING AREA:
2,031 SQ. FT.

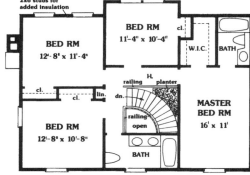

SECOND FLOOR

2x6 studs for added insulation

BED RM
12'-8" x 11'-4"

BED RM
11'-4" x 10'-4"

cl.

W.I.C.

BATH

cl.

cl.

lin.

railing

H. planter

dn.

MASTER BED RM
16' x 11'

BED RM
12'-8" x 10'-8"

railing open

BATH

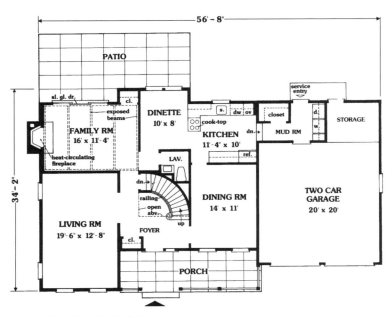

56'-8"

34'-2"

PATIO

sl. gl. dr.

cl.

exposed beams

DINETTE
10' x 8'

s.

dw ov

cook-top

closet

service entry

d.
w.

STORAGE

FAMILY RM
16' x 11'-4"

KITCHEN
11'-4" x 10'

dn.

MUD RM

heat-circulating fireplace

LAV.

ref.

dn.

railing open abv.

DINING RM
14' x 11'

TWO CAR GARAGE
20' x 20'

up

LIVING RM
19'-6" x 12'-8"

FOYER

cl.

PORCH

FIRST FLOOR

PRICE CODE E

VAULTED CEILINGS AND SKYLIT BATHS

No. 98727

- This plan features:
- — Three bedrooms
- — Three full baths with skylights
- A wrap-around country porch
- A formal Dining Room topped by a vaulted ceiling
- A first floor Master Suite that includes a walk-in closet and a full bath with double vanity
- An accommodating Swing Room that makes a perfect Den, Sewing or Guest Room
- A spacious fireplaced Family Room, divided from the Kitchen by an eating bar
- Six skylights add bright, natural light in the Sun Room
- A country Kitchen with a garden window, skylight, central cooktop island and a large walk-in pantry
- A Laundry Room with a laundry chute from the second floor

FIRST FLOOR — 2,171 SQ. FT.
SECOND FLOOR — 528 SQ. FT.

TOTAL LIVING AREA: 2,699 SQ. FT.

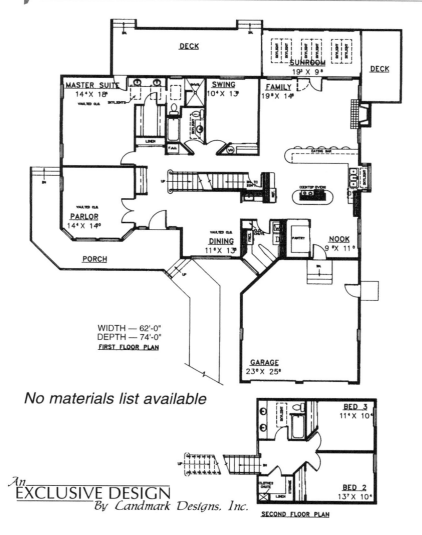

WIDTH — 62'-0"
DEPTH — 74'-0"
FIRST FLOOR PLAN

No materials list available

An
EXCLUSIVE DESIGN
By Landmark Designs, Inc.

SECOND FLOOR PLAN

PRICE CODE E

ELEGANT AND INVITING

No. 10689

■ This plan features:

— Five bedrooms

— Three and one half baths

■ Wrap-around verandas and a three-season porch

■ An elegant Parlor with a parquet floor and a formal Dining Room separated by a half-wall

■ An adjoining Kitchen with a Breakfast bar and nook

■ A Gathering Room with a fireplace, soaring ceilings and access to the porch

FIRST FLOOR — 1,580 SQ. FT.
SECOND FLOOR — 1,164 SQ. FT.
BASEMENT — 1,329 SQ. FT.
GARAGE — 576 SQ. FT.

TOTAL LIVING AREA: 2,744 SQ. FT.

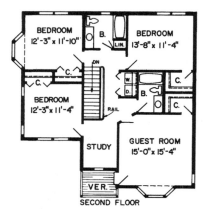

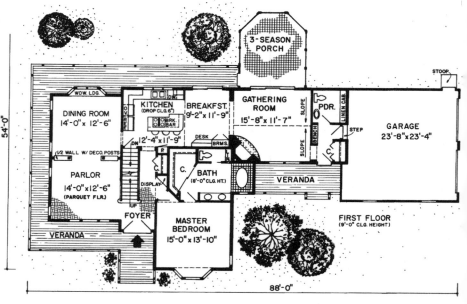

PRICE CODE D

FARMHOUSE FLAVOR

No. 20168

■ This plan features:

— Three or four bedrooms

— Two full and one half baths

■ A country-styled, three-sided porch, providing a warm welcome

■ A decorative ceiling treatment adding elegance to the formal Dining Room

■ A Den with built-in bookcases and a walk-in closet, may also be used as a fourth bedroom

■ A spacious island Kitchen with a pantry, and a cheerful Breakfast area with a decorative ceiling

■ A Sun Room highlighted by skylights and a plant shelf

■ A convenient first floor Master Suite with a skylit bath

■ Two additional bedrooms, sharing a full bath

FIRST FLOOR — 1,698 SQ. FT.
SECOND FLOOR — 601 SQ. FT.
BASEMENT — 1,681 SQ. FT.
GARAGE — 616 SQ. FT.

TOTAL LIVING AREA:
2,299 SQ. FT.

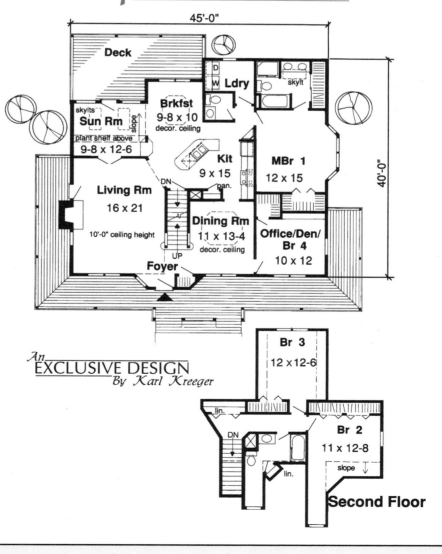

_An_ EXCLUSIVE DESIGN
By Karl Kreeger

PRICE CODE D

NINE SKYLIGHTS ADD NATURAL ILLUMINATION

No. 99780

■ This plan features:

— Three bedrooms

— Two full baths

■ Three skylights in the vaulted ceiling of the Dining Room, two skylights in the Eating Nook and four skylights in the Family Room

■ Soaring vaulted ceilings that add a feeling of openness to the Living and Dining Rooms

■ An island Kitchen with ample counter space to accommodate multiple cooks

■ A Master Bedroom with a bay window at the front and a small octagonal window at the side

■ Two bedrooms sharing a full bath

MAIN AREA — 2,564 SQ. FT.
BASEMENT — 2,564 SQ. FT.
GARAGE — 690 SQ. FT.

TOTAL LIVING AREA:
2,564 SQ. FT.

An
EXCLUSIVE DESIGN
By Landmark Designs, Inc.

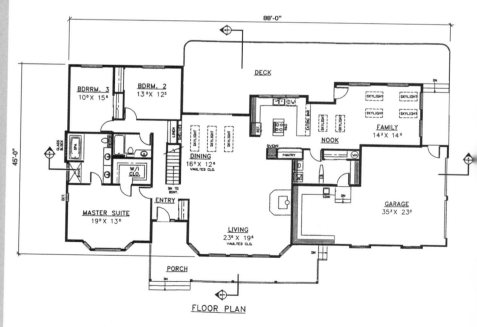

FLOOR PLAN

No materials list available

PRICE CODE C

FULL OF CHARM AND WARMTH

No. 99648

■ This plan features:

— Four bedrooms

— Two full and one half baths

■ A welcoming wrap-around porch and a covered rear porch and terrace

■ A large central Foyer directing traffic to all parts of the home

■ A formal Living Room enhanced by a bay window and seat

■ A formal Dining Room convenient to the Kitchen

■ An efficient Kitchen that includes an informal eating area

■ A fireplace adding warmth and atmosphere to the Family Room

■ An oversized Master Suite with a private Bath and a walk-in closet

■ Three additional bedrooms that share a full hall bath

FIRST FLOOR — 1,101 SQ. FT.
SECOND FLOOR — 1,065 SQ. FT.

**TOTAL LIVING AREA:
2,166 SQ. FT.**

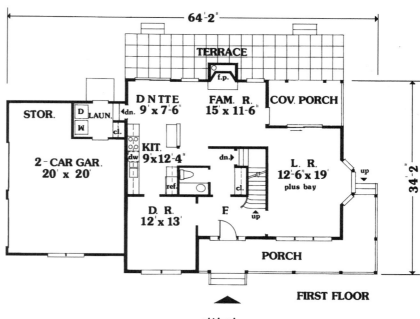

FIRST FLOOR

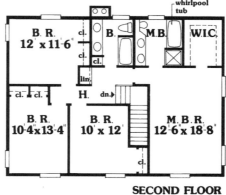

SECOND FLOOR

PRICE CODE D

No. 90424

■ This plan features:

— Three bedrooms

— Two full and one half baths

■ A covered porch in the front and a screened porch in the back to take advantage of seasonal weather

■ A Great Room with a stone fireplace that occupies the center of the home

■ An island Kitchen that flows directly into the Dining Room and the Breakfast Bay

■ A secluded Master Bedroom with a five-piece bath and his-n-her walk-in closets

■ Two upstairs bedrooms, each with plenty of closet space and private access to a shared bath

■ A slab foundation only

FIRST FLOOR — 1,535 SQ. FT.
SECOND FLOOR — 765 SQ. FT.
BASEMENT — 1,091 SQ. FT.

TOTAL LIVING AREA: 2,300 SQ. FT.

CALL THIS HOME

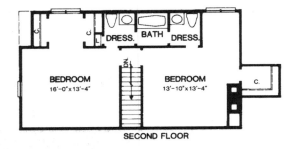

SECOND FLOOR

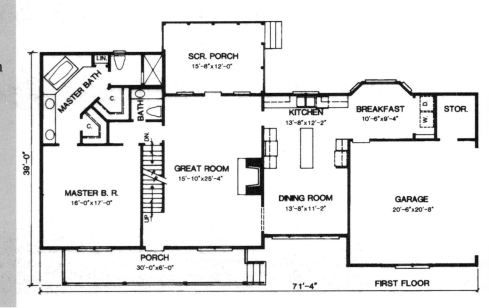

FIRST FLOOR

PRICE CODE C

A HINT OF VICTORIAN NOSTALGIA

No. 90909

- This plan features:
— Three bedrooms
— Two and one half baths
- A classic center stairwell
- A Kitchen with full bay window and built-in eating table
- A spacious Master Suite including a large walk-in closet and full bath

FIRST FLOOR — 1,206 SQ. FT.
SECOND FLOOR — 969 SQ. FT.
GARAGE — 471 SQ. FT.
BASEMENT — 1,206 SQ. FT.
WIDTH — 61'-0"
DEPTH — 44'-0"

TOTAL LIVING AREA: 2,175 SQ. FT.

An EXCLUSIVE DESIGN
By Westhome Planners, Ltd.

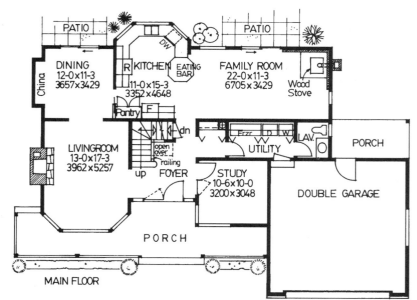

MAIN FLOOR

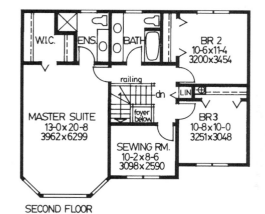

SECOND FLOOR

PRICE CODE F

No. 93321

- ■ This plan features:
- — Four bedrooms
- — Two full and one half baths
- ■ A Foyer with a vaulted ceiling, giving a great first impression
- ■ A Kitchen with a cooktop island and many built-in amenities
- ■ A Dinette with sliding glass doors to a wooden deck
- ■ A large Family Room with a beamed ceiling, bay window and a cozy fireplace
- ■ A tray ceiling in the formal Living Room, plus a fireplace
- ■ A Master Bedroom with a stepped ceiling, a double vanity private bath and a walk-in closet
- ■ Three additional bedrooms, with ample closet space, share use of a full hall Bath

FIRST FLOOR — 1,947 SQ. FT.
SECOND FLOOR — 1,390 SQ. FT.
BASEMENT — 1,947 SQ. FT.
GARAGE — 680 SQ. FT.
DECK — 322 SQ. FT.

TOTAL LIVING AREA: 3,337 SQ. FT.

TASTEFUL ELEGANCE

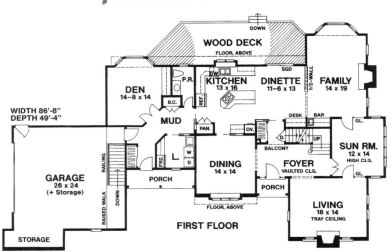

FIRST FLOOR

An EXCLUSIVE DESIGN
By Patrick Morabito, A.I.A. Architect

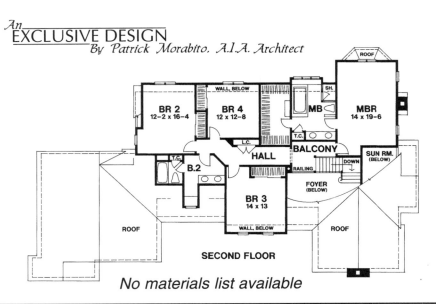

SECOND FLOOR

No materials list available

PRICE CODE D

SUITABLE FOR TODAY'S LIFESTYLE

No. 93253

■ This plan features:

— Four bedrooms

— Two full and one half baths

■ A large Family Room with a fireplace and access to the patio

■ A Breakfast Area that flows directly into the Family Room

■ A well-appointed Kitchen equipped with an eating bar, double sinks, built-in pantry and an abundance of counter and cabinet space

■ A Master Suite with a decorative ceiling and a private Bath

■ Three additional bedrooms that share a full bath

MAIN AREA — 2,542 SQ. FT.
GARAGE — 510 SQ. FT.

TOTAL LIVING AREA:
2,542 SQ. FT.

No materials list available

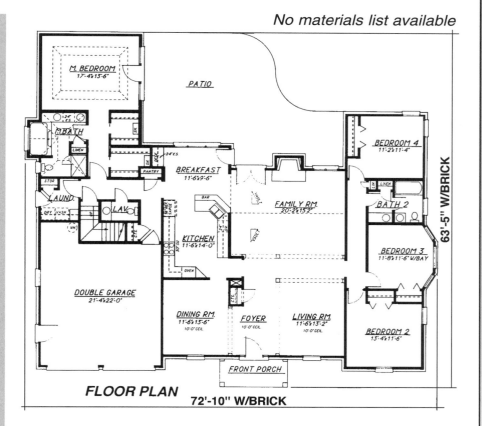

FLOOR PLAN

72'-10" W/BRICK

An
EXCLUSIVE DESIGN
By Jannis Vann & Associates, Inc.

PRICE CODE C

AN OLD-FASHIONED COUNTRY FEEL

No. 93212

■ This plan features:

— Three bedrooms

— Two and a half baths

■ A country-style porch and dormers lend charm

■ A large Living Room with a cozy fireplace

■ A formal Dining Room with a bay window and direct access to the Sun Deck

■ A sunny Breakfast Nook

■ A U-shaped Kitchen, efficiently arranged with ample work space

■ A first floor Master Suite with an elegant private bath complete with jacuzzi and a step-in shower

■ A second floor study or hobby room overlooking the deck

■ A future Bonus Room

FIRST FLOOR — 1,362 sq. ft.
SECOND FLOOR — 729 sq. ft.
BONUS ROOM — 384 sq. ft.
BASEMENT — 988 sq. ft.
GARAGE — 559 sq. ft.

TOTAL LIVING AREA:
2,091 sq. ft.

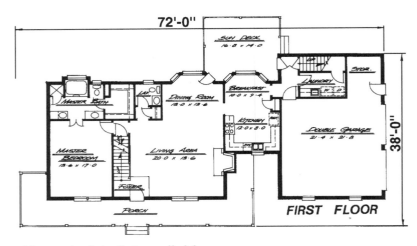

No materials list available

FIRST FLOOR

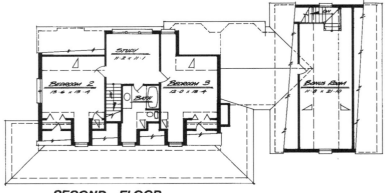

SECOND FLOOR

An
EXCLUSIVE DESIGN
By Jannis Vann & Associates, Inc.

PRICE CODE D

ROMANCE PERSONIFIED

No. 90439

■ This plan features:

— Three bedrooms

— Two full and one half baths

■ A spacious Family Room including a fireplace flanked by bookshelves

■ A sunny Breakfast Bay and adjoining country Kitchen with a peninsula counter

■ An expansive Master Suite spanning the width of the house including built-in shelves, walk-in closet, and a private bath with every amenity

■ A full bath that serves the two other bedrooms tucked into the gables at the front of the house

■ An optional basement or crawl space foundation — please specify when ordering

FIRST FLOOR — 1,366 SQ. FT.
SECOND FLOOR — 1,196 SQ. FT.
BASEMENT — 1,250 SQ. FT.
GARAGE — 484 SQ. FT.

**TOTAL LIVING AREA:
2,562 SQ. FT.**

SECOND FLOOR

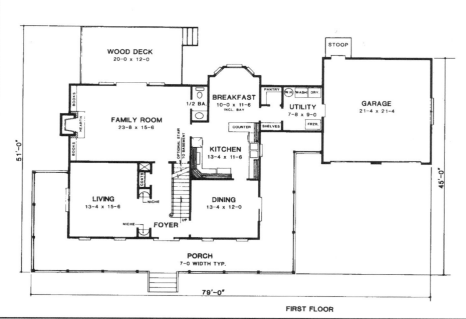

FIRST FLOOR

PRICE CODE D

COUNTRY STYLE FOR TODAY

No. 99620

■ This plan features:

— Four bedrooms

— Two full and one half baths

■ Two bay windows in the formal Living Room with a heat-circulating fireplace to enhance the mood and warmth

■ A spacious formal Dining Room with a bay window and easy access to the Kitchen

■ An octagon-shaped Dinette defined by columns, dropped beams and a bay window

■ An efficient island Kitchen with ample storage and counter space

■ A Master Suite equipped with a large whirlpool tub plus a double vanity

■ Three additional bedrooms that share a full hall bath

FIRST FLOOR — 1,132 SQ. FT.
SECOND FLOOR — 1,020 SQ. FT.
BASEMENT — 1,026 SQ. FT.
GARAGE & STORAGE — 469 SQ. FT.
LAUNDRY/MUDROOM — 60 SQ. FT.

TOTAL LIVING AREA:
2,212 SQ. FT.

FIRST FLOOR

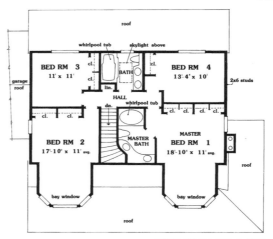

SECOND FLOOR

PRICE CODE D

ENTERTAIN WITH EASE

No. 10610

■ This plan features:

— Three bedrooms

— Two and one half baths

■ A Master Bedroom privately set with a sitting area, full bath and walk-in closet

■ An island Kitchen centered between the Dining Room and Breakfast area

■ A sunken Living Room with vaulted ceilings and a two-way fireplace

■ A covered porch and enormous deck

FIRST FLOOR — 1,818 SQ. FT.
SECOND FLOOR — 528 SQ. FT.
BASEMENT — 1,818 SQ. FT.

TOTAL LIVING AREA:
2,346 SQ. FT.

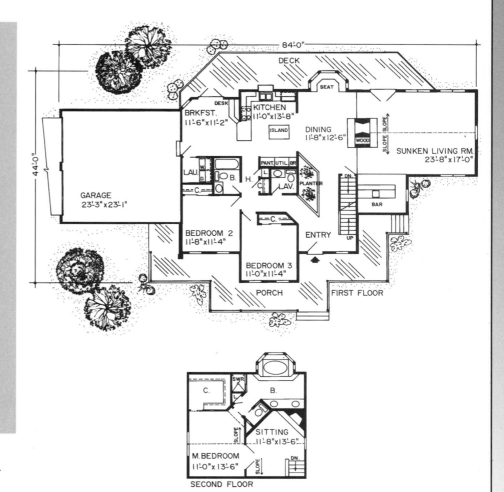

PRICE CODE C

A MAIN FLOOR MASTER RETREAT

No. 90992

- This plan features:
- — Three bedrooms
- — Two full and one half baths
- An island Kitchen with a built-in pantry, desk, double sinks, as well as ample cabinet space
- A corner gas fireplace in the Family Room for that cozy touch
- A built-in china cabinet in the Dining Room
- A second gas fireplace in the expansive Living Room
- First floor Master Bedroom with a private Master Bath
- Two additional bedrooms with dormers and window seats share a double vanity full bath
- Double garage has a workbench and an entry to both the Utility Room and the Lavatory

FIRST FLOOR — 1,306 SQ. FT.
SECOND FLOOR — 647 SQ. FT.
WIDTH — 62'-0"
DEPTH — 35'-6"

**TOTAL LIVING AREA:
1,953 SQ. FT.**

An EXCLUSIVE DESIGN
By Westhome Planners, Ltd.

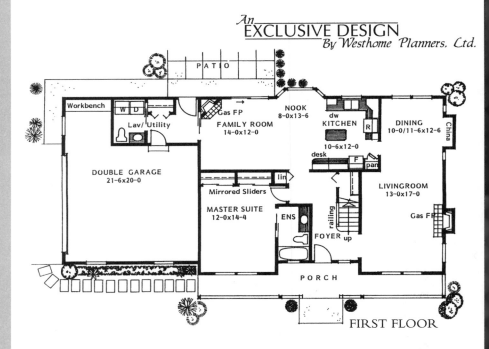

FIRST FLOOR

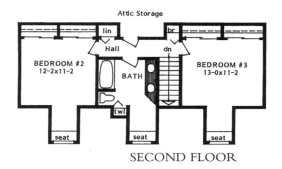

SECOND FLOOR

PRICE CODE F

BIG COUNTRY HOME HAS TRADITIONAL CHARM

No. 99239

■ This plan features:

— Three bedrooms

— Two full and two half baths

■ An elegant Living Room with a stone fireplace including an unusual Music Alcove, complete with custom built-ins for audio equipment

■ An adjoining Library having floor-to-ceiling, built-in bookcases and a second cozy fireplace

■ A formal Dining Room with a wall of windows and access to the back Porch

■ A wonderful Country Kitchen with its own fireplace, sitting/dining area, cooktop, snack bar and double sink

■ An incredible Master Suite with a large, luxurious Dressing/Bath equipped with a whirlpool tub, two vanities, an oversized shower, a walk-in closet and a wall closet

FIRST FLOOR — 2,026 SQ. FT.
SECOND FLOOR — 1,386 SQ. FT.
GARAGE — 576 SQ. FT.

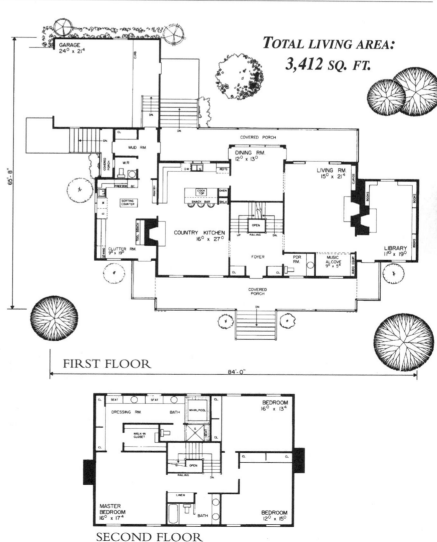

TOTAL LIVING AREA: 3,412 SQ. FT.

FIRST FLOOR

SECOND FLOOR

PRICE CODE D

TRADITIONAL FARMHOUSE

No. 99626

- This plan features:

— Four bedrooms

— Two full and one half baths

- A decorative circular stairway enhancing the Foyer

- A heat-circulating fireplace in both the Family Room and the formal Living Room

- An efficient, well-appointed Kitchen with a built-in pantry, double sinks and ample cabinet and counter space

- A Master Suite equipped with a walk-in closet, and a large Master Bath

- Three additional bedrooms that share a full hall bath

FIRST FLOOR — 1,183 SQ. FT.
SECOND FLOOR — 1,103 SQ. FT.
BASEMENT — 1,116 SQ. FT.
GARAGE & STORAGE — 467 SQ. FT.
PORCHES — 283 SQ. FT.

**TOTAL LIVING AREA:
2,286 SQ. FT.**

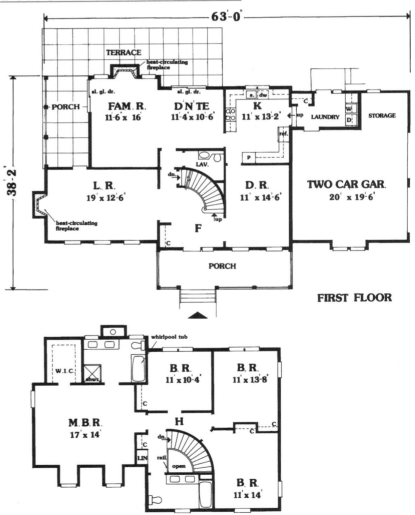

FIRST FLOOR

SECOND FLOOR

PRICE CODE B

FIREPLACE EQUIPPED FAMILY ROOM

An
EXCLUSIVE DESIGN
By Marshall Associates

No. 24326

■ This plan features:

— Four bedrooms

— Two full baths and one half bath

■ A lovely front porch shading the entrance

■ A spacious Living Room that opens into the Dining Area which flows into the efficient Kitchen

■ A Family Room equipped with a cozy fireplace and sliding glass doors to a patio

■ A Master Suite with a large walk-in closet and a private bath with a step-in shower

■ Three additional bedrooms that share a full hall bath

FIRST FLOOR — 692 SQ. FT.
SECOND FLOOR — 813 SQ. FT.
BASEMENT — 699 SQ. FT.
GARAGE — 484 SQ. FT.

TOTAL LIVING AREA:
1,505 SQ. FT.

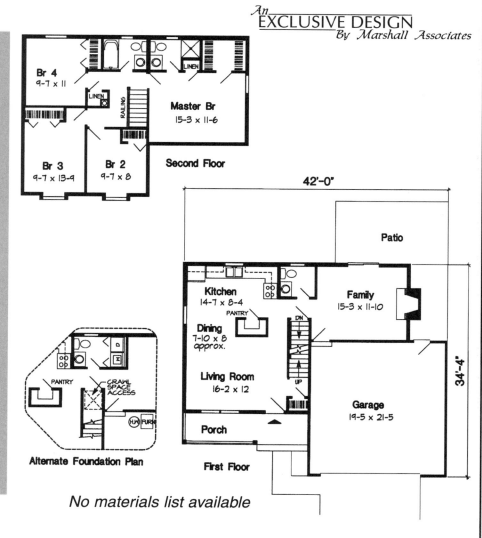

Second Floor

Alternate Foundation Plan

First Floor

No materials list available

PRICE CODE D

QUALITY COUNTRY LIVING

No. 99640

■ This plan features:

— Four bedrooms

— Two full and two half baths

■ A typical farmhouse front porch

■ A spacious central Foyer

■ A sunken formal living room, with a fireplace, a large windowed bay and a stepped ceiling

■ Dining Room with angled interior corners to form an octagon

■ A Kitchen with a central island

■ A second fireplace enhancing the Family Room

■ A Master Bedroom suite, with a large windowed bay sitting area, a walk-in closet, two additional linear closets and a deluxe bath

■ Three bedrooms share the full double vanity hall bath

■ A Studio area above the garage that includes a half-bath

FIRST FLOOR — 1,217 SQ. FT.
SECOND FLOOR — 1,249 SQ. FT.
BASEMENT — 1,249 SQ. FT.
GARAGE — 431 SQ. FT.

TOTAL LIVING AREA:
2,466 SQ. FT.

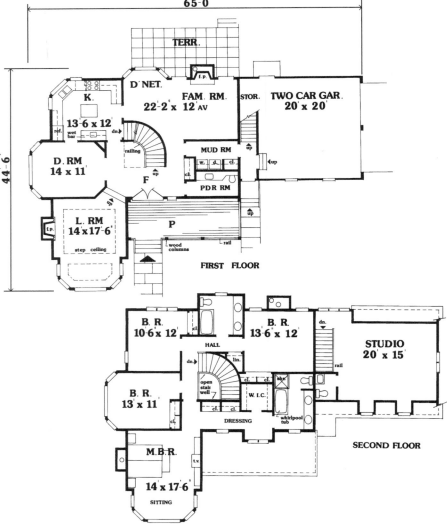

PRICE CODE D

TIMELESS COUNTRY HOME UPDATED

No. 93137

■ This plan features:

— Four bedrooms

— Two full and one half baths

■ A welcoming Foyer with a large coat closet

■ A formal Living Room and Dining Room flanking the Foyer, allowing for ease in entertaining

■ An open layout between the Kitchen, Nook and Family Room

■ Rich, ceramic tile throughout the Foyer, Kitchen areas, Sunroom and Baths

■ An efficient island Kitchen in close proximity to the Nook and the Dining Room

■ A bright Sun Room

■ An owner's retreat created by the lavish Master Suite

■ Three additional bedrooms that share a double vanity, and a compartmented bath

FIRST FLOOR — 1,333 SQ. FT.
SECOND FLOOR — 1,158 SQ. FT.

**TOTAL LIVING AREA:
2,491 SQ. FT.**

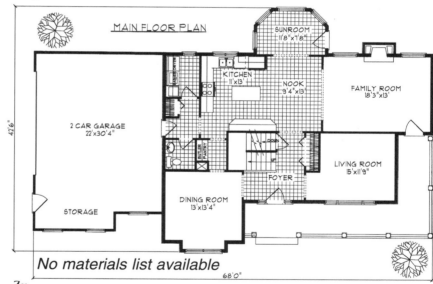

MAIN FLOOR PLAN

SUNROOM 11'8"x7'8"

KITCHEN 11'x13'

NOOK 9'4"x13'

FAMILY ROOM 18'3"x13'

2 CAR GARAGE 22'x30'4"

42'6"

STORAGE

BUTLER PANTRY

DOWN

LIVING ROOM 15'x11'9"

FOYER

DINING ROOM 13'x13'4"

No materials list available

68'0"

An **EXCLUSIVE DESIGN** *By Ahmann Design Inc.*

SECOND FLOOR PLAN

BEDROOM #3 10'6"x11'8"

BEDROOM #2 10'4"x11'8"

LINEN

DOWN

MASTER BEDROOM 15'x19'0"

OPEN TO FOYER

BEDROOM #4 13'x13'6"

PRICE CODE B

RUSTIC CHARMER

No. 90401

- This plan features:
— Three bedrooms
— Two full baths

- A first floor Master Suite with a large walk-in closet and a double vanity Master Bath

- An L-shaped Kitchen, well-equipped and efficiently laid out, flowing easily into a bayed Dining Room

- A Living Room with a raised-hearth fireplace to add warmth and a cozy atmosphere

- A second floor with two bedrooms, both with large walk-in closets

- An optional basement or crawl space foundation — please specify when ordering

FIRST FLOOR — 1,100 SQ. FT.
SECOND FLOOR — 660 SQ. FT.

**TOTAL LIVING AREA:
1,760 SQ. FT**

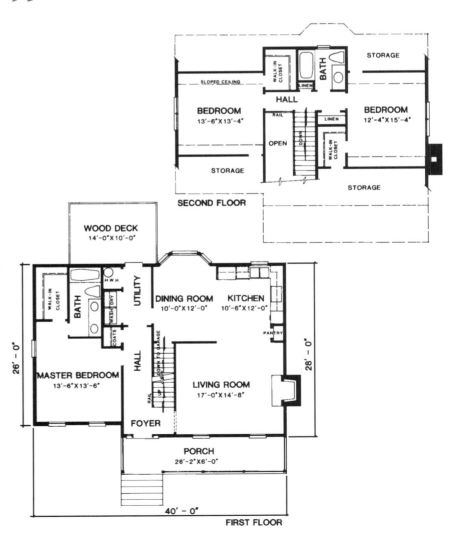

PRICE CODE C

Built in entertainment center for family fun

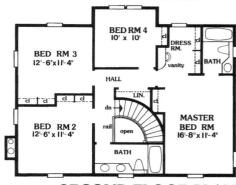

SECOND FLOOR PLAN

- BED RM 4 — 10' x 10'
- DRESS RM.
- vanity
- BATH
- BED RM 3 — 12'-6" x 11'-4"
- HALL
- LIN.
- cl
- dn
- rail — open
- MASTER BED RM — 16'-8" x 11'-4"
- BED RM 2 — 12'-6" x 11'-4"
- BATH

No. 90615

■ This plan features:

— Four bedrooms

— Two and one half baths

■ A heat-circulating fireplace in the Living Room framed by decorative pilasters that support dropped beams

■ A convenient mudroom providing access to the two-car Garage

■ A spacious Master Suite with a separate dressing area

■ An optional slab foundation

FIRST FLOOR — 1,094 SQ. FT.
SECOND FLOOR — 936 SQ. FT.
GARAGE — 441 SQ. FT.

TOTAL LIVING AREA:
2,030 SQ. FT.

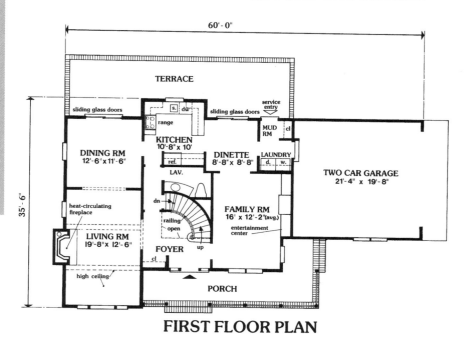

60'-0"

35'-6"

- TERRACE
- sliding glass doors
- s. dw
- range
- sliding glass doors
- service entry
- MUD RM
- cl
- KITCHEN — 10'-8" x 10'
- DINING RM — 12'-6" x 11'-6"
- ref.
- DINETTE — 8'-8" x 8'-8"
- LAUNDRY — d. w.
- TWO CAR GARAGE — 21'-4" x 19'-8"
- LAV.
- heat-circulating fireplace
- dn
- railing open
- FAMILY RM — 16' x 12'-2" (avg.)
- entertainment center
- LIVING RM — 19'-8" x 12'-6"
- FOYER
- up
- cl
- high ceiling
- PORCH

FIRST FLOOR PLAN

PRICE CODE D

VAULTED CEILINGS IN THE LIVING ROOM AND MASTER SUITE

No. 24269

■ This plan features:

— Three or four bedrooms

— Two full and one half baths

■ A vaulted ceiling in the Living Room adding to its spaciousness

■ A formal Dining Room with easy access to both the Living Room and the Kitchen

■ An efficient Kitchen with double sinks, and ample storage and counter space

■ An informal Eating Nook with a built-in pantry

■ A Master Suite with a vaulted ceiling and luxurious Master Bath and two walk-in closets

■ Two additional bedrooms share a full bath

FIRST FLOOR — 1,115 SQ. FT.
SECOND FLOOR — 1,129 SQ. FT.
BASEMENT — 1,096 SQ. FT.
GARAGE — 415 SQ. FT.

**TOTAL LIVING AREA:
2,244 SQ. FT.**

No materials list available

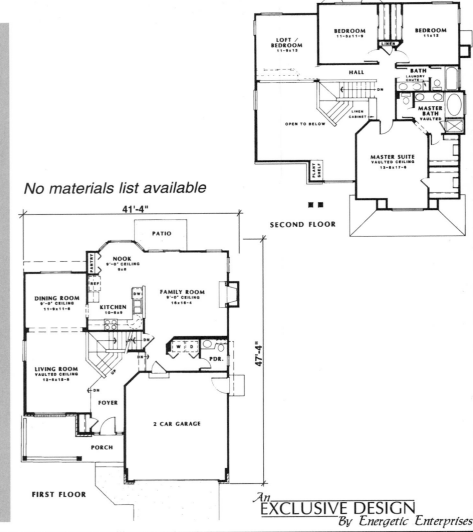

An
EXCLUSIVE DESIGN
By Energetic Enterprises

PRICE CODE E

LARGE WRAP-AROUND PORCH ADDS A TOUCH OF COUNTRY

No. 24403

■ This plan features:

— Three or four bedrooms

— Three full baths

■ A large welcoming, wrap-around porch adding an old-fashioned country feel

■ An elegant Dining Room topped by a decorative ceiling treatment

■ An expansive Family Room equipped with a massive fireplace with built-in bookshelves

■ An informal Breakfast Room conveniently enhanced by a built-in planning desk

■ Peninsula counter, a built-in pantry, and ample counter and cabinet space in the Kitchen

■ Two additional bedrooms sharing a full, compartmented hall bath

FIRST FLOOR — 1,378 SQ. FT.
SECOND FLOOR — 1,269 SQ. FT.
BASEMENT — 1,378 SQ. FT.
GARAGE — 717 SQ. FT.
PORCH — 801 SQ. FT.

TOTAL LIVING AREA:
2,647 SQ. FT.

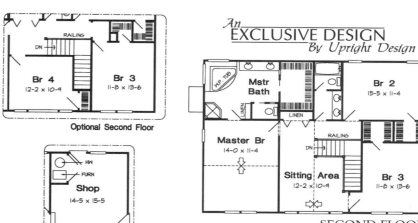

Br 4
12-2 x 10-9

Br 3
11-8 x 13-6

RAILING

DN

Optional Second Floor

Shop
14-5 x 15-5

HM

FURN

Crawl Space/Slab Option

An EXCLUSIVE DESIGN *By Upright Design*

Mstr Bath

W.P. TUB

LINEN

Br 2
15-5 x 11-4

LINEN

Master Br
14-0 x 11-4

RAILING

DN

Sitting Area
12-2 x 10-9

Br 3
11-8 x 13-6

SECOND FLOOR

No materials list available

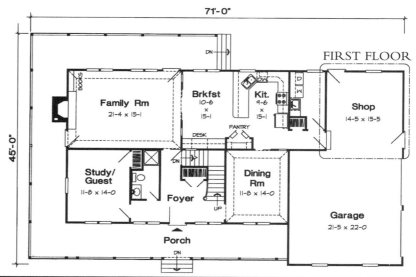

71'-0"

45'-0"

DN

FIRST FLOOR

BOOKS

Family Rm
21-4 x 15-1

Brkfst
10-6 x 15-1

Kit.
9-6 x 15-1

DW

Shop
14-5 x 15-5

PANTRY

DESK

Study/Guest
11-8 x 14-0

DN

Foyer

UP

Dining Rm
11-8 x 14-0

Garage
21-5 x 22-0

Porch

DN

An
EXCLUSIVE DESIGN
By Patrick Morabito, A.I.A. Architect

PRICE CODE E

No. 93335

■ This plan features:

— Four bedrooms

— Two full and one half baths

■ A sheltered Entry with welcoming sidelights, and an open Foyer with a landing staircase

■ A formal Dining Room crowned by a stepped ceiling, accenting its unique shape

■ A cozy, quiet Den with built-in book shelves, offering an at-home office

■ An expansive Great Room, with a tray ceiling accenting a two-way fireplace and windows on three sides, with an atrium door to deck

■ A private Master Suite equipped with a lavish Bath, including a corner window, whirlpool tub, a double vanity and two walk-in closets

■ Three additional bedrooms, on the second floor, with ample closet space, sharing a large hall bath

FIRST FLOOR — 2,164 SQ. FT.
SECOND FLOOR — 773 SQ. FT.

TOTAL LIVING AREA:
2,937 SQ. FT.

DECORATIVE CEILINGS ENHANCE INTERIOR

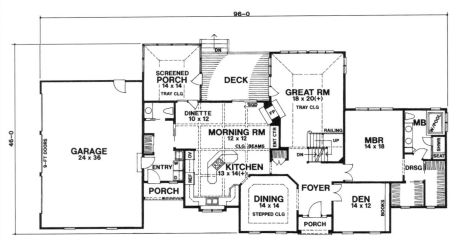

No materials list available

FIRST FLOOR

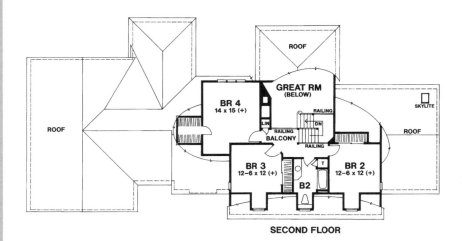

SECOND FLOOR

PRICE CODE E

No. 10628

■ This plan features:

— Three bedrooms

— Two full and one half baths

■ Shutter-trimmed, double hung windows, clapboard and brick siding, and a central entry flanked by side lights

■ Traditionally located formal Dining and Living Rooms, on either side of the entry

■ A spacious Kitchen/Dinette area with an island/breakfast bar, a pantry and ample counter and storage space

■ A beamed ceiling Family Room, with a fireplace that boasts built-in bookshelves and a charming window seat

■ A second floor Master Suite featuring a walk-in closet, raised tub and a separate shower

■ Two additional roomy bedrooms sharing a second full bath

FIRST FLOOR — 1,757 SQ. FT.
SECOND FLOOR — 1,075 SQ. FT.
BASEMENT — 1,757 SQ. FT.

**TOTAL LIVING AREA:
2,832 SQ. FT.**

A CAPE FOR THE COUNTRY

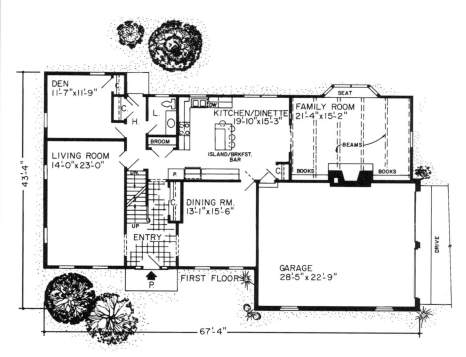

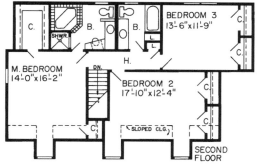

PRICE CODE D

COVERED PORCH ADDS CURB APPEAL

No. 91073

■ This plan features:

— Three bedrooms

— Two and one half baths

■ A large Living Room enhanced by a fireplace and an open entry to the formal Dining Room

■ An efficient L-shaped Kitchen with cooktop island and open layout to the Family Room and Nook area creating a feeling of spaciousness

■ Two generously sized bedrooms that share a full bath

■ A Master Suite that includes a walk-in closet and spa tub with garden windows

■ A large Bonus Room for you to decide on

FIRST FLOOR — 1,240 SQ. FT.
SECOND FLOOR — 969 SQ. FT.
BONUS ROOM — 254 SQ. FT.
GARAGE — 550 SQ. FT.

**TOTAL LIVING AREA:
2,209 SQ. FT.**

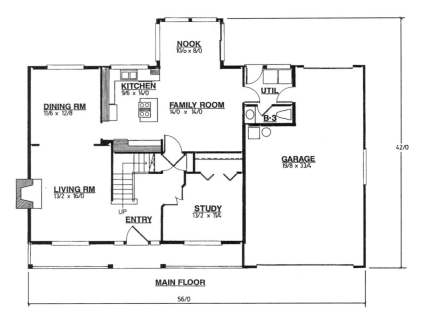

MAIN FLOOR

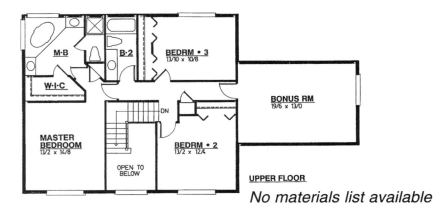

UPPER FLOOR

No materials list available

PRICE CODE D

COUNTRY STYLE FOR TODAY

No. 91700

- This plan features:
- — Three bedrooms
- — Two full and one half baths
- A wide wrap-around porch for a farmhouse style
- A spacious Living Room with double doors and a large front window
- A garden window over the double sink in the huge, country Kitchen with two islands, one a butcher block, and the other an eating bar
- A corner fireplace in the Family Room enjoyed throughout the Nook and Kitchen, thanks to an open layout
- A Master Suite with a spa tub, and a huge walk-in closet as well as a shower and double vanities

FIRST FLOOR — 1,785 SQ. FT.
SECOND FLOOR — 621 SQ. FT.

TOTAL LIVING AREA:
2,406 SQ. FT.

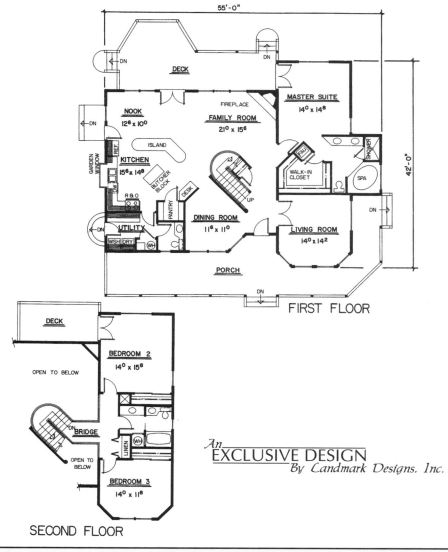

An
EXCLUSIVE DESIGN
By Landmark Designs, Inc.

RANCH WITH EVERYTHING

No. 20187

■ This plan features:

— Three bedrooms

— Two full baths

■ A decorative ceiling in the elegant formal Dining Room

■ A well-appointed Kitchen with built-in pantry, ample counter space and peninsula island that separates the Kitchen from the Breakfast room

■ A Living Room, with easy access to the deck, made cozy by a fireplace

■ A Master Bedroom with private Master Bath and walk-in closet

■ Two additional bedrooms that share a full hall bath

MAIN AREA — 1,416 SQ. FT.
BASEMENT — 1,416 SQ. FT.
GARAGE — 484 SQ. FT.

TOTAL LIVING AREA:
1,416 SQ. FT.

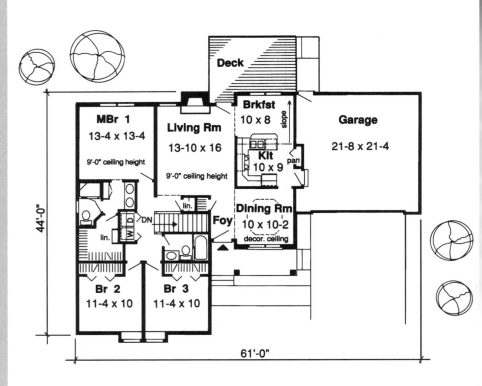

An
EXCLUSIVE DESIGN
By Karl Kreeger

PRICE CODE C

COZY HOMESTEAD

No. 24651

- This plan features:
— Three bedrooms
— Two full baths
- Multi-paned windows and a country porch
- A spacious Living Room, enhanced by the natural light and the fireplace with built-in book-shelves flanking one side
- An efficient U-shaped Kitchen, located next to the Dining Room, with a walk-in pantry, double sink and a Breakfast Nook
- A convenient first floor Laundry Room
- Private Master Suite with a whirlpool tub, separate shower, walk-in closet and tray ceiling
- Two additional bedrooms are located at the opposite side of the home and share a full hall bath with a skylight

MAIN AREA — 1,821 SQ. FT.
GARAGE — 1,075 SQ. FT.
BASEMENT — 742 SQ. FT.

**TOTAL LIVING AREA:
1,821 SQ. FT.**

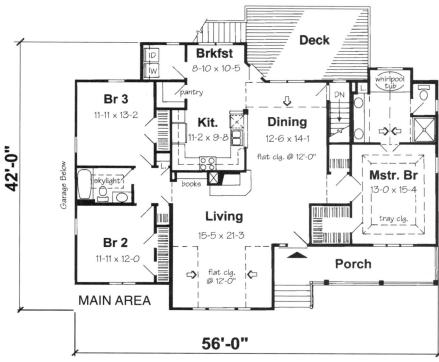

No materials list available

An
EXCLUSIVE DESIGN
By Plan One Homes, Inc.

PRICE CODE C

VARIED ROOF LINES ADD INTEREST

No. 93255

■ This plan features:

— Three bedrooms

— Two full and one half baths

■ A modern, convenient floor plan

■ Formal areas located at the front of the home

■ A decorative ceiling in the Dining Room

■ Columns accenting the Living Room

■ A large Family Room with a cozy fireplace and direct access to the deck

■ An efficient Kitchen located between the formal Dining Room and the informal Breakfast Room

■ A private Master Suite that includes a Master Bath and walk-in closet

■ Two additional bedrooms that share a full hall bath

MAIN AREA — 2,192 SQ. FT.
BASEMENT — 2,192 SQ. FT.
GARAGE — 564 SQ. FT.

TOTAL LIVING AREA:
2,192 SQ. FT.

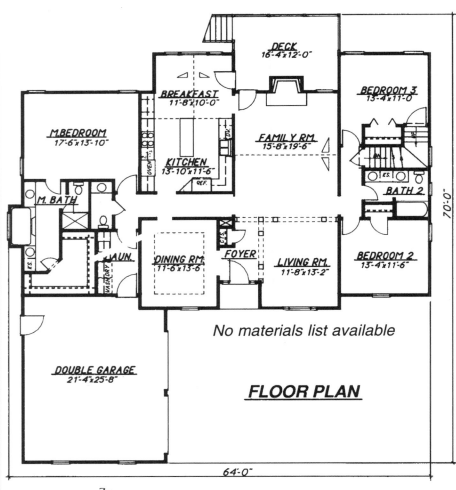

No materials list available

FLOOR PLAN

An
EXCLUSIVE DESIGN
By Jannis Vann & Associates, Inc.

PRICE CODE C

HOMEY COUNTRY PORCH

No. 24325

■ This plan features:

— Three bedrooms

— Two full and one half baths

■ A spacious Living Room with a cozy fireplace, triple front window and atrium door to Patio

■ A Family Room flowing into the Dining Room and Kitchen creates a comfortable gathering space

■ An efficient Kitchen including a peninsula counter, double sink, walk-in pantry and broom closet

■ A Master Suite with a walk-in closet, private Bath and a built-in audio/video center

■ A Laundry Room ideally located near the bedrooms

■ Two additional bedrooms that share a full hall bath

FIRST FLOOR — 908 SQ. FT.
SECOND FLOOR — 908 SQ. FT.
GARAGE — 462 SQ. FT.

TOTAL LIVING AREA:
1,816 SQ. FT.

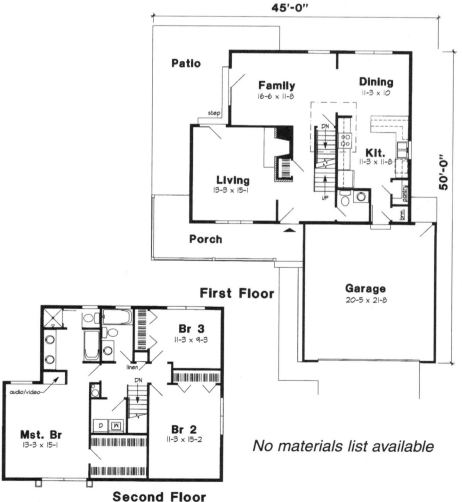

No materials list available

An
EXCLUSIVE DESIGN
By Marshall Associates

PRICE CODE B

OLD-FASHIONED COUNTRY PORCH

No. 93219

- ■ This plan features:
- — Three bedrooms
- — Two full and one half baths
- ■ A Traditional front Porch, with matching dormers above and a garage hidden below, leading into a open, contemporary layout
- ■ A Living Area with a cozy fireplace visible from the Dining Room for warm entertaining
- ■ A U-shaped, efficient Kitchen featuring a corner, double sink and pass-thru to the Dining Room
- ■ A convenient half bath with a laundry center on the first floor
- ■ A spacious, first floor Master Suite with a lavish Bath including a double vanity, walk-in closet and an oval, corner window tub
- ■ Two large bedrooms with dormer windows

FIRST FLOOR — 1,057 SQ. FT.
SECOND FLOOR — 611 SQ. FT.
BASEMENT — 511 SQ. FT.
GARAGE — 546 SQ. FT.

TOTAL LIVING AREA:
1,668 SQ. FT.

FIRST FLOOR

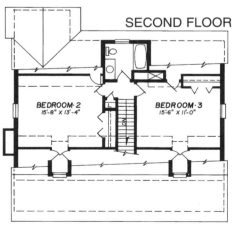

SECOND FLOOR

An
EXCLUSIVE DESIGN
By Jannis Vann & Associates, Inc.

PRICE CODE E

COUNTRY STYLE

No. 91750

■ This plan features:

— Four bedrooms

— Three full and one half baths

■ Easily adaptable for wheelchair accessibility

■ A cozy fireplace with a built-in wood box and bookshelves

■ A walk-in pantry, a Nook area, a cooktop island, and a corner double sink in the Kitchen

■ A spacious Family Room brightened by three skylights

■ A private Master Suite with two walk-in closets, a compartmented bath with a spa tub and a step-in shower

■ Two additional bedrooms with walk-in closets and private baths

■ Hobby Room/Office located off garage

MAIN AREA — 3,188 SQ. FT.
COVERED PORCH — 560 SQ. FT.
DECK — 324 SQ. FT.
GARAGE — 705 SQ. FT.
WIDTH — 84'-0"
DEPTH — 73'-6"

**TOTAL LIVING AREA:
3,188 SQ. FT.**

An EXCLUSIVE DESIGN
By Landmark Designs, Inc.

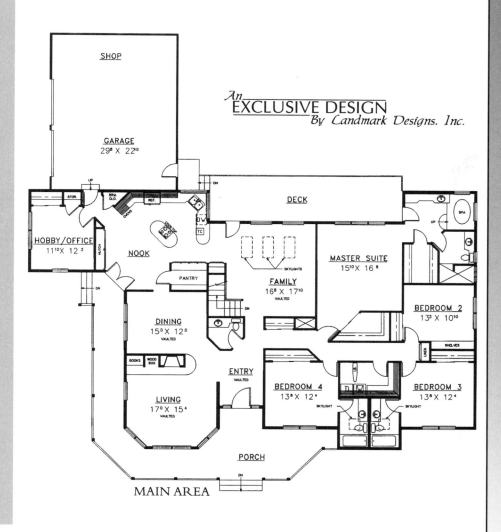

MAIN AREA

PRICE CODE C

HORIZONTAL DIMENSION

No. 99629

■ This plan features:

— Three bedrooms

— Two full and one half baths

■ A country farmhouse porch welcoming visitors

■ A large spacious Living Room with a cathedral ceiling flowing into the formal Dining Room

■ A spacious Family Room highlighted by a decorative heat-circulating fireplace and sliding glass doors to the deck

■ An U-shaped Kitchen, with lots of storage space, divides the Dinette with a peninsula counter

■ An informal Dinette Area graced by a handsome bay window

■ A Master Suite with three closets and a bath with a whirlpool tub

■ Two additional bedrooms sharing the full hall bath

MAIN AREA — 1,918 SQ. FT.
BASEMENT — 1,984 SQ. FT.
GARAGE — 706 SQ. FT.

TOTAL LIVING AREA:
1,918 SQ. FT.

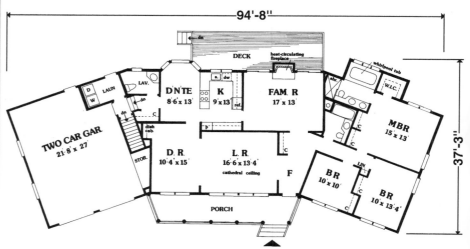

FLOOR PLAN

PRICE CODE E

A HINT OF COUNTRY STYLING

No. 98729

■ This plan features:

— Three bedrooms

— Two and a half baths

■ A wrap-around covered porch

■ A first floor Master Suite with a vaulted ceiling, front bay window, private bath and walk-in closet

■ A vast Living/Dining Room area enhanced by three skylights, a fireplace, and direct access to the rear deck

■ A U-shaped Kitchen with Nook Area, topped by a vaulted ceiling and equipped with a walk-in pantry

■ A Family Room with direct access to the patio and hot tub

■ Two additional bedrooms sharing a full bath on the lower level

■ A second floor Bonus Room for future expansion

MAIN AREA — 1,577 SQ. FT.
UPPER AREA — 1,090 SQ. FT.

TOTAL LIVING AREA:
2,667 SQ. FT.

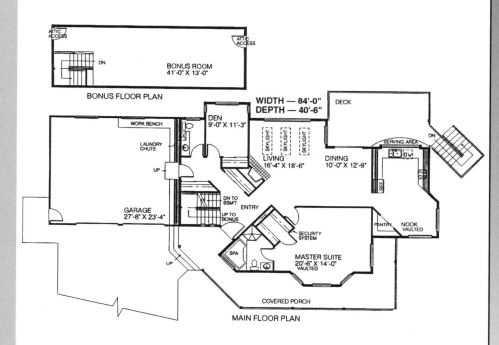

An
EXCLUSIVE DESIGN
By Landmark Designs, Inc.

PRICE CODE D

PLENTY OF SPACE FOR THE ACTIVE FAMILY

No. 98730

■ This plan features:

— Four bedrooms

— Three full baths

■ A bright Living Room with a vaulted ceiling

■ A country Kitchen stocked with built-in ovens, pantry, cooktop, garden window and an eating bar

■ A built-in hutch that also serves as a buffet in the Dining Room

■ A spacious family room leads to the rear deck

■ Lots of built-in storage space

■ A Guest Suite with a private bath

■ A luxurious Master Suite with a fireplace, vanity, spa, skylights, twin vanities and a conveniently located security system

■ Two secondary bedrooms sharing use of the twin basin, hall bath

■ A three car Garage with a workbench and sink

MAIN AREA — 2,596 SQ. FT.
GARAGE — 1,037 SQ. FT.

TOTAL LIVING AREA:
2,596 SQ. FT.

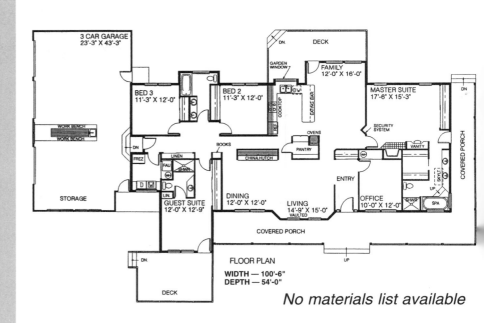

No materials list available

An
EXCLUSIVE DESIGN
By Candmark Designs, Inc.

PRICE CODE B

No. 98742

- ■ This plan features:
- — Three bedrooms
- — Two full baths
- ■ Covered porch and rear deck
- ■ A Foyer area with a convenient coat closet
- ■ Vaulted ceiling in the Nook with bay windows and natural illumination
- ■ A uniquely-designed Kitchen with a walk-in pantry, access to formal the Dining area and Nook
- ■ A focal point fireplace with windows on either side in the Living Room
- ■ A large walk-in closet, linen closet and a full private Bath highlight the Master Suite
- ■ Two additional bedrooms that share a full compartmented Bath
- ■ Two-car garage
- ■ Utility/Mud Room located between the Garage and Kitchen

MAIN AREA — 1,664 SQ. FT.

TOTAL LIVING AREA:
1,664 SQ. FT.

GAZEBO SHAPED NOOK

No materials list available

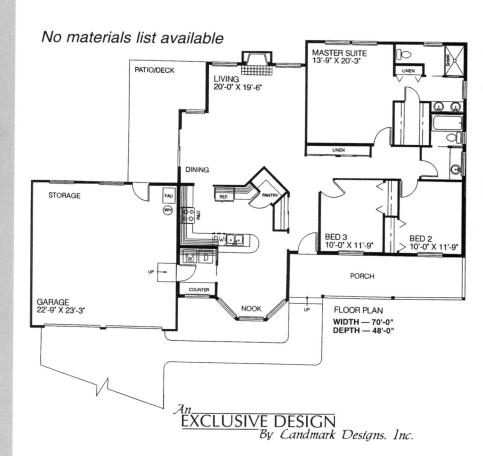

FLOOR PLAN
WIDTH — 70'-0"
DEPTH — 48'-0"

An
EXCLUSIVE DESIGN
By Landmark Designs, Inc.

PRICE CODE E

ROOM FOR A LARGE FAMILY

No. 24401

■ This plan features:

— Four or five bedrooms

— Three full baths

■ Tray ceilings in the formal Living Room and the Dining Room giving a touch of elegance to the rooms

■ An efficient Kitchen with a peninsula eating bar and a double sink

■ A cathedral ceiling in the Master Bedroom giving an air of spaciousness

■ A Master Bath with whirlpool tub, double vanities and a step-in shower

■ Three additional bedrooms share a full hall bath

FIRST FLOOR — 1,486 SQ. FT.
SECOND FLOOR — 1,213 SQ. FT.
GARAGE — 514 SQ. FT.

**TOTAL LIVING AREA:
2,699 SQ. FT.**

An EXCLUSIVE DESIGN
By Upright Design

First Floor

No materials list available

Second Floor

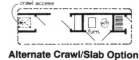

Alternate Crawl/Slab Option

PRICE CODE C

FROM TIMES GONE BY

No. 24301

■ This plan features:

— Four bedrooms

— Two and one half baths

■ A Family Room opening to a large deck in rear

■ A Master Bedroom with a private bath and ample closet space

■ A large Living Room with a bay window

■ A modern Kitchen with many amenities

FIRST FLOOR — 987 SQ. FT.
SECOND FLOOR — 970 SQ. FT.
BASEMENT — 985 SQ. FT.

TOTAL LIVING AREA:
1,957 SQ. FT.

An
EXCLUSIVE DESIGN
By Marshall Associates

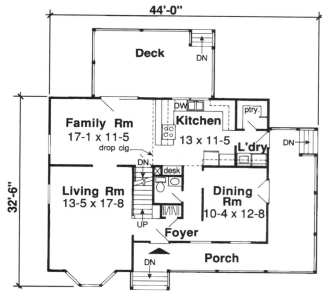

44'-0"

32'-6"

Deck
DN

Family Rm
17-1 x 11-5
drop clg.

Kitchen
13 x 11-5

DW ptry.

L'dry DN

Living Rm
13-5 x 17-8

DN
desk
UP

Dining Rm
10-4 x 12-8

Foyer

DN Porch

FIRST FLOOR

Br 2
11-1 x 11
lin.

Br 3
10-10 x 11

DN
railing

MBr
13-5 x 15

Br 4
13-1 x 10-10

SECOND FLOOR

PRICE CODE C

CURBSIDE APPEAL

No. 91069

■ This plan features:

— Three bedrooms

— Three full and one half baths

■ An attractive corner porch and a rear deck

■ A Great Room with double doors leading to the rear deck

■ A bright bayed Eating Nook for informal meals

■ A peninsula counter, double sink and ample counter and storage space in the Kitchen

■ A private Den area perfect for secluded study or late night work

■ A spacious Master Suite equipped with a walk-in closet, a spa tub, a double vanity and a step-in shower

■ Two roomy bedrooms that share a full, double vanity hall bath

■ Direct entrance from the garage

FIRST FLOOR — 1,059 SQ. FT.
SECOND FLOOR — 938 SQ. FT.

TOTAL LIVING AREA: 1,997 SQ. FT.

MAIN FLOOR PLAN

No materials list available

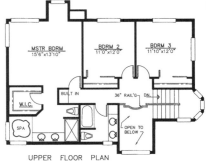

UPPER FLOOR PLAN

PRICE CODE B

COUNTRY STYLE AND CHARM

No. 91731

■ This plan features:

— Three bedrooms

— Two full baths

■ Brick accents, front facing gable, and railed wrap-around covered porch

■ A built-in range and oven in a dog-leg shaped Kitchen

■ A Nook with garage access for convenient unloading of groceries and other supplies

■ A bay window wrapping around the front of the formal Living Room

■ A Master Suite with French doors opening to the deck

MAIN AREA — 1,775 SQ. FT.
GARAGE — 681 SQ. FT.
WIDTH — 51'-6"
DEPTH — 65'-0"

**TOTAL LIVING AREA:
1,775 SQ. FT.**

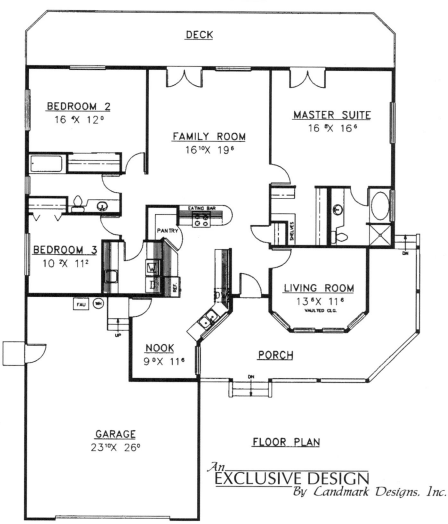

DECK

BEDROOM 2
16⁴X 12⁰

FAMILY ROOM
16¹⁰X 19⁶

MASTER SUITE
16⁸X 16⁶

EATING BAR

PANTRY

BEDROOM 3
10²X 11²

SHELVES

DN

LIVING ROOM
13⁶X 11⁶
VAULTED CLG.

FAU WH

UP

NOOK
9⁰X 11⁶

PORCH

DN

GARAGE
23¹⁰X 26⁰

FLOOR PLAN

An EXCLUSIVE DESIGN
By Landmark Designs, Inc.

PRICE CODE E

RELAX ON THE VERANDA

No. 91749

- ◼ This plan features:
- — Four bedrooms
- — Three full and one half baths
- ◼ A wrap-around veranda
- ◼ A sky-lit Master Suite with elevated custom spa, twin basins, a walk-in closet, and an extra vanity outside the bathroom
- ◼ A vaulted ceiling in the Den
- ◼ A fireplace in both the Family Room and the formal Living Room
- ◼ An efficient Kitchen with a peninsula counter and a double sink
- ◼ Two additional bedrooms with walk-in closets, served by a compartmentalized bath
- ◼ A Guest Suite with a private bath

MAIN AREA — 3,051 SQ. FT.
GARAGE — 646 SQ. FT.

TOTAL LIVING AREA:
3,051 SQ. FT.

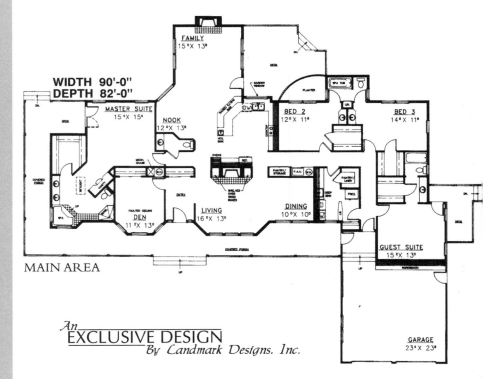

MAIN AREA

WIDTH 90'-0"
DEPTH 82'-0"

An
EXCLUSIVE DESIGN
By Landmark Designs, Inc.

PRICE CODE C

CONTEMPORARY WITH OLD-COUNTRY PORCH

No. 91757

■ This plan features:

— Three bedrooms

— Two and one half baths

■ A fireplaced Parlor with a built-in wood storage area

■ A Kitchen with a peninsula eating bar that runs into the Nook area

■ A vaulted ceiling in the fireplaced Family Room

■ A private, first floor Master Suite with a Master Bath and walk-in closet

FIRST FLOOR — 1,553 SQ. FT.
SECOND FLOOR — 531 SQ. FT.
GARAGE — 600 SQ. FT.
WIDTH — 55'-0"
DEPTH — 64'-0"

TOTAL LIVING AREA:
2,084 SQ. FT.

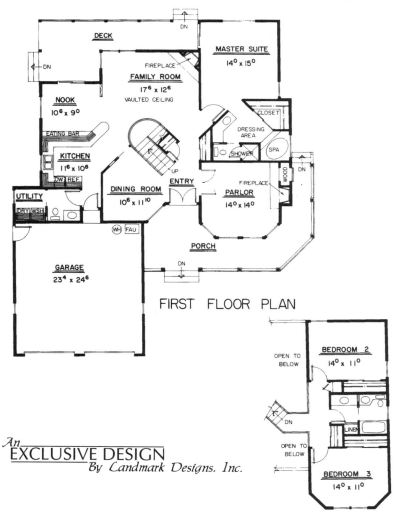

FIRST FLOOR PLAN

SECOND FLOOR PLAN

An
EXCLUSIVE DESIGN
By Landmark Designs, Inc.

PRICE CODE C

ATTRACTIVE, MULTI-PANED GLASS ENTRANCE

No. 93256

■ This plan features:

— Three bedrooms

— Two full and one half baths

■ An attractive use of multi-paned glass around the entrance

■ A large Living Room equipped with a beautiful fireplace and direct access to the patio

■ An elegant formal Dining Room accented with a bayed window

■ An efficient Kitchen with a built-in pantry, abundant counter and storage space, plus a peninsula counter with double sinks

■ A Breakfast Room connected to the Kitchen

■ A Master Suite with a decorative ceiling and private Master Bath

■ Two additional bedrooms served by a full hall bath

MAIN AREA — 2,033 SQ. FT.
BASEMENT — 1,902 SQ. FT.
GARAGE — 500 SQ. FT.

TOTAL LIVING AREA:
2,033 SQ. FT.

No materials list available

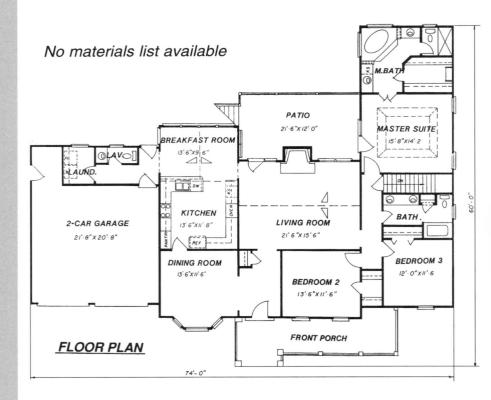

FLOOR PLAN

An EXCLUSIVE DESIGN
By Jannis Vann & Associates, Inc.

PRICE CODE E

TRADITIONAL WARMTH WITH A MODERN ACCENT

No. 10638

■ This plan features

— Four bedrooms

— Two and one half baths

■ Recessed ceilings in the Living, Dining and Master Bedrooms

■ Rustic beams, a fireplace and built-in shelves located in the Family Room

■ A Kitchen, with a laundry room close by, adjoins a cozy Breakfast area

■ A Master Suite complete with private bath and bay window sitting nook

FIRST FLOOR — 1,405 SQ. FT.
SECOND FLOOR — 1,364 SQ. FT.
GARAGE — 458 SQ. FT.

**TOTAL LIVING AREA:
2,769 SQ. FT.**

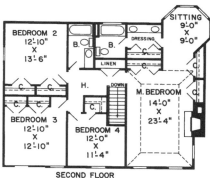

SECOND FLOOR

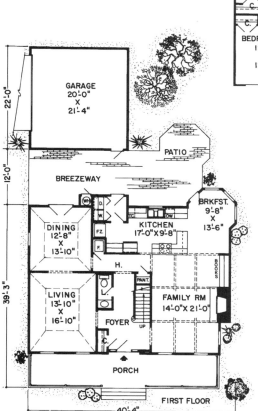

FIRST FLOOR

PRICE CODE B

*O*UTDOOR-LOVERS' DELIGHT

No. 10748

■ This plan features:

— Three bedrooms

— Two full baths

■ A roomy Kitchen and Dining Room

■ A massive Living Room with a fireplace and access to the wrap-around porch via double French doors

■ An elegant Master Suite and two additional spacious bedrooms closely located to the laundry area

MAIN AREA — 1,540 SQ. FT.
PORCHES — 530 SQ. FT.

TOTAL LIVING AREA:
1,540 SQ. FT.

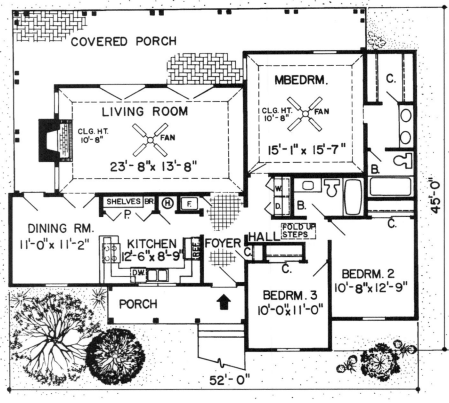

MAIN AREA

PRICE CODE B

No. 20350

■ This plan features:

— Three bedrooms

— Two full and one half baths

■ A wrap-around veranda adds charm and romance to the curb appeal of this home

■ Two fireplaces

■ An ample Foyer steps down to the Living Room crowned by a towering chimney and sloped ceiling

■ A Dining Room adjoining the fireplaced Living Room

■ An expansive family room, with a fireplace, is separated from the kitchen by an eating bar

■ A U-shaped Kitchen equipped with a pantry and a double sink

■ A spacious Master Suite with a private bath

■ Two additional bedrooms share the full hall bath

FIRST FLOOR — 972 SQ. FT.
SECOND FLOOR — 821 SQ. FT.
BASEMENT — 972 SQ. FT.

TOTAL LIVING AREA:
1,793 SQ. FT.

VERANDA CREATES ROMANCE

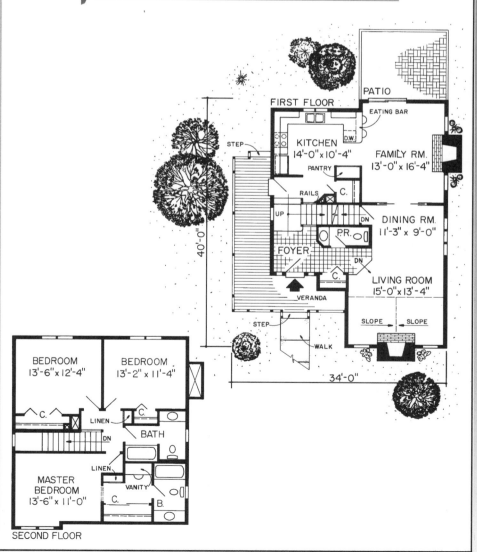

PRICE CODE F

A COUNTRY ESTATE

No. 93200

■ This plan features:

— Four bedrooms

— Four full and one half baths

■ A two-story Foyer, illuminated by side lights, a transom, and a second story window

■ Breakfast Room and Sun Room sharing a see-through fireplace

■ A gourmet Kitchen with two built-in pantries and an island with a vegetable sink

■ A second floor Master Suite, with a decorative ceiling, two walk-in closets, and a private balcony

■ Two additional bedrooms, with walk-in closets and private baths

■ A future Sitting Room option for the Master Suite

■ An optional basement, slab or crawl space foundation — please specify when ordering

FIRST FLOOR — 3,199 SQ. FT.
SECOND FLOOR — 2,531 SQ. FT.
BASEMENT — 3,199 SQ. FT.
GARAGE — 748 SQ. FT.
DECK — 652 SQ. FT.

**TOTAL LIVING AREA:
5,730 SQ. FT.**

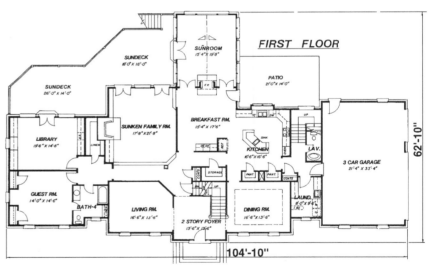

No materials list available

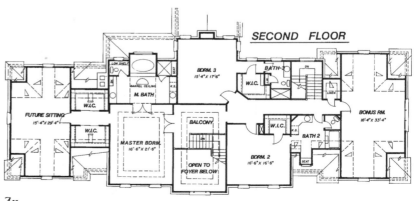

An EXCLUSIVE DESIGN
By Jannis Vann & Associates, Inc.

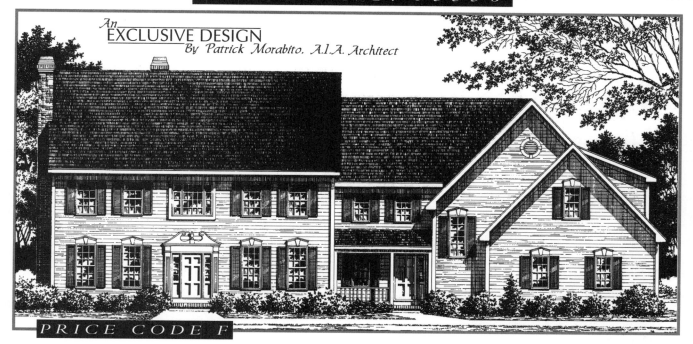

An
EXCLUSIVE DESIGN
By Patrick Morabito, A.I.A. Architect

PRICE CODE F

No. 93336

- This plan features:
- — Four bedrooms
- — Three and a half baths

- Two high ceiling Entries with landing staircases connecting a Hall/Balcony providing ease in accessing all areas of this expansive home

- Decorative beams highlighting a huge fireplace and a large bay window in the Family Room

- A well-equipped Kitchen with a cooktop island/eating bar, a double sink, built-in pantry and desk, and a Dinette with sliding glass doors to the Deck

- A private and plush Master Suite with an exclusive Screened Porch, dressing area with pocket doors into room size closet, a Bath with a platform, whirlpool tub, and Sitting Room, beyond the Kitchen/Bar alcove, with a corner fireplace and built-in book shelves

- Three additional bedrooms on the second floor, each with private access to a full bath, and a Bonus Room with many options

EXECUTIVE TREATMENT

FIRST FLOOR — 2,092 SQ. FT.
SECOND FLOOR — 1,934 SQ. FT.
BONUS — 508 SQ. FT.

TOTAL LIVING AREA:
4,026 SQ. FT.

No materials list available

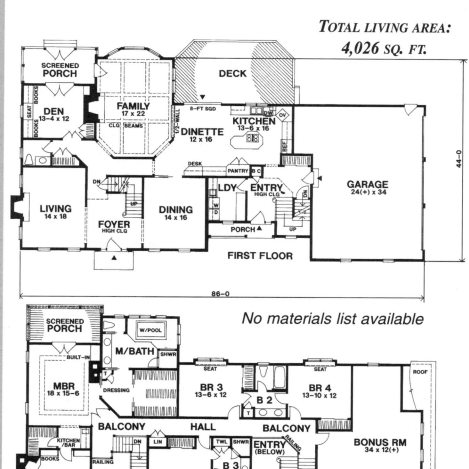

PRICE CODE C

COUNTRY HOME WITH MODERN UPDATES

No. 90187

- ■ This plan features:
- — Three bedrooms
- — Two full and one half baths
- ■ A grand, elevated porch running the entire width of the house
- ■ A Foyer area with a coat closet and a convenient half-bath
- ■ An efficient U-shaped Kitchen with a peninsula counter/eating bar
- ■ A magnificent cathedral ceiling in the Living and Recreation Rooms
- ■ A formal Dining Room
- ■ A Screened Porch adding living space throughout three seasons
- ■ A sloped ceiling in the Master Suite, with a walk-in closet and a private bath that features a compartmentalized commode
- ■ Two roomy bedrooms with plenty of storage space

FIRST FLOOR — 1,162 SQ. FT.
SECOND FLOOR — 847 SQ. FT.
COVERED PORCH — 345 SQ. FT

**TOTAL LIVING AREA:
2,009 SQ. FT.**

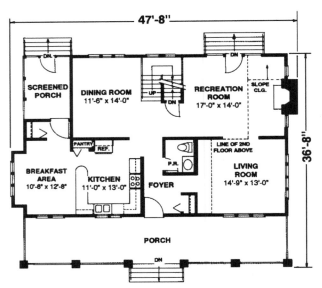

FIRST FLOOR

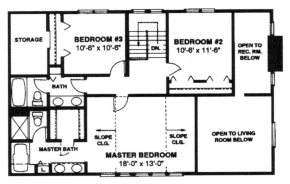

SECOND FLOOR

PRICE CODE A

FRONT SOLAR DESIGN ADDS DRAMA

No. 90414

- This plan features:
- — Three bedrooms
- — Two full baths
- Large front wooden deck
- A stone fireplace that collects and stores heat from the sunlight through tall Living/Family Room windows
- A cathedral ceiling crowning the Living/Family Room
- Direct access from the Dining Room to the rear deck
- A galley Kitchen adjoining the Dining Room
- A front Master Bedroom with siding glass doors to the front deck, a private bath and a walk-in closet
- Two additional bedrooms located at the opposite side of the home
- An optional basement, slab or crawl space foundation — please specify when ordering

MAIN AREA — 1,454 SQ. FT.

TOTAL LIVING AREA:
1,454 SQ. FT.

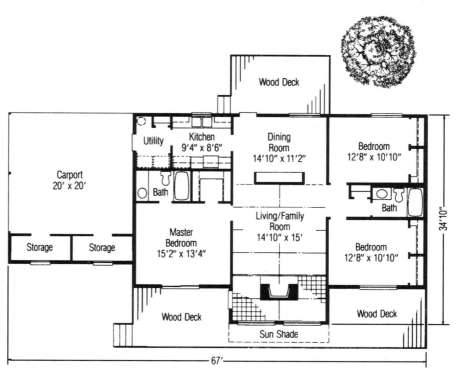

MAIN AREA

PRICE CODE F

SINGLE-LEVEL, FOUR BEDROOM HOME

No. 99777

■ This plan features:

— Four bedrooms

— Three full baths

■ A country-style porch, backed by a wealth of multi-paned windows that give this home a friendly, welcoming look

■ Two fireplaces; one in the Master Suite the other in the large Family Room, which also has a wetbar

■ A Living Room and Dining Room with a built-in hutch, that flow into each other

■ An efficient Kitchen with a sunny Eating Nook, large pantry, garden window and peninsula counter

■ A luxurious Master Suite with two walk-in closets and a bath

■ Two secondary bedrooms that share a full, double vanity bath, while the fourth bedroom has a private bath

MAIN AREA — 3,426 SQ. FT.
GARAGE — 598 SQ. FT.

TOTAL LIVING AREA:
3,426 SQ. FT.

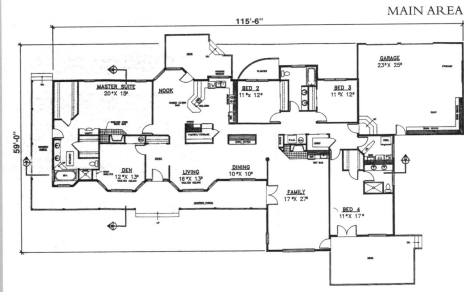

MAIN AREA

An
EXCLUSIVE DESIGN
By Landmark Designs, Inc.

PRICE CODE D

FARMHOUSE COLONIAL

No. 99632

■ This plan features:

— Four bedrooms

— Three full and one half baths

■ A front porch using columns to reflect the warmth of a farmhouse colonial

■ A Living/Dining Room area, with columns, warmed by a heat-circulating fireplace

■ Mud/Utility Room is accessible from the garage and rear entry

■ Kitchen has a bay window, a cooktop peninsula and a pantry

■ Second floor Studio with a full bath and a walk-in closet

■ Master Bedroom has a private bath with a whirlpool tub

■ Two-car garage

FIRST FLOOR — 1,925 SQ. FT.
SECOND FLOOR — 549 SQ. FT.
BASEMENT — 1,854 SQ. FT.
GARAGE — 494 SQ. FT.

TOTAL LIVING AREA:
2,474 SQ. FT.

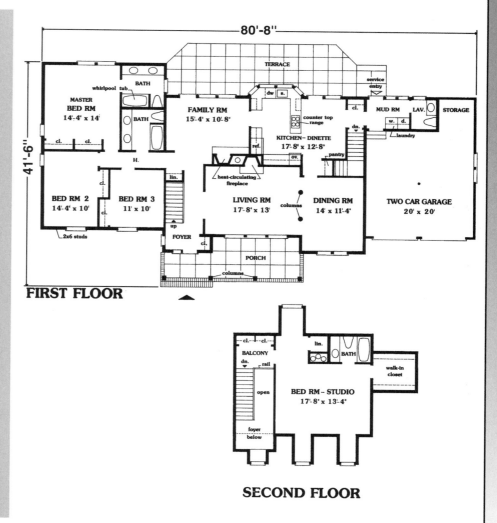

FIRST FLOOR

SECOND FLOOR

PRICE CODE C

ENJOY THIS COUNTRY FRONT PORCH

No. 93260

- ■ This plan features:
- — Three bedrooms
- — Two full and one half baths
- ■ An expansive Living Room with a cozy fireplace
- ■ A Sun Deck, expanding the living spaces outdoors
- ■ An efficient Kitchen with a peninsula counter that can be used as an eating bar
- ■ An informal Breakfast Room, with a Laundry Center, and a formal Dining Room
- ■ A Master Suite with a private Master Bath and a walk-in closet
- ■ Two additional bedrooms that share a full hall bath
- ■ An optional basement, slab or crawl space foundation — please specify when ordering

FIRST FLOOR — 892 SQ. FT.
SECOND FLOOR — 934 SQ. FT.
BONUS ROOM — 237 SQ. FT.
GARAGE — 520 SQ. FT.
BASEMENT — 870 SQ. FT.

**TOTAL LIVING AREA:
1,826 SQ. FT.**

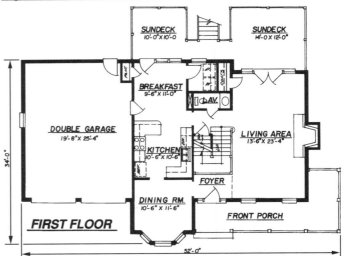

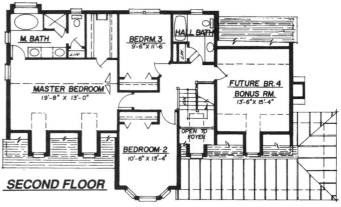

No materials list available

An
EXCLUSIVE DESIGN
By Jannis Vann & Associates, Inc.

PRICE CODE A

SIMPLY COMFORTABLE

No. 93400

■ This plan features:

— Three bedrooms

— Two full bath

■ An inviting front porch

■ A cozy fireplace in the Family Room

■ A versatile Dining Room with direct access to the rear porch

■ A comfortable Master Suite with a walk-in closet and a private bath

■ Two additional bedrooms that share a full hall bath

MAIN AREA — 1,496 SQ. FT.
BASEMENT — 752 SQ. FT.
GARAGE — 744 SQ. FT.

TOTAL LIVING AREA:
1,496 SQ. FT.

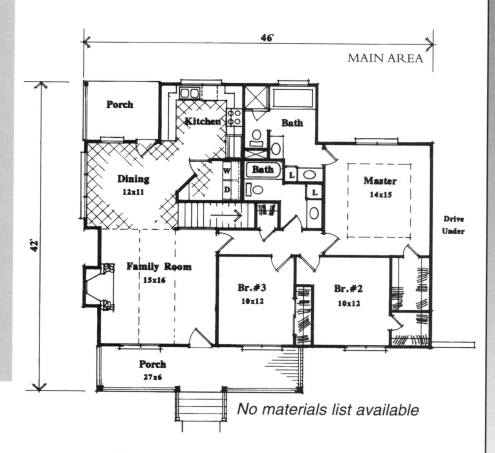

No materials list available

An
EXCLUSIVE DESIGN
By Greg Marquis

PRICE CODE E

SUNNY ATMOSPHERE PERVADES CLAPBOARD CLASSIC

No. 99206

- ■ This plan features:
- — Three bedrooms
- — Two full and one half baths
- ■ A front and rear covered porch
- ■ A centrally-located Kitchen equipped with a pass-through to the Family Room, built-in pantry and plenty of storage space
- ■ Formal Living and bayed Dining Rooms flow together
- ■ A Family Room enhanced by a bay window, raised hearth fireplace and a wetbar
- ■ A Master Bedroom Suite pampered by a luxurious private bath and two closets
- ■ Cozy gables highlight the secondary bedrooms, which share a full hall bath

FIRST FLOOR — 1,612 SQ. FT.
SECOND FLOOR — 1,356 SQ. FT.

TOTAL LIVING AREA:
2,968 SQ. FT.

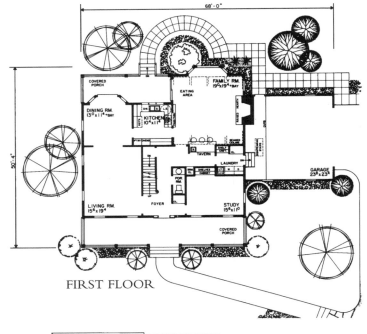

FIRST FLOOR

SECOND FLOOR

PRICE CODE D

A LARGE COUNTRY KITCHEN

No. 99776

■ This plan features:

— Three bedrooms

— Two full baths

■ Open layout between the large Kitchen, Great Room and Eating Nook gives the feeling that the area is even larger than it really is

■ Vaulted ceilings in the Entry, Great Room, Dining Room and the Master Suite

■ A country Kitchen that has a large walk-in pantry, separate vegetable sink, a garden window, and French doors that open onto a deck

■ A large walk-in closet and a private bath in the Master Suite

■ Two additional bedrooms that share a full hall bath

MAIN AREA — 2,282 SQ. FT.
BASEMENT — 1,980 SQ. FT.
GARAGE — 648 SQ. FT.

TOTAL LIVING AREA:
2,282 SQ. FT.

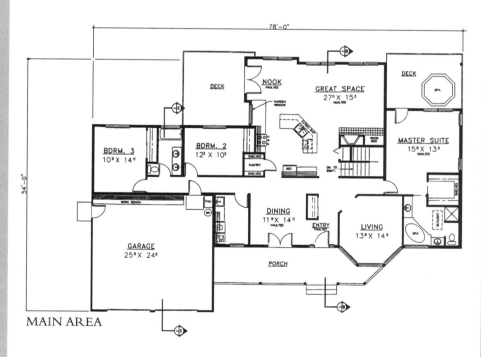

MAIN AREA

An
EXCLUSIVE DESIGN
By Landmark Designs, Inc.

PRICE CODE D

SPACIOUS COUNTRY HOME

No. 91701

■ This plan features:

— Three bedrooms

— Three full baths

■ A vaulted ceiling in the rambling Family Room/Nook/Kitchen combination

■ A vegetable sink in the work island of the large Kitchen which also has a walk-in pantry

■ A cozy, corner fireplace in the Family Room

■ A Master Suite with an L-shaped walk-in closet, private spa tub, separate shower, and double vanities

■ Two additional bedrooms that share a full, compartmentalized bath

FIRST FLOOR — 1,957 SQ. FT.
SECOND FLOOR — 531 SQ. FT.
GARAGE — 639 SQ. FT.

TOTAL LIVING AREA:
2,488 SQ. FT.

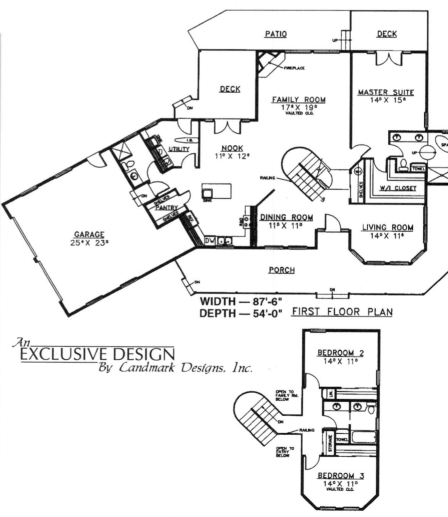

WIDTH — 87'-6"
DEPTH — 54'-0"   FIRST FLOOR PLAN

An
EXCLUSIVE DESIGN
By Landmark Designs, Inc.

SECOND FLOOR PLAN

PRICE CODE A

COUNTRY RANCH

No. 91797

■ This plan features:

— Three bedrooms

— Two full baths

■ A railed and covered wrap-around porch, adding charm to this country-styled home

■ A high vaulted ceiling in the Living Room

■ A smaller Kitchen with ample cupboard and counter space, that is augmented by a large pantry

■ An informal Family Room with access to the wood deck

■ A private Master Suite with a spa tub and a walk-in closet

■ Two family bedrooms that share a full hall bath

■ A shop and storage area in the two-car garage

MAIN AREA — 1,485 SQ. FT.
GARAGE — 701 SQ. FT.
WIDTH — 63'-0"
DEPTH — 51'-6"

TOTAL LIVING AREA:
1,485 SQ. FT.

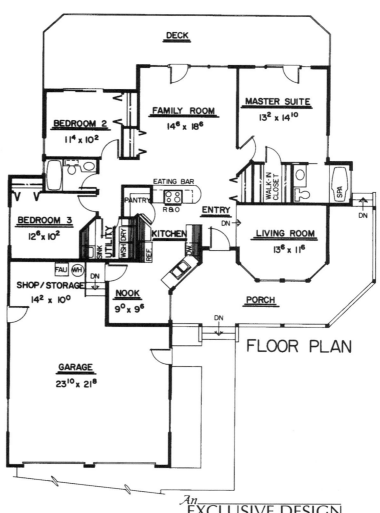

FLOOR PLAN

An
EXCLUSIVE DESIGN
By *Landmark Designs, Inc.*

PRICE CODE C

Moderate Ranch with Exciting Features

No. 90441

■ This plan features:

— Three bedrooms

— Two full baths

■ A large Great Room with a vaulted ceiling and a stone fireplace with bookshelves on either side

■ A spacious Kitchen with ample cabinet space, conveniently located next to the large Dining Room

■ A Master Suite having a large bath with a garden tub, double vanity and a walk-in closet

■ Two other large bedrooms, each with a walk-in closet and access to the full bath

■ An optional basement, slab or crawl space foundation — please specify when ordering

MAIN AREA — 1,811 SQ. FT.

TOTAL LIVING AREA:
1,811 SQ. FT.

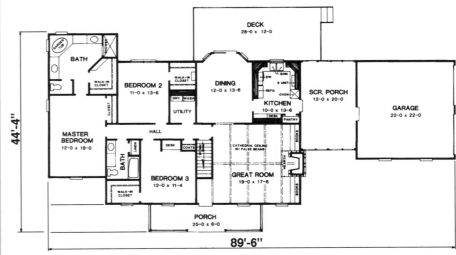

MAIN AREA

PRICE CODE D

A MODERN PLAN WITH A FARMHOUSE FLAVOR

No. 90201

■ This plan features:

— Four bedrooms

— Two full and one half baths

■ A sprawling covered porch

■ A cozy Family Room warmed by a fireplace with a raised hearth

■ A formal Dining Room with a large bay window

■ A handy Kitchen with built-ins including an eating bar

■ A Master Bedroom equipped with a dressing room, two closets and a private bath

FIRST FLOOR — 1,370 SQ. FT.
SECOND FLOOR — 969 SQ. FT.

TOTAL LIVING AREA:
2,339 SQ. FT.

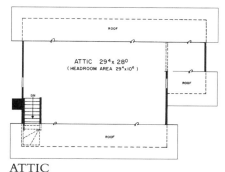

ATTIC 29⁴ x 28⁰
(HEADROOM AREA 29⁴ x 10⁶)

ATTIC

BED RM.
STUDY
11⁰ x 13²

MASTER
BED RM.
13⁰ x 13²

BED RM.
10⁰ x 10⁶

BED RM.
13⁰ x 10⁶

SECOND FLOOR

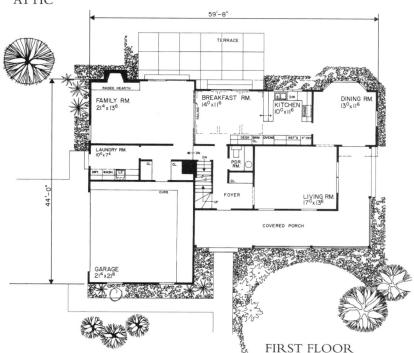

TERRACE

FAMILY RM.
21⁴ x 13⁶

BREAKFAST RM.
14⁰ x 11⁶

KITCHEN
10⁰ x 11⁶

DINING RM.
13⁰ x 11⁶

LAUNDRY RM.
10⁰ x 7⁶

PDR RM.

FOYER

LIVING RM.
17⁰ x 13⁶

COVERED PORCH

GARAGE
21⁴ x 21⁸

59'-8"

44'-0"

FIRST FLOOR

PRICE CODE D

FRIENDLY PORCH WELCOMES GUESTS

No. 91206

■ This plan features:

— Four bedrooms

— Two full and one half baths

■ A Master Suite with a huge, walk-in closet, a cozy window seat, double sinks and a garden tub

■ Three additional bedrooms that share a full hall bath

■ A sunken Family Room with French doors and a fireplace

■ A country Kitchen with a cook top island, a convenient Breakfast Bay and a large pantry

FIRST FLOOR — 1,346 SQ. FT.
SECOND FLOOR — 1,230 SQ. FT.
GARAGE AND STORAGE — 788 SQ. FT.

**TOTAL LIVING AREA:
2,576 SQ. FT.**

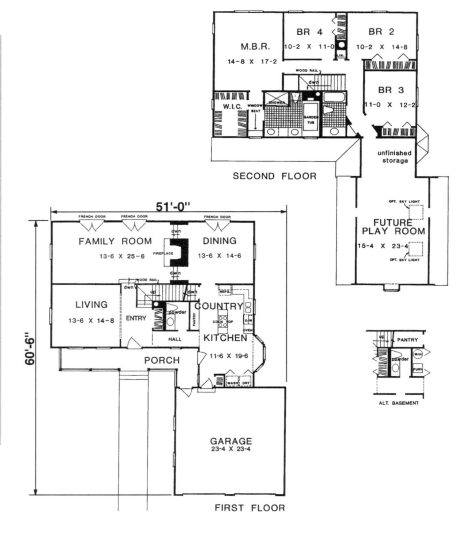

PRICE CODE B

COUNTRY STYLE CHARMER

No. 91903

■ This plan features:

— Three bedrooms

— Two full and one half baths

■ A classical symmetry and gracious front porch

■ Formal areas zoned towards the front of the house

■ A large Family Room with fireplace

■ A winder staircase located off the Family Room

■ A Master Bedroom with double vanities, separate glass shower and tub, and a built-in entertainment center

FIRST FLOOR — 910 SQ. FT.
SECOND FLOOR — 769 SQ. FT.
BASEMENT — 890 SQ. FT.

TOTAL LIVING AREA: 1,679 SQ. FT.

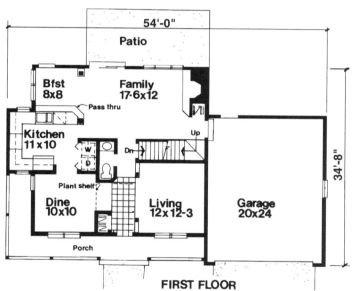

FIRST FLOOR

SECOND FLOOR

PRICE CODE A

COUNTRY HOME

No materials list available

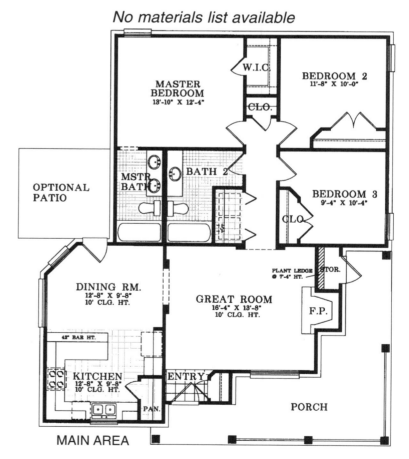

No. 93023

■ This plan features:

— Three bedrooms

— Two full baths

■ An American farmhouse with a corner wrap-around porch

■ A Great Room with ten foot ceilings and a focal point fire-place

■ Ten foot ceilings in the Kitchen and Dining Room that give the home a spacious feel

■ An eating bar, walk-in pantry and sink with a lovely window above, making the Kitchen efficient

■ A Master Suite with private Master Bath

■ Two additional bedrooms that share a second full bath

MAIN AREA — 1,249 SQ. FT.
WIDTH — 38'-6"
DEPTH — 46'-0"

**TOTAL LIVING AREA:
1,249 SQ. FT.**

An
EXCLUSIVE DESIGN
By Belk Home Designs

PRICE CODE D

HOME SWEET HOME

No. 93205

■ This plan features:

— Four bedrooms

— Two and a half baths

■ A wonderful wrap-around porch

■ Formal Living and Dining Rooms

■ A U-shaped Kitchen equipped with a peninsula counter, a double sink, and a pantry

■ A spacious Breakfast Room that is open to the Kitchen

■ An expansive Family Room with a large focal point fireplace, and access to the rear Deck and porch

■ A second floor Master Suite with a decorative ceiling, a lavish bath and a huge walk-in closet

■ Three additional bedrooms share a full, double vanity hall bath

■ A Bonus Room for future use

FIRST FLOOR — 1,320 SQ. FT.
SECOND FLOOR — 1,268 SQ. FT.
BONUS ROOM — 389 SQ. FT.
BASEMENT — 1,320 SQ. FT.
GARAGE — 482 SQ. FT.

TOTAL LIVING AREA:
2,588 SQ. FT.

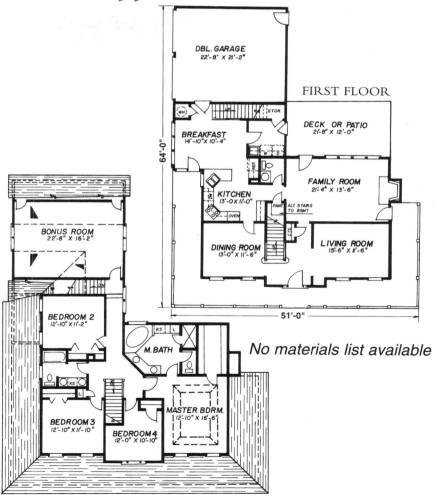

No materials list available

An
EXCLUSIVE DESIGN
By Jannis Vann & Associates, Inc.

PRICE CODE D

GINGERBREAD TREAT

No. 20500

■ This plan features:

— Three bedrooms

— Two full and one half baths

■ A wrap-around country porch

■ Twin palladium windows that add sun and character to both the Living and Game Rooms

■ A vaulted and fireplaced Living Room

■ A formal Dining Room that overlooks the porch

■ A kitchen conveniently located to both the Dining and Breakfast Rooms

■ A private, first floor Master Suite with his-n-her walk-in closets, and a luxury bath

■ Two second floor bedrooms share a full hall bath

■ A second floor Game Room which opens onto the second floor balcony, creating a distinctive family gathering place

FIRST FLOOR — 1,411 SQ. FT.
SECOND FLOOR — 856 SQ. FT.

TOTAL LIVING AREA:
2,267 SQ. FT.

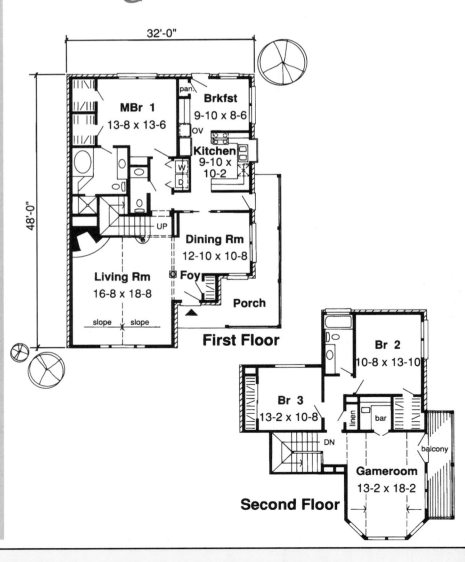

First Floor

Second Floor

PRICE CODE A

LARGE FRONT PORCH ADDS A COUNTRY TOUCH

No. 34601

■ This plan features:

— Three bedrooms

— Two full baths

■ A country-styled front porch

■ Vaulted ceiling in the Living Room which includes a fireplace

■ An efficient Kitchen with double sinks and peninsula counter that may double as an eating bar

■ Two first floor bedrooms with ample closet space

■ A second floor Master Suite with sloped ceiling, walk-in closet and private master Bath

FIRST FLOOR — 1,007 SQ. FT.
SECOND FLOOR — 408 SQ. FT.

**TOTAL LIVING AREA:
1,415 SQ. FT.**

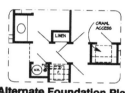

Alternate Foundation Plan

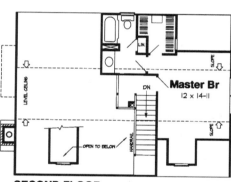

SECOND FLOOR

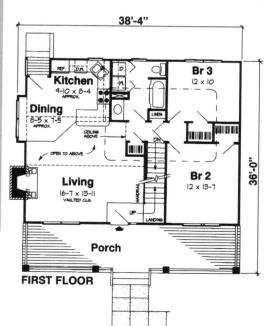

FIRST FLOOR

PRICE CODE C

STREETSIDE APPEAL

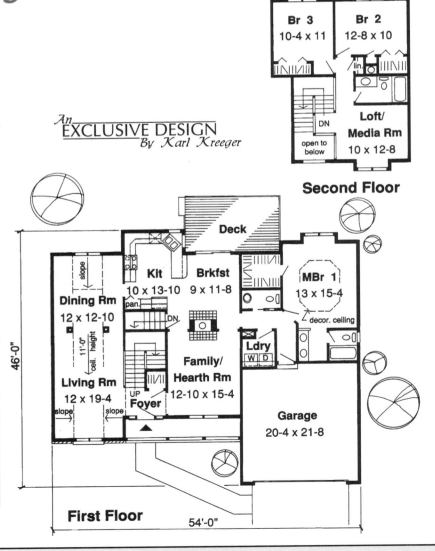

An
EXCLUSIVE DESIGN
By Karl Kreeger

Second Floor

Br 3 10-4 x 11

Br 2 12-8 x 10

lin.

DN

open to below

Loft/ Media Rm 10 x 12-8

First Floor

Deck

Kit 10 x 13-10

Brkfst 9 x 11-8

MBr 1 13 x 15-4

decor. ceiling

Dining Rm 12 x 12-10

pan.

DN

Ldry W D

Living Rm 12 x 19-4

UP **Foyer**

Family/ Hearth Rm 12-10 x 15-4

Garage 20-4 x 21-8

slope

11'-0" ceil. height

46'-0"

54'-0"

No. 20160
- This plan features:
  - — Three bedrooms
  - — Two full and one half baths
- An elegant Living and Dining Room combination that is divided by columns
- A Family/Hearth Room with a two-way fireplace to the Breakfast room
- A well-appointed Kitchen with built-in pantry, peninsula counter and double corner sink
- A Master Suite with decorative ceiling, walk-in closet and private bath
- Two additional bedrooms that share a full hall bath

FIRST FLOOR — 1,590 SQ. FT.
SECOND FLOOR — 567 SQ. FT.
BASEMENT — 1,576 SQ. FT.
GARAGE — 456 SQ. FT.

TOTAL LIVING AREA:
2,157 SQ. FT.

PRICE CODE D

VERSATILITY GALORE

No. 26781

■ This plan features:

— Four bedrooms

— Two full and one half baths

■ Southern exposed windows including a bay, half-round, and dormers

■ An optional Solarium entrance

■ A Family Room with a bay window and a corner fireplace

■ An efficient Kitchen, serving the Morning Room with ease

■ A roomy formal Living Room, with a bay window

■ A Master Suite with a private double vanity bath and an optional Sitting Room

■ Three additional bedrooms sharing a full hall bath

FIRST FLOOR — 1,339 SQ. FT.
SECOND FLOOR — 1,219 SQ. FT.
BASEMENT — 1,250 SQ. FT.
GARAGE — 521 SQ. FT.
SOLARIUM (UNHEATED) — 279 SQ. FT.

TOTAL LIVING AREA:
2,558 SQ. FT.

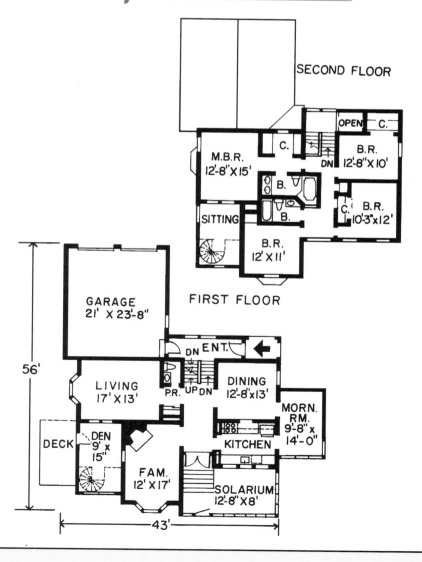

SECOND FLOOR

M.B.R. 12'-8"X15'
C.
OPEN
C.
B.R. 12'-8"X10'
DN
B.
B.
SITTING
B.
C.
B.R. 10'-3"x12'
B.R. 12'X11'

FIRST FLOOR

GARAGE 21' X 23'-8"

56'

DN ENT.

LIVING 17'X13'
P.R.
UP DN
DINING 12'-8'x13'

DECK

DEN 9' x 15"

FAM. 12'X17'

KITCHEN

MORN. RM. 9'-8" x 14'-0"

SOLARIUM 12'-8"X8'

43'

PRICE CODE D

No. 99756

■ This plan features:

— Four bedrooms

— Three full baths

■ An old-fashioned covered porch giving a country flavor

■ A balcony that overlooks the Living Room

■ A fireplace with a wide, tiled hearth spanning the corner directly under the balcony

■ Four skylights and a wealth of windows that combine to make the Sun Nook brighter than the rest of the home

■ A central work island in the large Kitchen

■ A large walk-in closet and private bathroom with an enclosed toilet and shower in the Master Suite

■ Three bedrooms located on the second floor that share a full hall bath

FIRST FLOOR — 1,830 SQ. FT.
SECOND FLOOR — 644 SQ. FT.
GARAGE — 846 SQ. FT.
WIDTH — 92'-0"
DEPTH — 44'-0"

TOTAL LIVING AREA:
2,474 SQ. FT.

SPECIAL TOUCHES THROUGHOUT

An EXCLUSIVE DESIGN
By Landmark Designs. Inc.

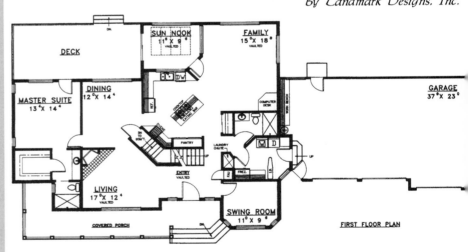

FIRST FLOOR PLAN

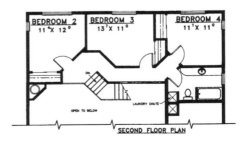

SECOND FLOOR PLAN

PRICE CODE E

ANGLED GEM

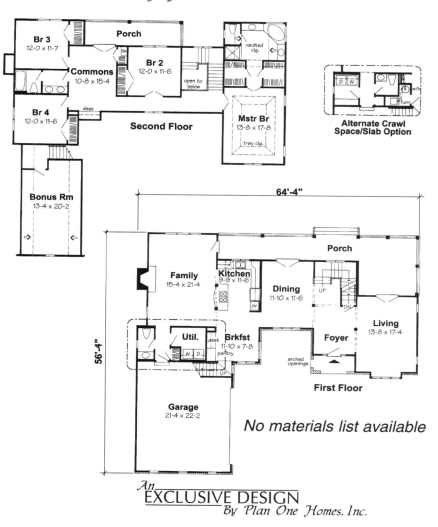

No. 24655

■ This plan features:

— Four bedrooms

— Two full and one half baths

■ An appealing elevation, combining siding, brick and an arched entrance

■ A formal Living Room and Dining Room, each with access to the rear porch

■ An efficient Kitchen

■ A built-in pantry and planning desk in the Breakfast Room

■ A fireplaced Family Room

■ A tray ceiling Master Bedroom with two walk-in closets and a vaulted ceiling in the private bath

■ Three addition bedrooms sharing a double vanity, full hall bath

■ A Commons Area with a built-in desk and access to a second floor porch

■ A Bonus Room for future needs

FIRST FLOOR — 1,427 SQ. FT.
SECOND FLOOR — 1,451 SQ. FT.
BONUS ROOM — 364 SQ. FT.

**TOTAL LIVING AREA:
2,878 SQ. FT.**

No materials list available

An
EXCLUSIVE DESIGN
By Plan One Homes, Inc.

PRICE CODE D

GINGERBREAD GEM

No. 10766

- This plan features:
- — Three bedrooms
- — Two and one half baths
- Warm weather living space afforded by a wrap-around covered porch, second floor balcony, and a huge rear deck
- Large windows adding a sunny glow to every room
- The family areas flowing together for a wide open atmosphere that's warmed by the Family Room fireplace
- A large Master Suite with an abundance of closet space and an expansive bath area

FIRST FLOOR — 1,311 SQ. FT.
SECOND FLOOR — 968 SQ. FT.
BASEMENT — 968 SQ. FT.

TOTAL LIVING AREA:
2,279 SQ. FT.

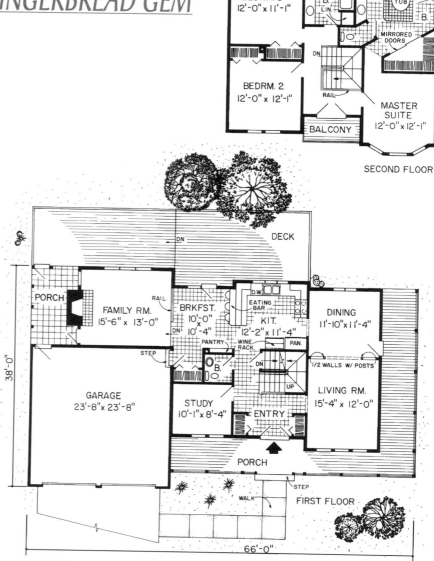

PRICE CODE D

VICTORIAN CHARMER

No. 90188

■ This plan features:

— Three bedrooms

— Two full and one half bath

■ A octagonal gazebo off the wrap-around front porch connecting directly to the Dining Room

■ An octagonal Foyer area with angled steps leading upstairs

■ An Activity(Family) Room with a fireplace open to the rear family living areas

■ A bright Breakfast area for informal meals

■ A Kitchen with a peninsula counter and ample storage space

■ A Master Bedroom with his-n-her closets, a sitting area, and a double vanity bath

■ Two additional bedrooms with ample storage that share a double vanity hall bath

FIRST FLOOR — 1,281 SQ. FT.
SECOND FLOOR — 1,089 SQ. FT.
COVERED PORCH — 424 SQ. FT.
GARAGE — 464 SQ. FT.

TOTAL LIVING AREA: 2,370 SQ. FT.

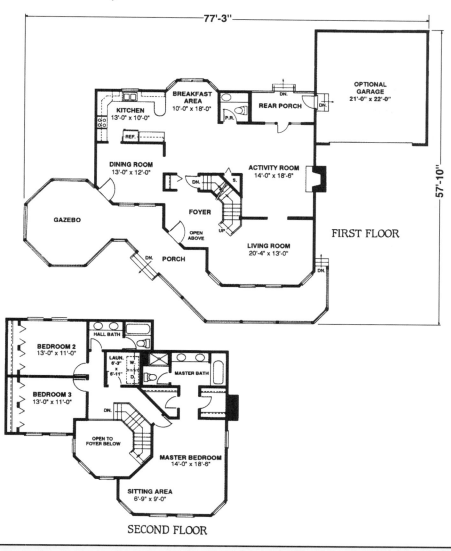

PRICE CODE D

No. 92013

■ This plan features:

— Three bedrooms

— Two full and one half baths

■ A large, island Kitchen with a built-in pantry, built-in desk and a double sink

■ A vaulted ceiling in the Sun Room

■ A tray ceiling in the formal Dining Room with easy access to the Kitchen

■ A fireplace and a built-in wetbar in the informal Family Room

■ A vaulted ceiling in the Master Suite which is equipped with his -n-her walk-in closets and a private full Bath

■ A barrel vaulted ceiling in the front bedroom

■ A convenient second floor Laundry Room

FIRST FLOOR — 1,336 SQ. FT.
SECOND FLOOR — 1,015 SQ. FT.
BASEMENT — 1,336 SQ. FT.
GARAGE — 496 SQ. FT.

TOTAL LIVING AREA:
2,351 SQ. FT.

WARM WELCOME UPON ENTERING

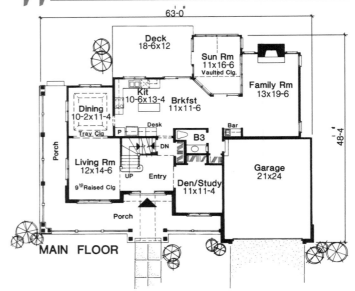

MAIN FLOOR

UPPER FLOOR

PRICE CODE C

FARMHOUSE FOR TODAY'S FAMILY

No. 90619

- This plan features:
— Four bedrooms
— Two full and one half baths
- Country porch giving warmth and charm to an American tradition
- A spacious central Foyer leads to the Dining, Living and Family Rooms
- A fireplaced Living Room
- A Family Room with a rustic exposed beam ceiling and a second fireplace
- An L-shaped Kitchen/Dinette with direct access to the Mud and Laundry Rooms
- A Mudroom entrance from the garage or side porch area
- A Master Suite with his-n-her closets and a private bath
- Three additional roomy bedrooms that share use of a hall bath

FIRST FLOOR — 1,162 SQ. FT.
SECOND FLOOR — 920 SQ. FT.

TOTAL LIVING AREA:
2,082 SQ. FT.

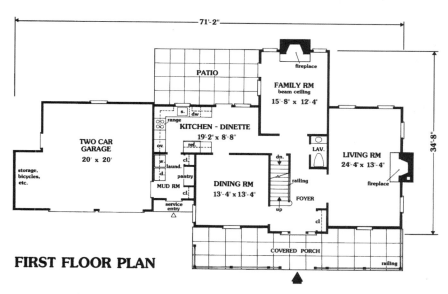

FIRST FLOOR PLAN

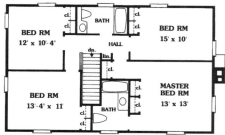

SECOND FLOOR PLAN

PRICE CODE B

Bay Windows and a Terriffic Front Porch

No. 93261

■ This plan features:

— Three bedrooms

— Two full baths

■ A country front porch

■ An expansive Living Area that includes a fireplace

■ A Master Suite with a private Master Bath and a walk-in closet, as well as a bay window view of the front yard

■ An efficient Kitchen that serves the sunny Breakfast Area and the Dining Room with equal ease

■ A built-in pantry and a desk add to the conveniences in the Breakfast Area

■ Two additional bedrooms that share the full hall bath

■ A convenient main floor Laundry Room

MAIN AREA — 1,778 SQ. FT.
BASEMENT — 1,008 SQ. FT.
GARAGE — 728 SQ. FT.

**TOTAL LIVING AREA:
1,778 SQ. FT.**

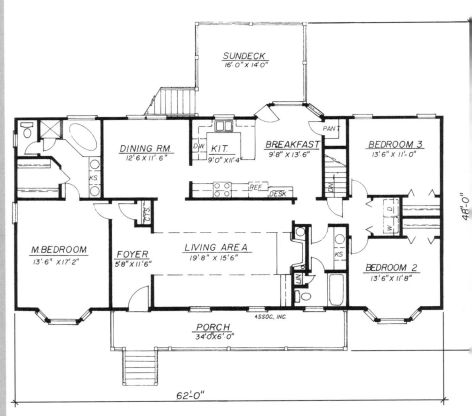

An
EXCLUSIVE DESIGN
By Jannis Vann & Associates, Inc.

PRICE CODE D

CATHEDRAL CEILING IN THE MASTER SUITE

No. 93308

■ This plan features:

— Four bedrooms

— Two full and one half baths

■ A vaulted ceiling in the Foyer

■ A formal Living Room and Dining Room that open into each other

■ A Kitchen that is situated to efficiently serve the Dinette and the Dining Room

■ Direct access from the Dinette to the Wood Deck, expanding living space to the outdoors

■ A cathedral ceiling in the luxurious Master Suite which boasts a Master Bath

■ Four additional bedrooms that share a full hall bath

FIRST FLOOR — 1,190 SQ. FT.
SECOND FLOOR — 1,061 SQ. FT.
BASEMENT — 1,190 SQ. FT.
GARAGE — 532 SQ. FT.

TOTAL LIVING AREA:
2,251 SQ. FT.

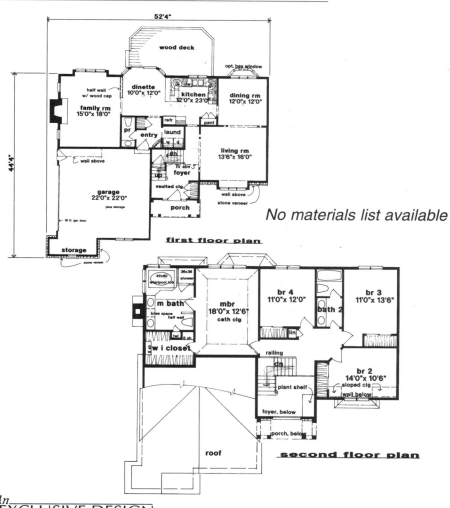

No materials list available

An EXCLUSIVE DESIGN
By Patrick Morabito, A.I.A. Architect

PRICE CODE E

GORGEOUS AND LIVABLE

No. 20196

■ This plan features:

— Four bedrooms

— Three full baths

■ A bay window that enhances the Living Room with natural light

■ A decorative ceiling accentuating the formal Dining Room

■ A Breakfast room with an incredible shape

■ An island Kitchen with an efficient layout and in close proximity to both the formal Dining Room and the informal Breakfast Room

■ A spacious Family Room that is warmed by a cozy fireplace

■ A fantastic Master Suite with a decorative ceiling, private Master Bath and a large walk-in closet

■ Three additional bedrooms, with walk-in closets, that share a full hall bath

FIRST FLOOR — 1,273 SQ. FT.
SECOND FLOOR — 1,477 SQ. FT.
BASEMENT — 974 SQ. FT.
GARAGE — 852 SQ. FT.

TOTAL LIVING AREA:
2,750 SQ. FT.

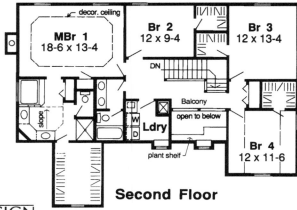

An EXCLUSIVE DESIGN
By Karl Kreeger

Second Floor

- decor. ceiling
- MBr 1 18-6 x 13-4
- Br 2 12 x 9-4
- Br 3 12 x 13-4
- DN
- Balcony open to below
- Ldry
- plant shelf
- Br 4 12 x 11-6

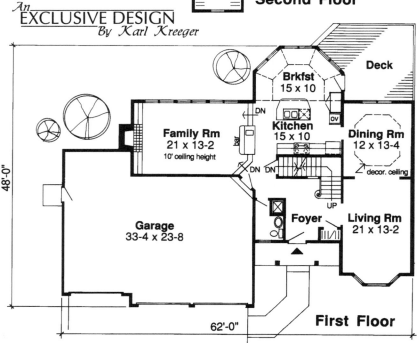

First Floor

- Deck
- Brkfst 15 x 10
- Kitchen 15 x 10
- Family Rm 21 x 13-2 (10' ceiling height)
- bar
- DN / DN DN
- Dining Rm 12 x 13-4 (decor. ceiling)
- UP
- Garage 33-4 x 23-8
- Foyer
- Living Rm 21 x 13-2
- 48'-0"
- 62'-0"

PRICE CODE F

PAST LUXURIES REVISITED

No. 20405

■This plan features:

— Four bedrooms (with optional fifth bedroom)

— Four and one half baths

■ An arched entry to the formal Living and Dining Rooms, divided by columns for an open feeling

■ A short hall leading past the sunny Library to the private Master Suite with a luxurious garden spa and private access to the veranda

■ An open arrangement of the Kitchen, Breakfast area, and Family Room creating a spacious atmosphere

■ A lofty Game Room on the second floor, perfect for recreation or just relaxing

FIRST FLOOR — 2,423 SQ. FT.
SECOND FLOOR — 1,235 SQ. FT.
GARAGE — 507 SQ. FT.

TOTAL LIVING AREA: 3,658 SQ. FT.

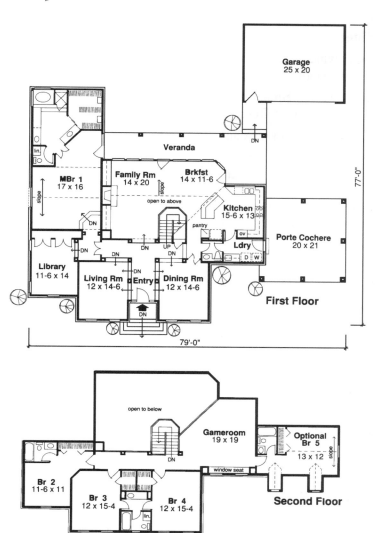

PRICE CODE F

No. 93320

■ This plan features:

— Four bedrooms

— Three full and one half baths

■ A Library with a spiral staircase to the loft above and a cozy fireplace to read by

■ An elegant formal Dining Room with a beautiful bay window

■ A U-shaped Kitchen equipped with a cooktop island, built-in pantry and a built-in desk

■ A vaulted ceiling crowning the Dinette which has sliding glass doors to the wooden deck

■ A luxurious hot tub in the Sun Room

■ A Master Suite with a walk-in closet, and a supurb master bath

FIRST FLOOR — 2,397 SQ. FT.
SECOND FLOOR — 1,612 SQ. FT.
BASEMENT — 2,397 SQ. FT.
GARAGE — 1,197 SQ. FT.
WIDTH — 90'-0"
DEPTH — 66'-0"

TOTAL LIVING AREA:
4,009 SQ. FT.

LIBRARY WITH A SPIRAL STAIRCASE

No materials list available

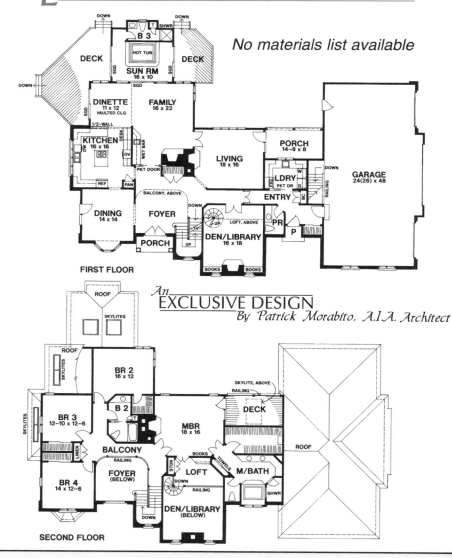

An EXCLUSIVE DESIGN
By Patrick Morabito, A.I.A. Architect

PRICE CODE F

No. 93301

This plan features:

— Four bedrooms

— Three full and one half baths

■ A formal Living Room accented by the large front window, separated from the formal Dining Room by a half wall

■ A large country Kitchen with a center cooktop island, built-in pantry and plenty of work space

■ An informal Dinette area with access to the rear yard

■ A large Family Room with a cozy fireplace and a large rear window

■ A sloped ceiling in the Master Suite enhanced by a luxurious bath and a huge walk-in closet

■ Three additional bedrooms enhanced by walk-in closets and private access to full baths

■ Laundry/Mud Room accessed from the front porch or garage

FIRST FLOOR — 1,778 SQ. FT.
SECOND FLOOR — 1,498 SQ. FT.

TOTAL LIVING AREA: 3,276 SQ. FT.

RELAXED FAMILY LIVING

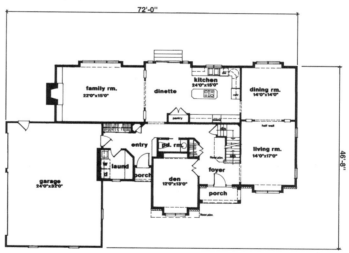

FIRST FLOOR

No materials list available

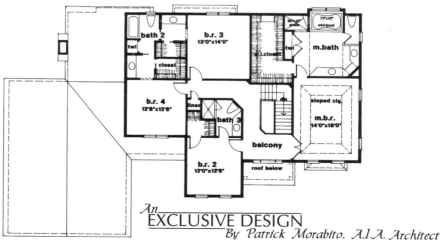

SECOND FLOOR

An EXCLUSIVE DESIGN
By Patrick Morabito, A.I.A. Architect

PRICE CODE C

VICTORIAN TOUCHES DISGUISE MODERN DESIGN

No. 90616

■ This plan features:

— Three bedrooms

— Two full and one half baths

■ A Master Suite with a high ceiling, an arched window, a private bath, and a tower sitting room with an adjoining roof deck

■ Two additional bedrooms that share a full hall bath

■ A Living Room accentuated by a brick fireplace

■ A well-equipped Kitchen with a built-in pantry and peninsula counter

■ A sky-lit Family Room with a built-in entertainment center

FIRST FLOOR — 1,146 SQ. FT.
SECOND FLOOR — 846 SQ. FT.
BASEMENT — 967 SQ. FT.
GARAGE — 447 SQ. FT.

**TOTAL LIVING AREA:
1,992 SQ. FT.**

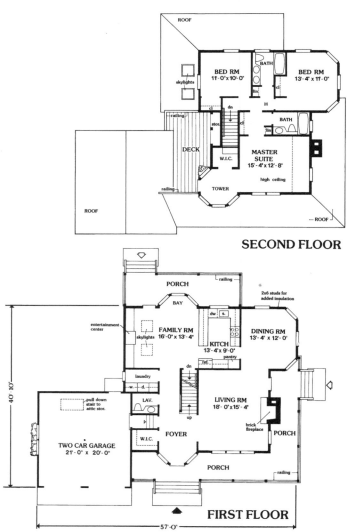

SECOND FLOOR

FIRST FLOOR

PRICE CODE C

COZY WINDOW SEAT COMMANDS FRONT YARD VIEW

No. 90517

■ This plan features:

— Three bedrooms

— Two full and one half baths

■ A covered front porch and rear deck provide outdoor living space

■ Easy traffic flow design with central staircase in the Foyer

■ Kitchen door that separates dinner guests from the cook

■ A Kitchen with a peninsula counter/eating bar, a built-in pantry and planning desk and an informal Nook

■ An expansive Family Room that flows from the Nook and is enhanced by a fireplace

■ A Master Bedroom Suite served by a private bath and a large walk-in closet

FIRST FLOOR — 1,065 SQ. FT.
SECOND FLOOR — 813 SQ. FT.

TOTAL LIVING AREA:
1,878 SQ. FT.

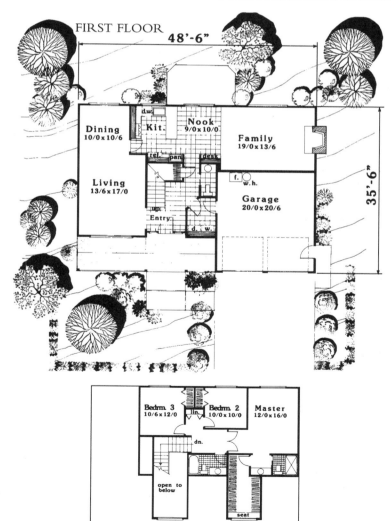

FIRST FLOOR 48'-6"

Dining 10/0 x 10/6
Kit.
Nook 9/0 x 10/0
Family 19/0 x 13/6
d.w.
ref. pan. desk
Living 13/6 x 17/0
f. w.h.
Garage 20/0 x 20/6
up
Entry
d. w.

35'-6"

Bedrm. 3 10/6 x 12/0
Bedrm. 2 10/0 x 10/0
Master 12/0 x 16/0
ln.
dn.
open to below
seat

SECOND FLOOR

PRICE CODE C

A TOUCH OF COUNTRY

No. 99012

■ This plan features:

— Three bedrooms

— Two full and one half baths

■ A front wrap-around porch dominating the exterior

■ A corner Dining Room accented by a front bay window and sliding glass doors to the porch

■ A cozy Family Room with a bay window and easy access to the powder and laundry rooms

■ A well-appointed galley Kitchen efficiently serves the formal Dining Room and the informal Dinette

■ A fourth bay window in the Master Suite equipped with a full bath and walk-in closet

■ Laundry Room with garage entry

■ Two additional bedrooms sharing the full bath in the hall

FIRST FLOOR — 975 SQ. FT.
SECOND FLOOR — 864 SQ. FT.
BASEMENT — 871 SQ. FT.
GARAGE — 250 SQ. FT.

**TOTAL LIVING AREA:
1,839 SQ. FT.**

No materials list available

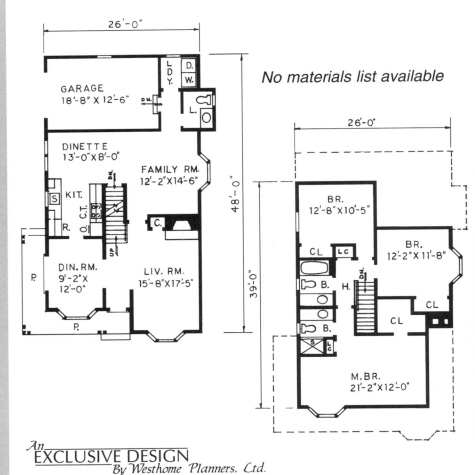

An
EXCLUSIVE DESIGN
By Westhome Planners, Ltd.

PRICE CODE A

APPEAL EVERYONE WANTS

No. 92016

■ This plan features:

— Three bedrooms

— Two and one half baths

■ Repeating front gables, shuttered windows, and wrap-around front porch

■ A large Family/Kitchen opening to a screened porch and private side deck

■ A Master Bedroom with private Bath and one wall of closet space

■ Second floor laundry facilities

FIRST FLOOR — 760 SQ. FT.
SECOND FLOOR — 728 SQ. FT.
BASEMENT — 768 SQ. FT.

TOTAL LIVING AREA: 1,488 SQ. FT.

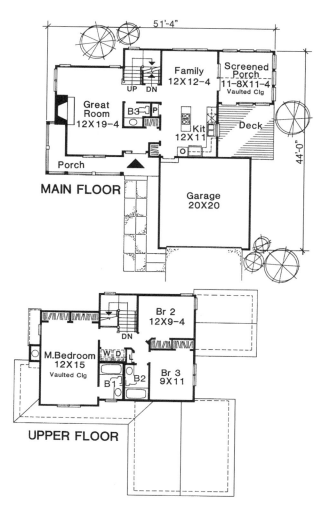

PRICE CODE B

RELAX AND ENJOY THE TERRACE

No. 90649

- This plan features:
- — Four bedrooms
- — Two full baths
- Covered Porch
- Clapboard siding, shuttered and double-hung windows
- A convenient floor plan that allows you to finish the second floor later
- An L-shaped Living/Dining Room combination with sliding glass doors to the rear porch, enhanced by an energy efficient heat-circulating fireplace
- A Kitchen that opens directly into the sunny Dinette area
- Two bedrooms with full bath access
- Optional greenhouse

FIRST FLOOR — 1,127 SQ. FT.
SECOND FLOOR — 578 SQ. FT.

TOTAL LIVING AREA:
1,705 SQ. FT.

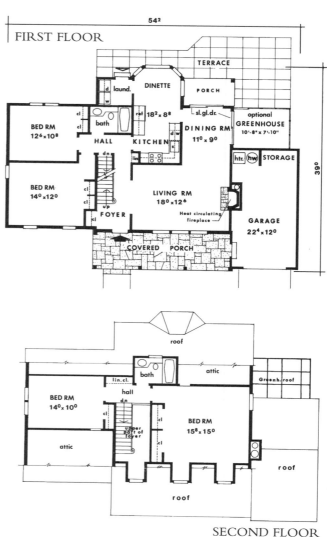

FIRST FLOOR

SECOND FLOOR

PRICE CODE B

YOUR CLASSIC HIDEAWAY

No. 90423

■ This plan features:

— Three bedrooms

— Two full baths

■ A lovely fireplace in the Living Room, which is both cozy and a source of heat for the core area

■ An efficient country Kitchen connecting the large Dining and Living Rooms

■ A lavish Master Suite enhanced by a step-up sunken tub, more than ample closet space, and separate shower

■ A screened porch and patio area for outdoor living

■ An optional basement, slab or crawl space foundation — please specify when ordering

MAIN AREA — 1,773 SQ. FT.
SCREENED PORCH — 240 SQ. FT.

TOTAL LIVING AREA:
1,773 SQ. FT.

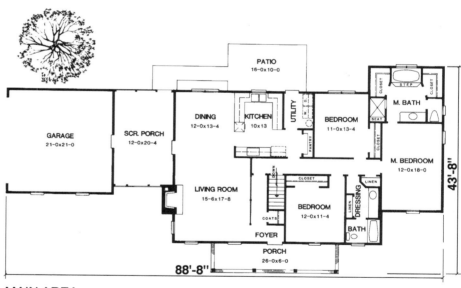

MAIN AREA

PRICE CODE E

ROOM TO GROW

No. 90838

- This plan features:
- — Three bedrooms
- — Three full baths
- A corner gas fireplace in the spacious Living Room
- A Master Suite including a private Bath with a whirlpool tub, separate shower and a double vanity
- An island Kitchen that is well-equipped to efficiently serve both formal Dining Room and informal Nook
- Two additional bedrooms sharing a full bath on the second floor

FIRST FLOOR — 1,837 SQ. FT.
SECOND FLOOR — 848 SQ. FT.
BASEMENT — 1,803 SQ. FT.
BONUS ROOM(OVER GARAGE) — 288 SQ. FT.

TOTAL LIVING AREA:
2,685 SQ. FT.

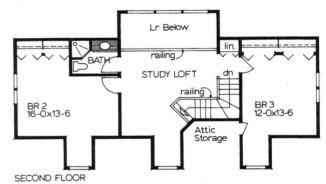

SECOND FLOOR

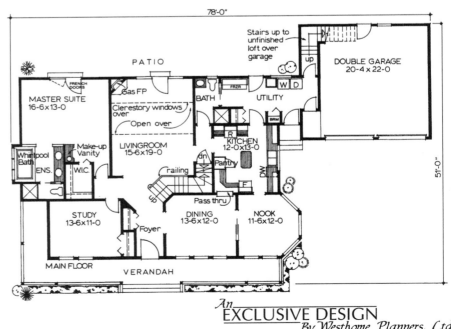

An
EXCLUSIVE DESIGN
By Westhome Planners, Ltd.

PRICE CODE D

No. 91707

■ This plan features:

— Three bedrooms

— Two full and one half baths

■ A wrap-around country porch provides a warm welcome

■ A vaulted ceiling to the second floor in the formal Living Room and the entryway adds a feeling of vastness

■ An efficient and spacious island Kitchen with both a garden window and a bay window

■ A built-in hutch tucked into an angle of the elegant Dining Room

■ A cozy corner fireplace

■ An oversized tub and a shower brightened by a skylight and glass blocks in the luxurious Master Suite

■ Two additional bedrooms that share use of a full bath

FIRST FLOOR — 1,940 SQ. FT.
SECOND FLOOR — 552 SQ. FT.
GARAGE — 608 SQ. FT.
WIDTH — 54'-6"
DEPTH — 66'-0"

**TOTAL LIVING AREA:
2,492 SQ. FT.**

GOOD USE OF SPACE

An
EXCLUSIVE DESIGN
By Landmark Designs, Inc.

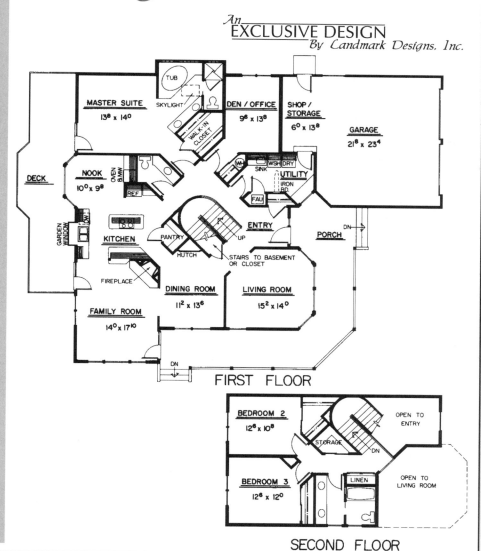

FIRST FLOOR

SECOND FLOOR

PRICE CODE B

CAREFREE ONE-LEVEL CONVENIENCE

No. 10674

■ This plan features:

— Three bedrooms

— Two full baths

■ A galley Kitchen, centrally-located between the Dining, Breakfast and Living Room areas

■ A huge Family Room which exits onto the patio

■ The Master Suite with double closets and vanities

MAIN AREA — 1,600 SQ. FT.
GARAGE — 465 SQ. FT.

TOTAL LIVING AREA:
1,600 SQ. FT.

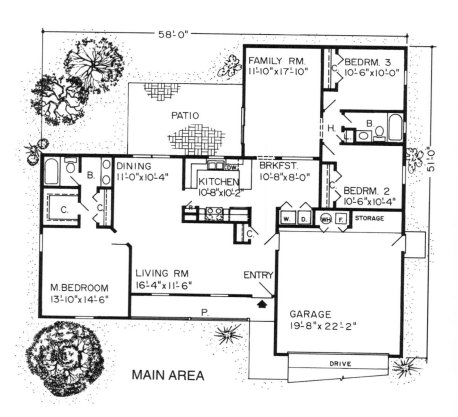

MAIN AREA

PRICE CODE E

No. 34025

■ This plan features:

— Four bedrooms

— Two full and one half baths

■ A charming front porch

■ A two-way fireplace with built-in shelves

■ A large open Kitchen with a central cook-top island, built-in desk and pantry and a bright Breakfast Nook open to the Family Room

■ A wetbar separating the Breakfast Nook from the Family Room

■ A screened porch adding living space for three seasons

■ A Master Suite equipped with a large walk-in closet and a private bath

■ Three additional bedrooms, each with walk-in closets, share a full hall bath

■ An optional basement, slab or crawl space foundation — please specify when ordering

FIRST FLOOR — 1,450 SQ. FT.
SECOND FLOOR — 1,341 SQ. FT.

TOTAL LIVING SPACE:
2,791 SQ. FT.

CHARMING PORCH SHELTERS ENTRY

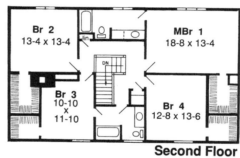

Br 2
13-4 x 13-4

MBr 1
18-8 x 13-4

Br 3
10-10 x 11-10

Br 4
12-8 x 13-6

Second Floor

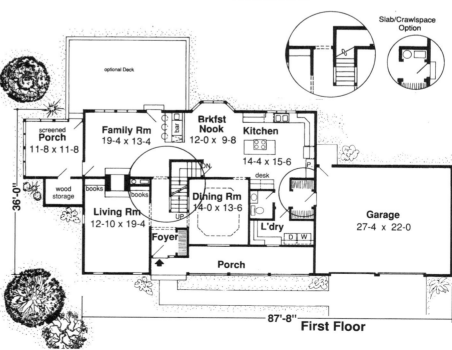

Slab/Crawlspace Option

optional Deck

screened Porch
11-8 x 11-8

Family Rm
19-4 x 13-4

Brkfst Nook
12-0 x 9-8

Kitchen
14-4 x 15-6

wood storage

books

books

Living Rm
12-10 x 19-4

Dining Rm
14-0 x 13-6

desk

L'dry

Garage
27-4 x 22-0

Foyer

Porch

36'-0"

87'-8"

First Floor

PRICE CODE C

COUNTRY FARMHOUSE

No. 90639

■ This plan features:

— Three bedrooms

— Three full baths

■ An old-fashioned Porch surrounding this Saltbox design with two convenient entrances

■ A central Foyer with a curved staircase opening to a Sunken Living Room with a heat-circulating fireplace

■ A formal Dining Room with a sliding glass door to the Terrace and separated from Living Room by a railing

■ A comfortable Family Room with a built-in entertainment center is conveniently located near the Mudroom and Foyer

■ An efficient, U-shaped Kitchen serving both the Dining Room and Dinette with ease

■ An expansive Master Suite with two closets, a dressing area, and a private Bath highlighted by skylights

■ Two additional, roomy bedrooms sharing a full hall bath

FIRST FLOOR — 1,238 SQ. FT.
SECOND FLOOR — 797 SQ. FT.
BASEMENT — 1,159 SQ. FT.
GARAGE — 439 SQ. FT.

TOTAL LIVING AREA:
2,035 SQ. FT.

SECOND FLOOR

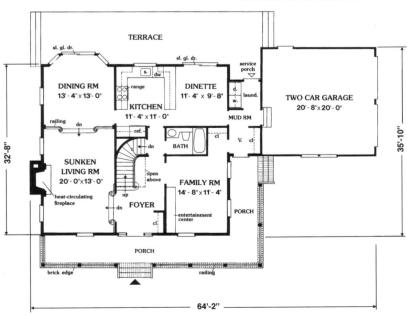

FIRST FLOOR

PRICE CODE D

*L*ARGE LIVING SPACES ABOUND WITHIN

No. 90189

■ This plan features:

— Four bedrooms

— Two full and one half baths

■ A country styled front porch

■ Double entry doors leading into a two-story Foyer

■ A spacious fireplaced Living Room emphasized with a sloped ceiling

■ A formal Dining Room accented by a bay window

■ An efficient Kitchen with a peninsula counter, separating it from the Breakfast Area

■ A large Master Suite served by a double vanity bath and a walk-in closet

■ Three additional bedrooms sharing a full bath in the hall

■ A convenient second floor laundry area

FIRST FLOOR — 1,231 SQ. FT.
SECOND FLOOR — 1,049 SQ. FT.

**TOTAL LIVING AREA:
2,280 SQ. FT.**

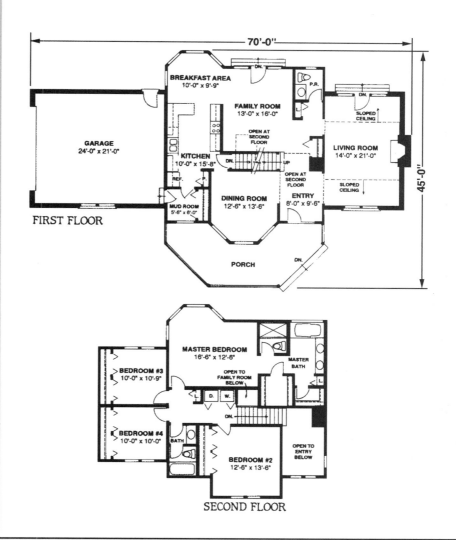

FIRST FLOOR

SECOND FLOOR

PRICE CODE C

NEAT AND TIDY FLOOR PLAN

No. 93266

■ This plan features:

— Three bedrooms

— Two full and one half baths

■ A large Family Room includes a huge fireplace and double doors opening to the front porch

■ A Breakfast area with direct access to the Sun Deck, expanding your living space in the warmer weather

■ A formal Living Room

■ An efficiently located Kitchen

■ A large Master Suite with a decorative ceiling, a walk-in closet and a private Master Bath

■ Two additional bedrooms that share a full hall bath

■ A second floor laundry center

FIRST FLOOR — 990 SQ. FT.
SECOND FLOOR — 976 SQ. FT.
BASEMENT — 431 SQ. FT.
GARAGE — 559 SQ. FT.

TOTAL LIVING AREA: 1,966 SQ. FT.

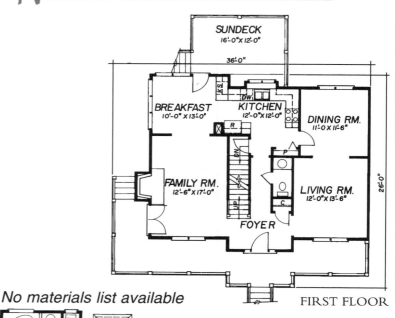

No materials list available

FIRST FLOOR

SECOND FLOOR

An EXCLUSIVE DESIGN
By Jannis Vann & Associates, Inc.

PRICE CODE F

No. 93268

■ This plan features:

— Five bedrooms

— Four full baths and two half baths

■ A Grand Staircase and a Music Hall beyond the two-story Foyer

■ A Living Room with a decorative ceiling and a fireplace

■ Center island cooktop Kitchen includes Butlers pantry and bayed Breakfast area

■ A large bayed Family Room with a wetbar and a fireplace

■ A Master Suite with a decorative ceiling, a fireplace, three walk-in closets and a Master Bath

■ Three additional bedrooms have private baths and walk-in closets

■ A Guest Suite or maid's quarters

FIRST FLOOR — 3,418 SQ. FT.
SECOND FLOOR — 2,131 SQ. FT.
BONUS ROOM — 404 SQ. FT.
BASEMENT — 2,280 SQ. FT.
GARAGE — 624 SQ. FT.

TOTAL LIVING AREA:
5,549 SQ. FT.

GRAND STAIRCASE AND A MUSIC ROOM

An
EXCLUSIVE DESIGN
By Jannis Vann & Associates, Inc.

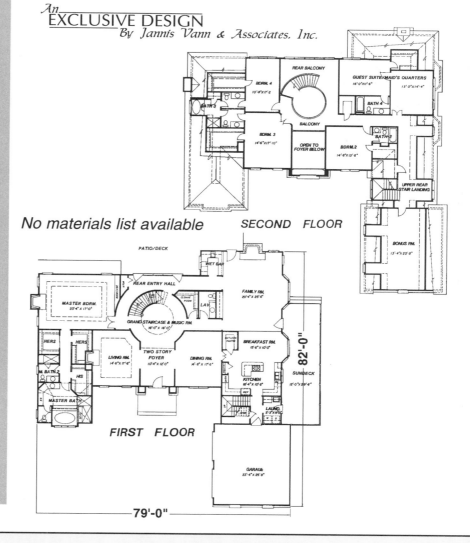

No materials list available

SECOND FLOOR

FIRST FLOOR

PRICE CODE C

TWO-STORY CONTEMPORARY

No. 20505

■ This plan features:

— Three bedrooms

— Two full and one half baths

■ Sloped ceilings in the Living Room and the Foyer

■ A cozy, focal point fireplace in the Living Room

■ A vaulted ceiling in the formal Dining Room which is also enhanced by floor-to-ceiling windows

■ A vaulted ceiling in the luxurious Master Suite with oval tub, step-in shower, and a long vanity with two basins

■ A well-equipped Kitchen with an island and a peninsula counter

■ An informal Breakfast Room that is convenient to the Kitchen and the Living Room

■ Two upstairs bedrooms that share a full hall bath

FIRST FLOOR — 1,580 SQ. FT.
SECOND FLOOR — 534 SQ. FT.
BASEMENT — 1,573 SQ. FT.
PORCH/PATIO — 340 SQ. FT.

TOTAL LIVING AREA: 2,114 SQ. FT.

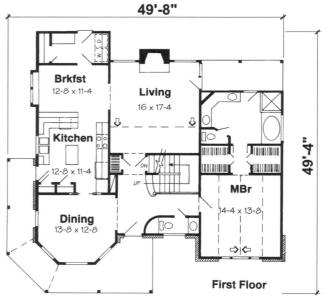

First Floor

No materials list available

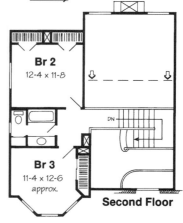

Second Floor

PRICE CODE D

CLASSIC FARMHOUSE WITH ELEGANT AMENITIES

No. 99608

■ This plan features:

— Four bedrooms

— Two full and one half baths

■ A decorative curved stairway in the roomy foyer

■ A Living Room with an ornamental heat-circulating fireplace

■ A Dining Room enhanced by a large bay window

■ A sky-lit Family Room with a heat-circulating fireplace and sliding glass doors to the terrace

■ An efficient well-equipped Kitchen with a window over the sink and a peninsula counter

■ A Master Suite with a Master Bath equipped with a whirlpool tub and double vanities

FIRST FLOOR — 1,364 SQ. FT.
SECOND FLOOR — 1,083 SQ. FT.
BASEMENT — 854 SQ. FT.
GARAGE — 403 SQ. FT.

TOTAL LIVING AREA: 2,447 SQ. FT.

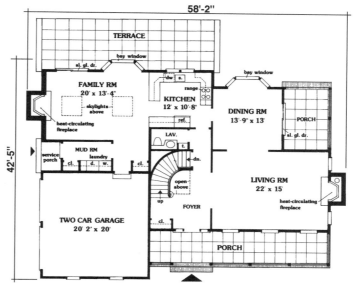

FIRST FLOOR PLAN

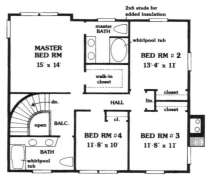

SECOND FLOOR PLAN

PRICE CODE E

EXPANDABLE, HANDICAP ACCESSIBLE

An EXCLUSIVE DESIGN
By Landmark Designs, Inc.

No. 91751

■ This plan features:

— Six bedrooms

— Three full and one half baths

■ A ramp providing wheelchair accessibility and wide inner doors

■ Kitchen with a center cooktop/eating bar island, double ovens and a garden window over the double sinks

■ A corner fireplace in the Family/Nook area

■ A Master Suite with a walk-in closet, a compartmented bath, a double vanity and a step-in shower

■ Two additional bedrooms on the opposite side of the house, sharing a full hall bath

■ Second floor plan offers three bedrooms, a vaulted ceiling, and a full hall bath

MAIN AREA — 2,199 SQ. FT.
SECOND FLOOR — 999 SQ. FT.
COVERED PORCH — 462 SQ. FT.
BASEMENT — 2,199 SQ. FT.
GARAGE — 606 SQ. FT.
STORAGE — 72 SQ. FT.

**TOTAL LIVING AREA:
3,198 SQ. FT.**

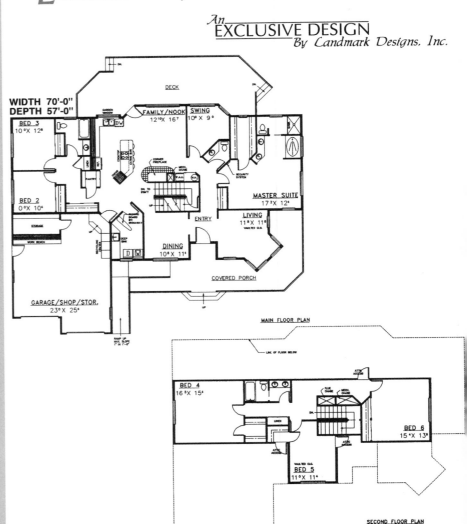

WIDTH 70'-0''
DEPTH 57'-0''

MAIN FLOOR PLAN

SECOND FLOOR PLAN

PRICE CODE A

ONE STORY COUNTRY HOME

No. 99639

■ This plan features:

— Three bedrooms

— Two full baths

■ A Living Room with an imposing, high ceiling that slopes down to a normal height of eight feet, focusing on the decorative heat-circulating fireplace at the rear wall

■ An efficient Kitchen that adjoins the Dining Room that views the front Porch

■ A Dinette Area for informal eating in the Kitchen that can comfortably seat six people

■ A Master Suite arranged with a large dressing area that has a walk-in closet plus two linear closets and space for a vanity

■ Two family bedrooms that share a full hall bath

MAIN AREA — 1,367 SQ. FT.
BASEMENT — 1,267 SQ. FT.
GARAGE — 431 SQ. FT.

TOTAL LIVING AREA:
1,367 SQ. FT.

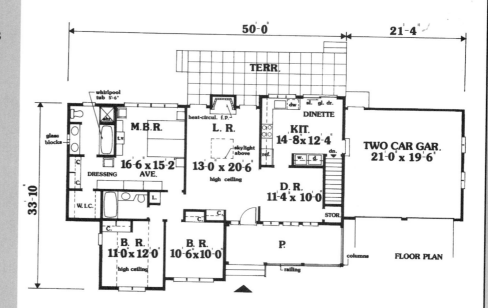

FLOOR PLAN

PRICE CODE F

MODERN TUDOR IS HARD TO RESIST

No. 10737

■ This plan features:

— Four bedrooms

— Three and one half baths

■ A seven-sided Breakfast room, an island Kitchen adjoining the Formal Dining Room

■ A beamed Family Room with private Study

■ A Master Suite complete with sauna, whirlpool, double vanity and fireplace

First floor — 2,457 sq. ft.
Second floor — 1,047 sq. ft.
Basement — 2,457 sq. ft.
Garage — 837 sq. ft.
Sun room — 213 sq. ft.

Total living area: 3,504 sq. ft.

An EXCLUSIVE DESIGN
By Karl Kreeger

PRICE CODE E

PORCH RECALLS ROMANTIC ERA

No. 20098

■ This plan features

— Four bedrooms

— Two and one half baths

■ A Kitchen serving a hexagonal Breakfast room, a formal Dining Room and adjoining deck

■ A Master Bedroom just off the Living Room and steps away from the parlor

■ The deck is accessed through the Dining Room

FIRST FLOOR — 1,843 SQ. FT.
SECOND FLOOR — 1,039 SQ. FT.
BASEMENT — 1,843 SQ. FT.
GARAGE — 484 SQ. FT.

TOTAL LIVING AREA:
2,882 SQ. FT.

An
EXCLUSIVE DESIGN
By Karl Kreeger

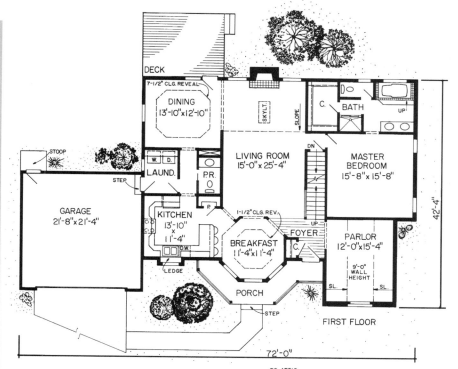

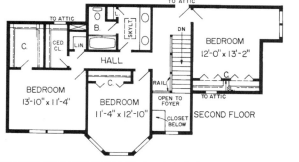

PRICE CODE C

ENERGY-SAVING CAPE

No. 90696

■ This plan features:

— Four bedrooms

— Two full baths

■ A large Living Room with an exposed wood beam ceiling, heat-circulating fireplace and a bay window

■ A sunny Dining and Family Room enlarged by a bay window with sliding glass doors to a rear deck

■ A country Kitchen with generous cabinet and counter space

■ A first floor Master Bedroom with his-n-her closets

■ Two additional upstairs bedrooms with sitting areas and skylights

FIRST FLOOR — 1,382 SQ. FT.
SECOND FLOOR — 688 SQ. FT.
BASEMENT — 1,202 SQ. FT.

TOTAL LIVING AREA:
2,070 SQ. FT.

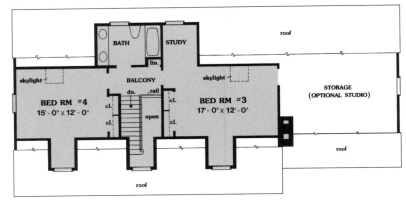

SECOND FLOOR PLAN

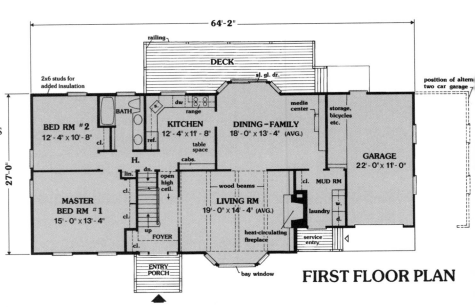

FIRST FLOOR PLAN

PRICE CODE C

No. 91053

■ This plan features:

— Three bedrooms

— Two and a half baths

■ A classic Victorian exterior design accented by a wonderful turret room and second floor covered porch above a sweeping veranda

■ A spacious formal Living Room leading into a formal Dining Room for ease in entertaining

■ An efficient, U-shaped Kitchen with loads of counter space and a peninsula snackbar, opens to an eating Nook and Family Room for informal gatherings and activities

■ An elegant Master Suite with a unique, octagon Sitting area, a private Porch, an oversized, walk-in closet and private Bath with a double vanity and a window tub

■ Two additional bedrooms with ample closets sharing a full hall bath

FIRST FLOOR — 1,150 SQ. FT.
SECOND FLOOR — 949 SQ. FT.
GARAGE — 484 SQ. FT.

UPDATED VICTORIAN

TOTAL LIVING AREA:
2,099 SQ. FT.

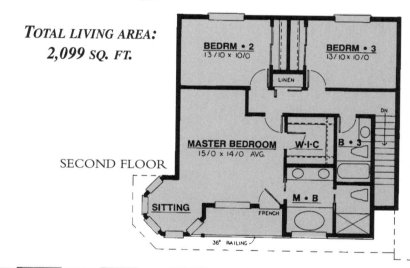

SECOND FLOOR

BEDRM • 2
13/10 x 10/0

BEDRM • 3
13/10 x 10/0

LINEN

MASTER BEDROOM
15/0 x 14/0 AVG.

W·I·C

B · 3

DN

SITTING

FRENCH

M · B

36" RAILING

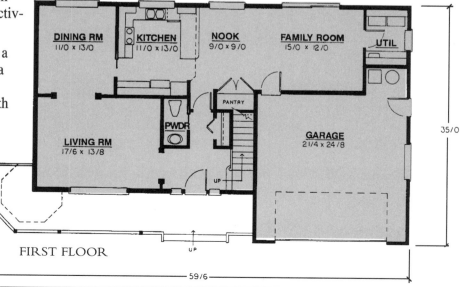

DINING RM
11/0 x 13/0

KITCHEN
11/0 x 13/0

NOOK
9/0 x 9/0

FAMILY ROOM
15/0 x 12/0

UTIL

PANTRY

PWDR

LIVING RM
17/6 x 13/8

GARAGE
21/4 x 24/8

UP

UP

FIRST FLOOR

59/6

35/0

PRICE CODE C

A LITTLE BIT OF COUNTRY FLAIR

No. 99774

■ This plan features:

— Three bedrooms

— Three full baths

■ Front-facing dormers, cedar shake roofing, and a wide front porch add a country flavor to an otherwise contemporary style

■ Vaulted ceilings

■ Four skylights in the Kitchen and the Family Room

■ A bay window in the Living Room that juts out onto the wrap-around porch

■ A Master Suite with a walk-in closet, a compartmented with skylights, an oversized shower, a spa tub and two vanities

■ Two additional bedrooms that share a full hall bath

MAIN AREA — 2,192 SQ. FT.
GARAGE — 800 SQ. FT.

TOTAL LIVING AREA:
2,192 SQ. FT.

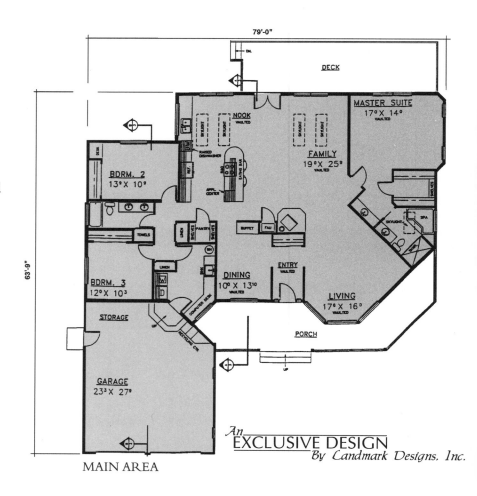

MAIN AREA

An
EXCLUSIVE DESIGN
By Landmark Designs, Inc.

PRICE CODE E

No. 99649

■ This plan features:

— Four or five bedrooms

— Three full and one half baths

■ A welcoming wrap-around porch leading to a striking two-story Foyer

■ A heat-circulating fireplace and a wetbar in the Family Room

■ An U-shaped Kitchen with a pantry and an adjacent Utility/Mud Room

■ A Master Bedroom Suite with a double walk-in closet, optional fireplace and a Private Bath with a double vanity, whirlpool tub and a separate shower

■ Three bedrooms, two with walk-in closets, share a full bath

■ An All Purpose Room on the third floor is equipped with a full bath

FIRST FLOOR — 1,293 SQ. FT.
SECOND FLOOR — 1,138 SQ. FT.
THIRD FLOOR — 575 SQ. FT.
BASEMENT — 1,293 SQ. FT.

TOTAL LIVING AREA:
3,006 SQ. FT.

CHARMING AND DIGNIFIED

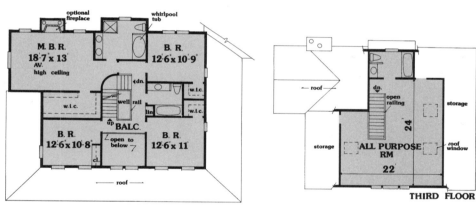

SECOND FLOOR

THIRD FLOOR

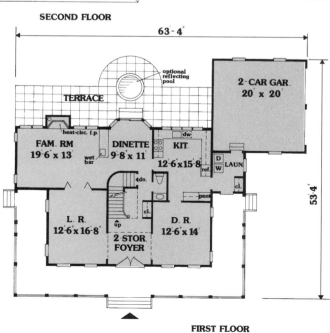

FIRST FLOOR

PRICE CODE C

HOME FILLED WITH COUNTRY COMFORTS

No. 90687

■ This plan features:

— Four bedrooms

— Two and one half baths

■ A covered porch, window boxes, and two chimneys

■ Cozy Living and Dining Rooms

■ Cabinets and a greenhouse bay separate the Kitchen, dinette, and Family Room overlooking the backyard

■ A covered porch just off the fire-placed Family Room

FIRST FLOOR — 1,065 SQ. FT.
SECOND FLOOR — 1,007 SQ. FT.
LAUNDRY/MUDROOM — 88 SQ. FT.
GARAGE — 428 SQ. FT.

TOTAL LIVING AREA:
2,160 SQ. FT.

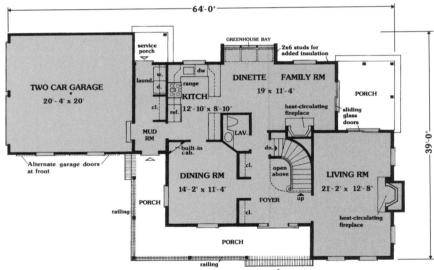

FIRST FLOOR PLAN

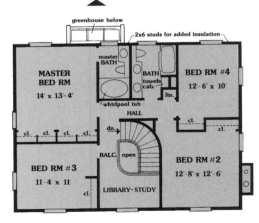

SECOND FLOOR PLAN

PRICE CODE C

SKYLIGHT BRIGHTENS BREAKFAST NOOK

No. 24251

■ This plan features:

— Three bedrooms

— Two full and one half bath

■ A covered porch entry

■ A vaulted ceiling and bay window in the Dining Room

■ A center island Kitchen, with a double basin sink, efficiently using space

■ A skylight adds natural light to the Breakfast Nook

■ Built-in bookshelves or an entertainment center around the fireplace in the Family Room

■ A wetbar convenient to the entertainment areas

■ A Master Suite with a cathedral ceiling has a walk-in closet, a double vanity, separate shower and tub in the bathroom

■ Two additional bedrooms share a full hall bath

FIRST FLOOR — 1,157 SQ. FT.
SECOND FLOOR — 907 SQ. FT.

**TOTAL LIVING AREA:
2,064 SQ. FT.**

An
EXCLUSIVE DESIGN
By Energetic Enterprises

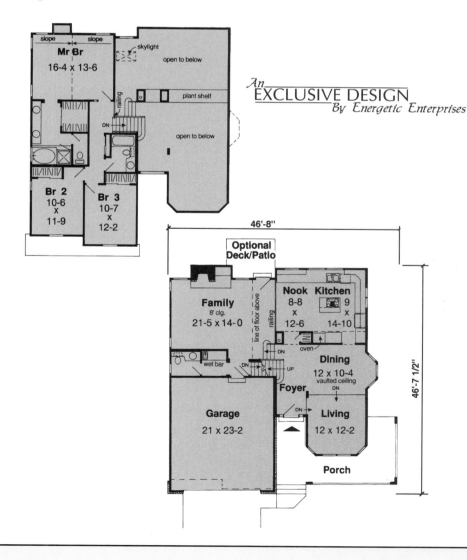

PRICE CODE C

FARMHOUSE INFLUENCE

No. 10829

■ This plan features:

— Four bedrooms

— Two full and one half bath

■ Clapboard siding, a covered rear porch and colonial windows convey an old-fashioned warmth

■ Formal Living and Dining Rooms

■ An efficient U-shaped Kitchen, equipped with double sinks, a built-in pantry and a peninsula counter/eating bar that separates it from the Breakfast area

■ A cozy fireplace enhancing the Family Room while adding warmth and atmosphere

■ A second floor Master Suite with a private bath

■ Three additional bedrooms which share a full bath

FIRST FLOOR — 1,116 SQ. FT.
SECOND FLOOR — 825 SQ. FT.
BASEMENT — 1,116 SQ. FT.
GARAGE — 576 SQ. FT.

TOTAL LIVING AREA:
1,941 SQ. FT.

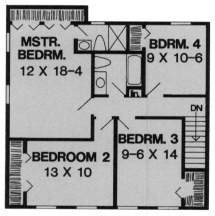

SECOND FLOOR

MSTR. BEDRM. 12 X 18-4

BDRM. 4 9 X 10-6

BEDRM. 3 9-6 X 14

BEDROOM 2 13 X 10

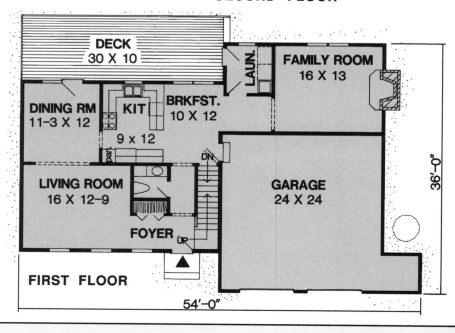

DECK 30 X 10

DINING RM 11-3 X 12

KIT 9 x 12

BRKFST. 10 X 12

LAUN.

FAMILY ROOM 16 X 13

LIVING ROOM 16 X 12-9

GARAGE 24 X 24

FOYER

UP

FIRST FLOOR

36'-0"

54'-0"

PRICE CODE B

CHARMING EXTERIOR DELIGHTS WITHIN

No. 34376

■ This plan features:

— Three bedrooms

— Two full baths

■ An arched window and covered porch entry

■ An open Living Room and Dining Room arrangement spanning the depth of the home

■ A Kitchen, including a corner sink, with a window overlooking the backyard

■ Twin bay windows adding light and space to the informal Dining area and Master Suite

■ An attached street-side Garage adding a sound buffer for the three bedrooms

MAIN AREA — 1,748 SQ. FT.
BASEMENT — 1,693 SQ. FT.
GARAGE — 541 SQ. FT.

TOTAL LIVING AREA:
1,748 SQ. FT.

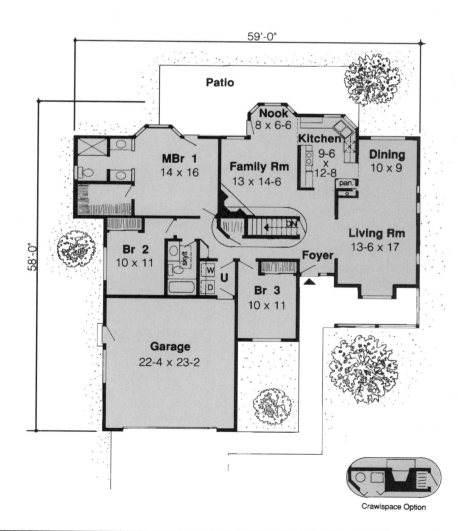

Crawlspace Option

PRICE CODE F

A MASTER SUITE TO LOVE

No. 99240

■ This plan features:

— Three bedrooms

— Two full and two half baths

■ A large Sun Room with a cathedral ceiling and floor-to-ceiling windows

■ An enormous country Kitchen with a center range, double wall ovens, more than ample counter space, and a snackbar

■ A Clutter Room with a walk-in pantry, half-bath, and laundry/work area

■ A double-sided fireplace that opens the Kitchen to the Living Room with a wall-length raised hearth

■ A huge Master Suite with his-n-her walk-in closets, dressing or exercise room and a private Master Bath

FIRST FLOOR — 3,511 SQ. FT.
SECOND FLOOR — 711 SQ. FT.
GARAGE — 841 SQ. FT.
WORKSHOP/THIRD GARAGE BAY —
231 SQ. FT.

TOTAL LIVING AREA:
4,222 SQ. FT.

SECOND FLOOR

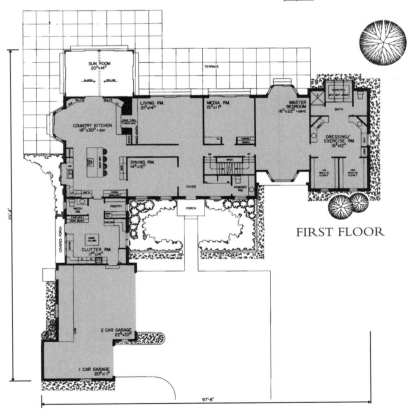

FIRST FLOOR

PRICE CODE F

COLONIAL CLASSIC

No. 99210

■ This plan features:

— Three bedrooms

— Three full and one half baths

■ A dramatic cathedral ceiling entry with balcony overlook

■ A two-story Family Room with a divided window wall

■ A well-planned Kitchen that opens onto a sunny, "greenhouse" Breakfast Room

■ Separate his-n-her dressing/bath suites in the Master Bedroom

FIRST FLOOR — 2,116 SQ. FT.
SECOND FLOOR — 1,848 SQ. FT.
GARAGE — 667 SQ. FT.

TOTAL LIVING AREA:
3,964 SQ. FT.

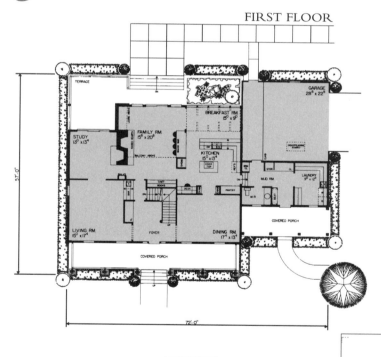

FIRST FLOOR

SECOND FLOOR

PRICE CODE E

FAMILY ROOM WITH EXPOSED BEAMS

No. 93307

■ This plan features:

— Three bedrooms

— Two full and one half baths

■ An attractive elevation using stone veneer and shingles with multi-paned windows

■ A two-story Foyer with a balcony above

■ A Kitchen with a cooktop island, added space for an eating bar, and ample pantry and cabinet space

■ An informal Dinette Area

■ Exposed beams and a fireplace enhance the Family Room

■ A formal Living Room and Dining Room

■ A Master Suite with a sitting area, lavish Bath and walk-in closet

■ Two additional bedrooms that share a full hall bath

FIRST FLOOR — 1,685 SQ. FT.
SECOND FLOOR — 1,187 SQ. FT.
BASEMENT — 1,685 SQ. FT.
GARAGE — 576 SQ. FT.

**TOTAL LIVING AREA:
2,872 SQ. FT.**

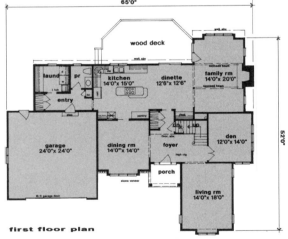

first floor plan

No materials list available

second floor plan

An
EXCLUSIVE DESIGN
By Patrick Morabito, A.I.A. Architect

PRICE CODE D

No. 93283

■ This plan features:

— Four bedrooms

— Two and a half baths

■ A Victorian accented porch with an octagonal sitting area

■ A central Foyer area highlighted by a decorative staircase

■ An elegant bay window in the formal Dining Room

■ A formal Living Room

■ A large Kitchen with a central work island and an open layout into the cheery Breakfast Bay

■ An expansive Family Room equipped with a cozy fireplace and two sets of French doors leading to the Sun deck

■ A grand Master Suite with a sitting alcove, a walk-in closet, a bath and a private balcony

■ Three additional bedrooms, one with an attractive bay window

■ Second floor laundry area

FIRST FLOOR — 1,155 SQ. FT.
SECOND FLOOR — 1,209 SQ. FT.

TOTAL LIVING AREA: 2,364 SQ. FT.

COUNTRY VICTORIAN

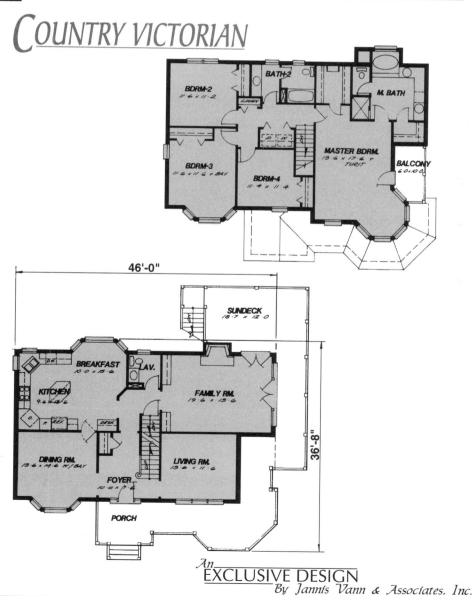

An
EXCLUSIVE DESIGN
By Jannis Vann & Associates. Inc.

PRICE CODE B

OLD-FASHIONED CHARM

No. 21124

■ This plan features:

— Two bedrooms

— Two full baths

■ An old-fashioned, homespun flavor created by the use of lattice work, horizontal and vertical placement of wood siding, and full-length porches

■ An open Living Room, Dining Room and Kitchen

■ A Master Suite finishing the first level

■ Wood floors throughout adding a touch of country

FIRST FLOOR — 835 SQ. FT.
SECOND FLOOR — 817 SQ. FT.
WIDTH — 45'-4"
DEPTH — 34'-0"

TOTAL LIVING AREA: 1,652 SQ. FT.

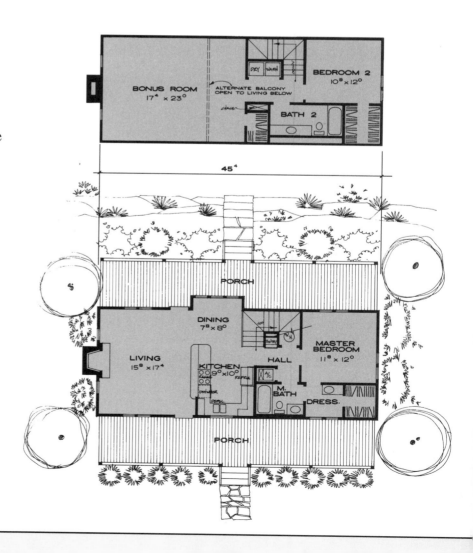

PRICE CODE B

A TOUCH OF VICTORIAN

An
EXCLUSIVE DESIGN
By Greg Stafford

No. 24611

■ This plan features:

— Three bedrooms

— Two full and one half baths

■ A cozy fireplace enhancing the Living Room

■ A formal Dining Room that can easily view and enjoy the Living Room's fireplace, adding ambience to entertaining

■ A efficient, well-appointed, U-shaped Kitchen

■ A sunny Breakfast Nook that views the rear yard

■ A second floor Master Suite with a sloped ceiling, private bath and a walk-in closet

■ Two additional bedrooms that share a full hall bath

FIRST FLOOR — 857 SQ. FT.
SECOND FLOOR — 829 SQ. FT.
GARAGE — 484 SQ. FT.
PORCH — 120 SQ. FT.

TOTAL LIVING AREA:
1,686 SQ. FT.

No materials list available

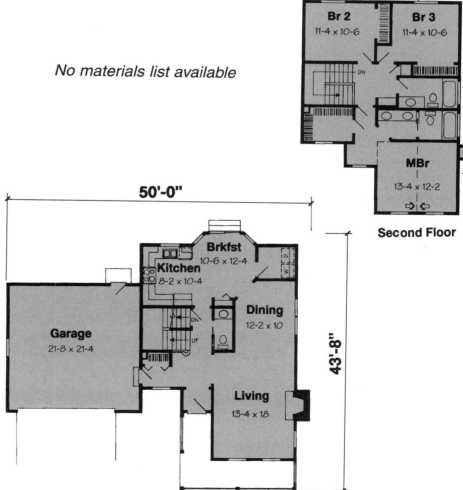

PRICE CODE D

Lots of room to grow

No. 93237

■ This plan features:

— Three bedrooms

— Two full and one half baths

■ A formal Living Room adjoining the Dining Room, perfectly arranged for entertaining

■ A Kitchen with an abundance of work space and a peninsula counter/eating bar

■ A Breakfast Bay with access to the Sun Deck and a pantry

■ A spacious Family Room enhanced by a cozy fireplace

■ A second floor Master Suite with a decorative ceiling, a private bath and two walk-in closets

■ Two additional bedrooms sharing use of the full hall bath

■ Second floor Laundry Room

■ A Bonus Room for future growth

FIRST FLOOR — 1,128 SQ. FT.
SECOND FLOOR — 1,180 SQ. FT.
BONUS ROOM — 254 SQ. FT.
BASEMENT — 1,114 SQ. FT.
GARAGE — 484 SQ. FT.

TOTAL LIVING AREA: 2,308 SQ. FT.

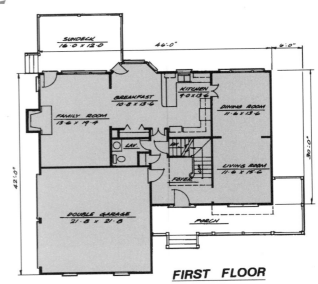

FIRST FLOOR

No materials list available

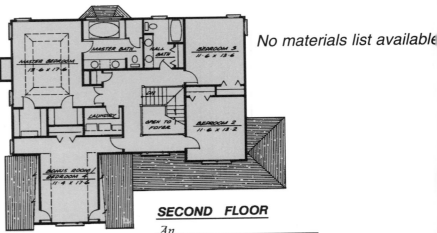

SECOND FLOOR

An EXCLUSIVE DESIGN
By Jannis Vann & Associates, Inc.

192

PRICE CODE F

A FITTING EXECUTIVE DWELLING

No. 93331

■ This plan features:

— Four bedrooms

— Two full and one half baths

■ A fireplace in the formal Living Room

■ A high ceiling and balcony overlooking the Foyer

■ A formal Dining Room with a bump-out window

■ A wonderful gourmet Kitchen with a cooktop island/snack bar and a built-in pantry

■ An informal Dinette area with direct access to the wood deck

■ A tray ceiling and fireplace enhance the Family Room

■ A tray ceiling and lavish bath in the large Master Suite

■ Three additional bedrooms share a full hall bath

FIRST FLOOR — 1,946 SQ. FT.
SECOND FLOOR — 1,484 SQ. FT.
BASEMENT — 1,946 SQ. FT.
GARAGE — 816 SQ. FT.

**TOTAL LIVING AREA:
3,430 SQ. FT.**

No materials list available

An
EXCLUSIVE DESIGN
By Patrick Morabito, A.I.A. Architect

PRICE CODE C

OPEN LAYOUT FOR AN EFFICIENT RANCH

No. 20103

■ This plan features:

— Three bedrooms

— Two full baths

■ A country porch sheltering a recessed entry

■ High ceilings and angled fireplace flanked by built-in bookcases in the Living Room

■ A spacious Kitchen adjoining a sunny Breakfast Nook with sliding glass doors to the rear deck

■ A formal Dining Room with a decorative ceiling overlooking the rear yard

■ A Master Suite that includes a full bath with double vanities and a walk-in shower

■ Two additional bedrooms sharing A second full bath

■ Two-car garage with Kitchen access

MAIN AREA — 1,927 SQ. FT.
GARAGE — 477 SQ. FT.

**TOTAL LIVING AREA:
1,927 SQ. FT.**

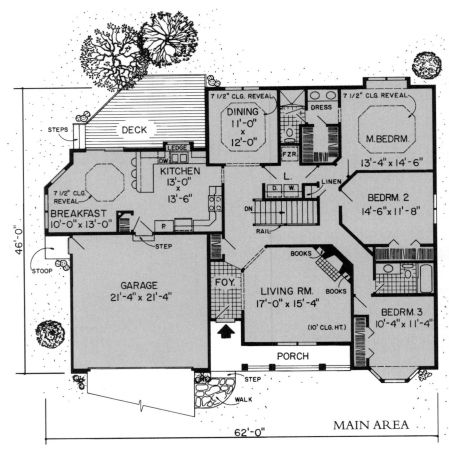

An
EXCLUSIVE DESIGN
By Karl Kreeger

PRICE CODE E

GABLES PROVIDE COZY SITTING NOOKS

No. 20117

■ This plan features:

— Three bedrooms

— Two and one half baths

■ An expansive Living and Dining Room arrangement tucked right off the central foyer

■ A Kitchen and Breakfast area overlooking the rear deck

■ An elegant Master Suite with a huge, walk-in closet and double vanities

■ Two upstairs bedrooms with an adjoining full bath, a handy cedar closet for winter storage, and a loft tucked above the rest of the house

FIRST FLOOR — 1,766 SQ. FT.
SECOND FLOOR — 999 SQ. FT.
BASEMENT — 1,730 SQ. FT.
GARAGE — 504 SQ. FT.

**TOTAL LIVING AREA:
2,765 SQ. FT.**

An
EXCLUSIVE DESIGN
By Karl Kreeger

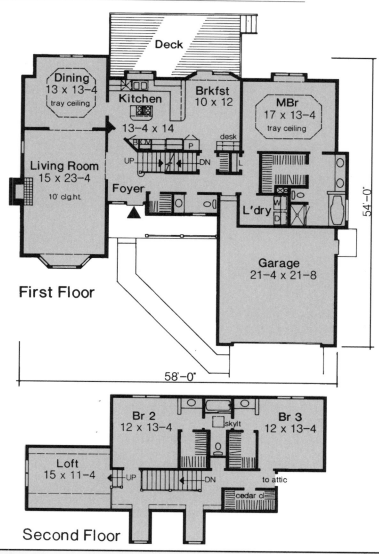

First Floor

Second Floor

PRICE CODE D

DIGNIFIED GRACE AND STYLE

No. 93305

■ This plan features:

— Three bedrooms

— Two full and one half baths

■ A two-story Foyer with an overlooking balcony

■ An expansive Great Room with a tray ceiling and a sensational fireplace

■ A first floor Master Suite that includes a walk-in closet and a Master Bath

■ An island Kitchen and Dinette area with more than ample cabinet and closet space

■ Sliding glass doors that lead to a wood deck

■ A formal Dining Room with direct access to the Great Room

■ Two bedrooms on the second floor that share a full bath

FIRST FLOOR — 1,542 SQ. FT.
SECOND FLOOR — 685 SQ. FT.
BASEMENT — 1,542 SQ. FT.
GARAGE — 576 SQ. FT.

**TOTAL LIVING AREA:
2,227 SQ. FT.**

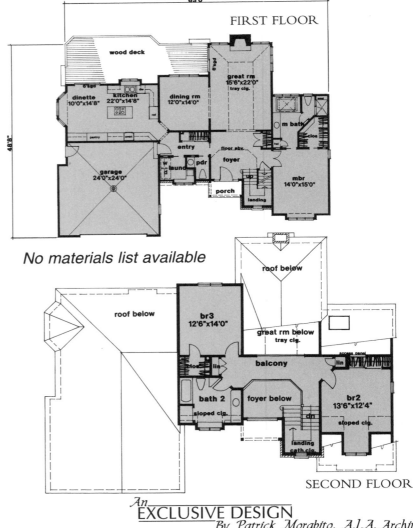

No materials list available

An
EXCLUSIVE DESIGN
By Patrick Morabito, A.I.A. Architect

PRICE CODE B

A TOUCH OF VICTORIAN STYLING

No. 93230

■ This plan features:

— Three bedrooms

— Two full and one half baths

■ A covered porch and a pointed roof on the sitting alcove of the Master Suite giving this home a Victorian look

■ A formal Living Room directly across from the Dining Room for ease in entertaining

■ An efficient Kitchen with a bright bayed Breakfast area

■ The Family Room has a cozy fireplace nestled in a corner

■ A large Master Suite with a cozy sitting alcove and double vanity bath

■ Two additional bedrooms serviced by a full hall bath

FIRST FLOOR — 887 SQ. FT.
SECOND FLOOR — 877 SQ. FT.
BASEMENT — 859 SQ. FT.
GARAGE — 484 SQ. FT.

**TOTAL LIVING AREA:
1,764 SQ. FT.**

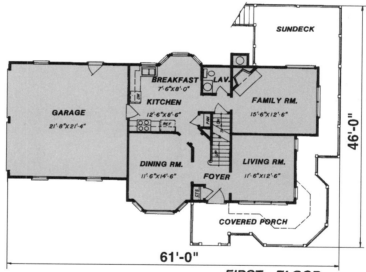

FIRST FLOOR

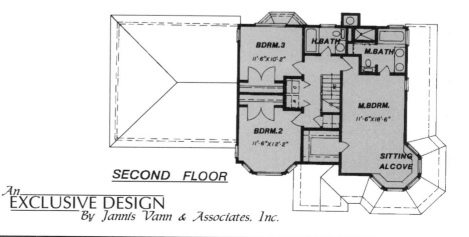

SECOND FLOOR

An
EXCLUSIVE DESIGN
By Jannis Vann & Associates, Inc.

PRICE CODE D

DEN DOUBLES AS HOME OFFICE

No. 90816

- ■ This plan features:
- — Four bedrooms
- — Two full and one half baths
- ■ A sunken Living Room for formal entertaining
- ■ A built-in china cabinet in the Dining Room which also has a bay window
- ■ A built-in pantry and planning area in the efficient Kitchen
- ■ A sunken Family Room with a cozy fireplace
- ■ A Master Suite with a Jacuzzi tub and a separate shower

FIRST FLOOR — 1,252 SQ. FT.
SECOND FLOOR — 1,117 SQ. FT.
BASEMENT — 1,245 SQ. FT.
GARAGE — 564 SQ. FT.
WIDTH — 71'-0"
DEPTH — 35'-0"

TOTAL LIVING AREA: 2,369 SQ. FT.

An
EXCLUSIVE DESIGN
By Westhome Planners, Ltd.

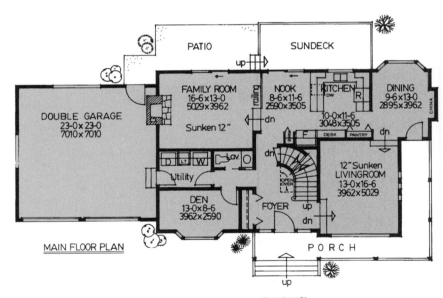

MAIN FLOOR PLAN

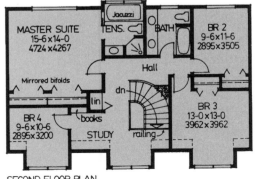

SECOND FLOOR PLAN

PRICE CODE D

No. 92012

■ This plan features:

— Three bedrooms

— Two full and one half baths

■ A two-story Entry

■ A formal Living Room with a large front picture window with a half-circle transom above

■ A Den with a decorative ceiling to use as an office, study or fourth bedroom

■ A formal dining room crowned by a decorative ceiling

■ A large island Kitchen with a Breakfast area that is open to the fireplaced Family Room

■ A Master Suite with his-n-her closets, a double vanity bath and a separate shower and tub

■ Two additional bedrooms with a full bath

FIRST FLOOR — 1,264 SQ. FT.
SECOND FLOOR — 940 SQ. FT.
BASEMENT — 1,252 SQ. FT.
GARAGE — 455 SQ. FT.

TOTAL LIVING AREA:
2,204 SQ. FT.

IRRESTIBLE COUNTRY CHARM

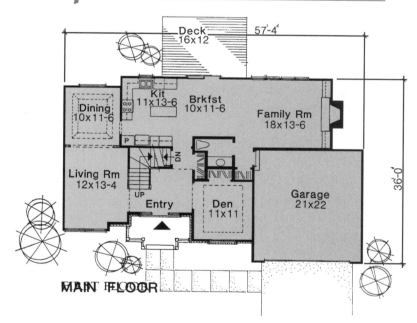

MAIN FLOOR

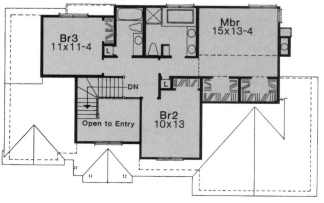

SECOND FLOOR

PRICE CODE E

DESIGNED FOR A LARGER FAMILY

No. 91710

■ This plan features:

— Four or five bedrooms

— Two full and one half baths

■ Country wrap-around porch, with two entrances: one into the Foyer, the other into the Eating Nook

■ Formal Living and Dining Rooms with charming bay windows

■ An efficient Kitchen open to the Nook and Family Room, with two peninsula counters

■ A bright Eating Nook with a convenient walk-in pantry

■ A cozy corner fireplace

■ A bay window gracing the Master Suite, with a double vanity bath and a walk-in closet

■ Three additional bedrooms sharing a full hall bath

FIRST FLOOR — 1,654 SQ. FT.
SECOND FLOOR — 1,526 SQ. FT.
GARAGE — 700 SQ. FT.

**TOTAL LIVING AREA:
3,180 SQ. FT.**

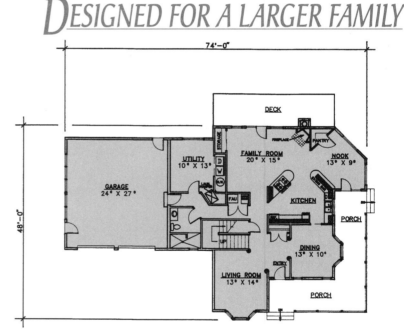

MAIN LEVEL

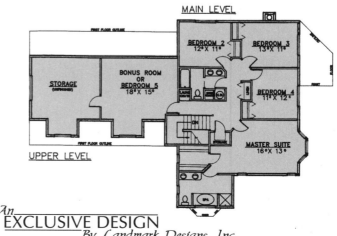

UPPER LEVEL

An EXCLUSIVE DESIGN
By Landmark Designs, Inc.

PRICE CODE D

No. 91784

■ This plan features:

— Three bedrooms

— Two full and one half baths

■ A second floor balcony overlooking the entry area and Family Room

■ A roomy Living Room graced with a bay window area

■ A brick-faced fireplace in the expansive Family Room

■ An efficient Kitchen equipped with a cooktop island and an informal eating nook with a large walk-in pantry

■ A Master Suite with a bay window area, a walk-in closet and an extravagant bath

■ Two additional bedrooms that share a full hall bath with a laundry chute to the Laundry room below

MAIN AREA — 2,487 SQ. FT.
GARAGE — 779 SQ. FT.
WIDTH — 76'-0"
DEPTH — 50'-0"

TOTAL LIVING AREA:
2,487 SQ. FT.

ATTRACTIVE DETAILING AND ANGLES

An
EXCLUSIVE DESIGN
By Landmark Designs. Inc.

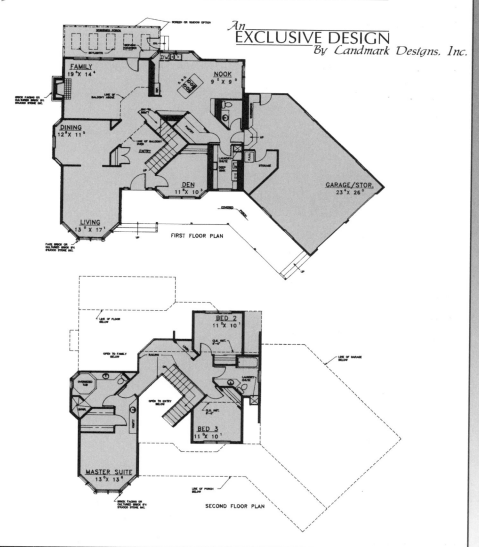

PRICE CODE A

RUSTIC EXTERIOR COMPLETES HOME

No. 34600

■ This plan features:

— Three bedrooms

— Two full baths

■ A two-story, fireplaced Living Room with exposed beams adds to the rustic charm

■ An efficient, modern Kitchen with ample work and storage space

■ Two first floor bedrooms with individual closet space share a full bath

■ A Master Bedroom secluded on the second floor with its own full bath

■ A welcoming front Porch adding to the living space

FIRST FLOOR — 1,013 SQ. FT.
SECOND FLOOR — 315 SQ. FT.
BASEMENT — 1,008 SQ. FT.

TOTAL LIVING AREA:
1,328 SQ. FT.

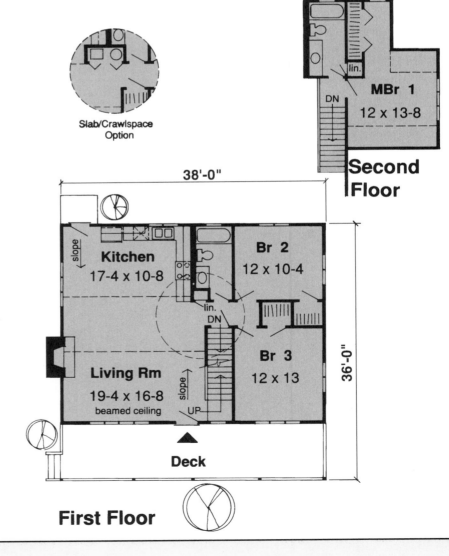

Slab/Crawlspace Option

First Floor

PRICE CODE C

Beautiful family home

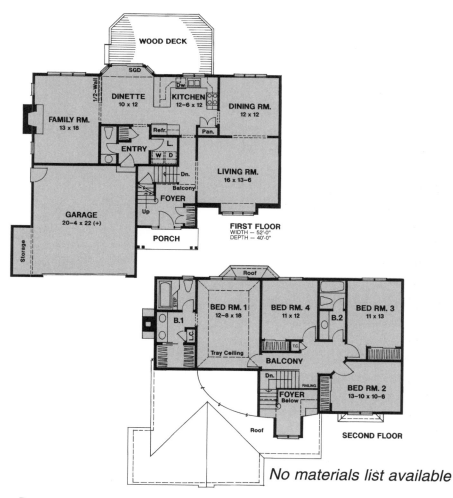

No. 93314

■ This plan features:

— Four bedrooms

— Two full and one half baths

■ A tray ceiling and private Bath in the Master Suite

■ A formal Living Room and Dining Room that flow into each other for ease in entertaining

■ A U-shaped Kitchen with a built-in pantry and an eating bar

■ A fireplace in the cozy Family Room

■ A entrance from the garage keeping muddy shoes and dirty clothing away from living areas

■ Three smaller bedrooms that share a full hall bath

FIRST FLOOR — 1,145 SQ. FT.
SECOND FLOOR — 1,004 SQ. FT.
BASEMENT — 1,145 SQ. FT.
GARAGE — 480 SQ. FT.

TOTAL LIVING AREA:
2,149 SQ. FT.

No materials list available

An
EXCLUSIVE DESIGN
By Patrick Morabito, A.I.A. Architect

PRICE CODE D

A BIT OF NINETEENTH CENTURY

No. 99716

■ This plan features:

— Three bedrooms

— Three full baths

■ Twin front gables, bay windows and a large, wrap-around, covered front porch giving a feeling of the nineteenth century

■ A country Kitchen with a central island and an attached pantry

■ A Dining Area that is located at the back of the Living Room

■ A cozy fireplace in the Living Room

■ A Master Suite with a walk-in closet and a private bath that includes a raised tub

■ Two smaller bedrooms that share a bath and vanity between them

FIRST FLOOR — 1,370 SQ. FT.
SECOND FLOOR — 1,162 SQ. FT.
GARAGE — 657 SQ. FT.
WIDTH — 70'-0"
DEPTH — 34'-0"

TOTAL LIVING AREA:
2,532 SQ. FT.

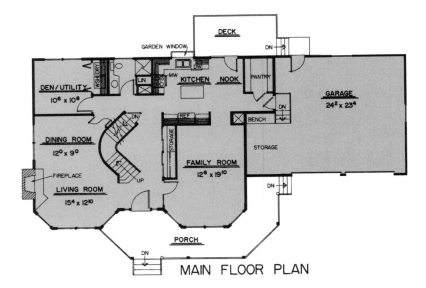

MAIN FLOOR PLAN

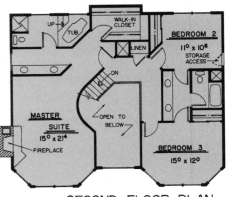

SECOND FLOOR PLAN

PRICE CODE C

PASSIVE SOLAR HEATING

No. 99739

■ This plan features:

— Three bedrooms

— Two full baths

■ A spacious uniquely shaped Living Room with a wood stove

■ A Family Room with four skylights and direct deck access

■ An efficient Kitchen with a cooktop, eating bar island, and a garden window above the sink

■ A private Master Suite that is equipped with a walk-in closet, oval tub, step-in shower, skylight and double vanity.

■ Two additional bedrooms that share a full hall bath

MAIN AREA — 1,979 SQ. FT.
GARAGE — 628 SQ. FT.
WIDTH — 60'-0"
DEPTH — 66'-0"

TOTAL LIVING AREA:
1,979 SQ. FT.

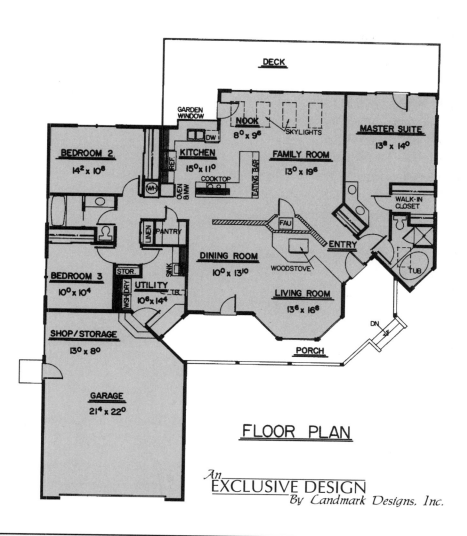

FLOOR PLAN

An
EXCLUSIVE DESIGN
By Landmark Designs, Inc.

PRICE CODE D

LONG, CLEAN LINES

No. 98744

■ This plan features:

— Three bedrooms

— Two full baths

■ A long porch sweeping across most of the front facade

■ Formal Living and Dining Room areas that open to each other with a fireplace for partial separation

■ A Family Theater area with a built-in entertainment center accessible on either side of the wall

■ Two secondary bedrooms that share a full bath in the hall

■ An efficient Kitchen separated from the Nook by a peninsula counter/eating bar

■ A splendid Master Suite with a private bath, sitting area and two sets of glass doors open to porches

MAIN FLOOR — 2,424 SQ. FT.
GARAGE — 962 SQ. FT.
WIDTH — 86'-0"
DEPTH — 72'-0"

TOTAL LIVING AREA:
2,424 SQ. FT.

An
EXCLUSIVE DESIGN
By Landmark Designs, Inc.

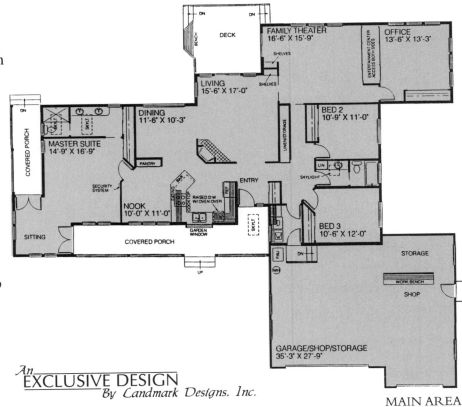

MAIN AREA

PRICE CODE D

LARGE OPEN LIVING SPACES

No. 98745

■ This plan features:

— Three bedrooms

— Two full and one half baths

■ A covered veranda that sweeps around to the side of the house

■ A cozy Family Room open to the Dining Room and the Kitchen

■ A formal Dining area efficiently served by the Kitchen

■ A charming Master Suite enhanced by a private bath and a huge walk-in closet

■ Two additional bedrooms served by a full bath in the hall

■ Mud/Utility Room has outside entrance and easy access from the garage

FIRST FLOOR — 1,830 SQ. FT.
SECOND FLOOR — 582 SQ. FT.
WIDTH — 57'-0"
DEPTH — 65'-0"

TOTAL LIVING AREA:
2,412 SQ. FT.

An
EXCLUSIVE DESIGN
By Landmark Designs, Inc.

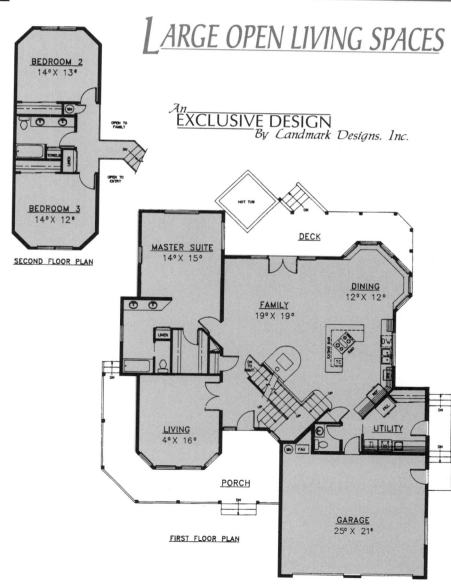

SECOND FLOOR PLAN

BEDROOM 2
14⁰ X 13⁰

OPEN TO FAMILY

OPEN TO ENTRY

BEDROOM 3
14⁰ X 12⁸

FIRST FLOOR PLAN

HOT TUB

DECK

MASTER SUITE
14⁰ X 15⁰

DINING
12⁰ X 12⁰

FAMILY
19⁰ X 19⁰

LINEN

LIVING
4⁰ X 16⁰

UTILITY

PORCH

GARAGE
25⁰ X 21⁸

PRICE CODE E

PLENTY OF ROOM FOR ALL

No. 93249

■ This plan features:

— Four bedrooms

— Three full and one half baths

■ An extensive Living Area with a fireplace, built-in shelves, double doors to the rear porch and an embellished ceiling

■ A U-shaped Kitchen that includes a double sink, a peninsula counter and an island

■ A sunny bayed Breakfast Room and a formal Dining Room on separate sides of the Kitchen

■ A main floor Master Suite with a decorative ceiling and a luxurious private Bath

■ Three bedrooms on the lower level, one with a private bath and one with private access to a full bath

■ Two-car garage

MAIN LEVEL — 1,871 SQ. FT.
LOWER LEVEL — 1,015 SQ. FT.
BASEMENT — 826 SQ. FT.
GARAGE — 558 SQ. FT.

TOTAL LIVING AREA:

An
EXCLUSIVE DESIGN
By Jannis Vann & Associates, Inc.

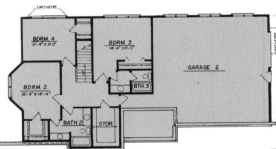

LOWER LEVEL

MAIN LEVEL

No materials list available

PRICE CODE F

ALL THE AMENITIES YOU NEED

No. 93329

■ This plan features:

— Four bedrooms

— Two full and one half baths

■ A sunken Living Room with a focal point fireplace

■ A bayed window and stepped ceiling in the Dining Room

■ A sunken Den with built-in bookshelves and a storage closet

■ A focal point fireplace, beamed ceiling and window seat in the Family Room

■ A gourmet Kitchen with work island and built-in pantry

■ A Master Suite that includes a tray ceiling and a large walk-in closet

■ A compartmented Master Bath with a separate tub and shower

■ Three additional bedrooms that share a full bath

FIRST FLOOR — 1,823 SQ. FT.
SECOND FLOOR — 1,492 SQ. FT.
BASEMENT — 1,823 SQ. FT.
GARAGE — 832 SQ. FT.

TOTAL LIVING AREA:
3,315 SQ. FT.

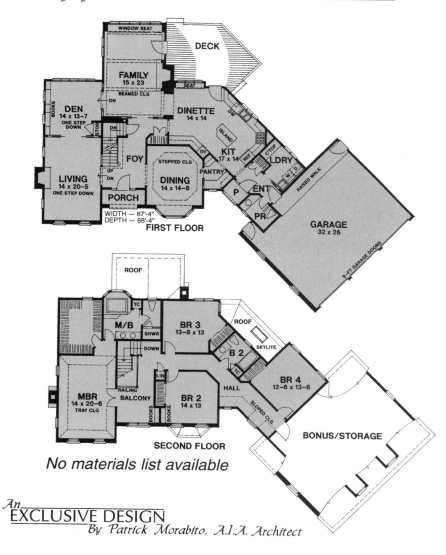

No materials list available

An EXCLUSIVE DESIGN
By Patrick Morabito, A.I.A. Architect

PRICE CODE C

ABUNDANT WINDOWS ADD AN OUTDOOR FEELING

No. 99310

- This plan features:
- — Three bedrooms
- — Two and one half baths
- A Traditional front porch
- A breakfast bay overlooking the patio
- A built-in bar in the Dining Room
- An efficient Kitchen with range top island, built-in planning desk, and pantry
- A Living Room with fireplace, vaulted ceilings, and windows on three sides
- A Master Suite with a private, double vanity bath

FIRST FLOOR — 1,160 SQ. FT.
SECOND FLOOR — 797 SQ. FT.

TOTAL LIVING AREA:
1,957 SQ. FT.

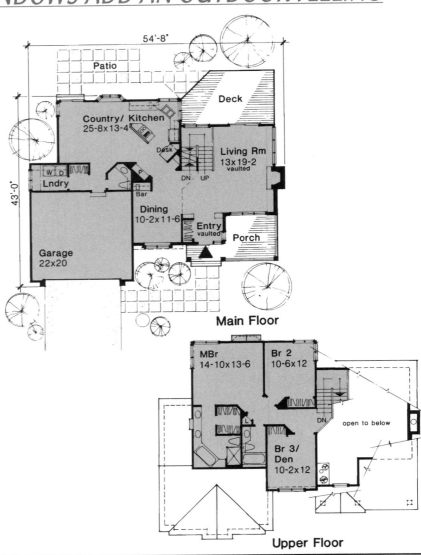

Main Floor

Upper Floor

PRICE CODE E

PLENTY OF CURB APPEAL

No. 99348

■ This plan features:

— Four bedrooms

— Two full and one half baths

■ A country porch leading to a two-story ceramic tiled Foyer

■ A spacious Family Room

■ Three skylights illuminating the Sun Room

■ A decorative coffered ceiling in the formal Dining Room

■ A Kitchen with ceramic tile, a peninsula counter/eating bar and a walk-in pantry

■ An luxurious Master Bath and a walk-in closet in the Master Suite which also has a vaulted ceiling

■ Three additional bedrooms, one with a cozy window seat

FIRST FLOOR — 1,363 SQ. FT.
SECOND FLOOR — 1,357 SQ.FT.
SUN ROOM — 146 SQ. FT.
OFFICE SPACE — 300 SQ. FT.
BASEMENT — 1,663 SQ. FT.
GARAGE — 504 SQ. FT.

**TOTAL LIVING AREA:
3,166 SQ. FT.**

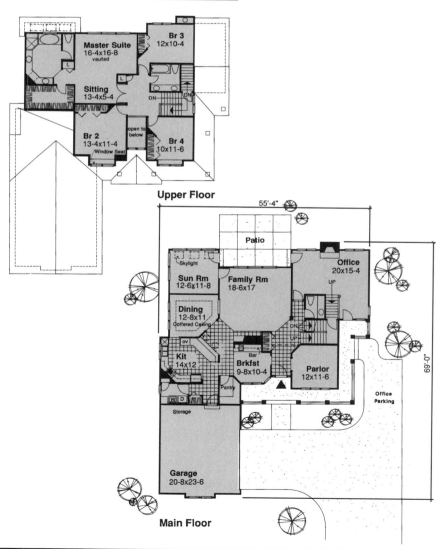

PRICE CODE D

No. 90826

■ This plan features:

— Three or four bedrooms

— Three full and one half baths

■ A large wrap-around porch

■ An immense Living Room, highlighted by a fieldstone fireplace

■ A Study or Guest Room with easy access to a full bath

■ A central work island Kitchen

■ Open floor plan between the Kitchen and the Family Room

■ A formal Dining Room with direct access to the Kitchen

■ A Sewing room and a Utility Room

■ A large Master Suite served by a private bath and huge walk-in closet

FIRST FLOOR — 1,463 SQ. FT.
SECOND FLOOR — 981 SQ. FT.
BASEMENT — 814 SQ. FT.

TOTAL LIVING AREA:
2,444 SQ. FT.

An
EXCLUSIVE DESIGN
By Westhome Planners, Ltd.

WATCH THE WORLD GO BY

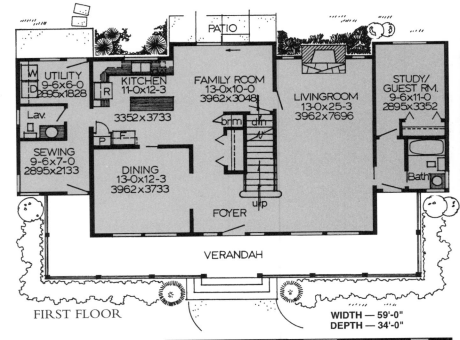

WIDTH — 59'-0"
DEPTH — 34'-0"

FIRST FLOOR

SECOND FLOOR

PRICE CODE E

No. 93304

◼ This plan features:

— Three bedrooms

— Two full and one half baths

◼ A country porch accenting the Victorian details of this home

◼ A two-story Foyer

◼ Octagonal shaped Living Room

◼ A Family Room highlighted by a fireplace, a vaulted ceiling and access to the rear wooden deck

◼ Kitchen with a center cooktop island and a peninsula counter

◼ A formal Dining Room

◼ A large Master Suite served by a private bath and a walk-in closet

◼ Two more bedrooms share use of a full double vanity hall bath

◼ Mudroom sandwiched between the Kitchen and the garage

◼ Convenient second floor laundry

FIRST FLOOR — 1,612 SQ. FT.
SECOND FLOOR — 1,172 SQ. FT.
BASEMENT — 1,612 SQ. FT.
GARAGE — 156 SQ. FT.

**TOTAL LIVING AREA:
2,784 SQ. FT**

OLD FASHIONED COUNTRY HOME

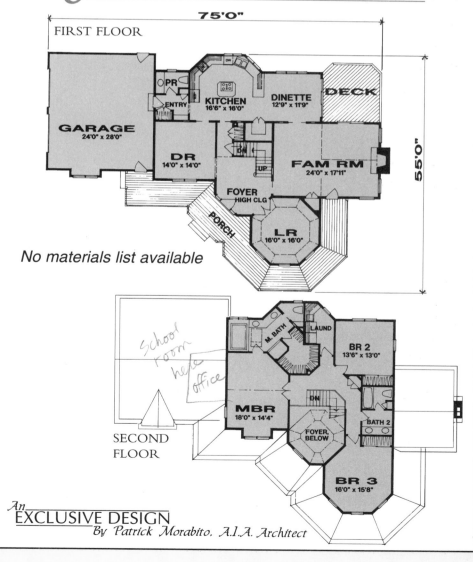

No materials list available

An
EXCLUSIVE DESIGN
By Patrick Morabito, A.I.A. Architect

PRICE CODE D

HOME FOR TODAY AND TOMORROW

No. 92009

■ This plan features:

— Four bedrooms

— Two full and one half baths

■ A covered porch entrance

■ A formal Living Room to the left of the Entry Hall

■ A formal Dining Room with direct access from the Kitchen

■ A spacious fireplaced Family Room, open to the Kitchen yet separated by an eating bar

■ A country Kitchen equipped with a cooktop island peninsula counter, a double sink eating bar, and a built-in pantry

■ A roomy second floor Master Suite with two closets, a double vanity and a compartmented bath

■ Three more bedrooms sharing a full double hall vanity bath

■ A second floor laundry area

FIRST FLOOR — 1,059 SQ. FT.
SECOND FLOOR — 1,248 SQ. FT.
BASEMENT — 1,071 SQ. FT.
GARAGE — 468 SQ. FT.

TOTAL LIVING AREA:
2,307 SQ. FT.

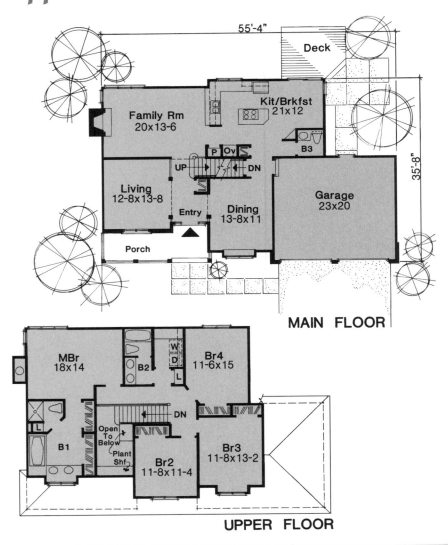

MAIN FLOOR

UPPER FLOOR

PRICE CODE A

QUAINT STARTER HOME

No. 92400

■ This plan features:

— Three bedrooms

— Two full baths

■ A vaulted ceiling giving an airy feeling to the Dining and Living Rooms

■ A streamlined Kitchen with a comfortable work area, a double sink and ample cabinet space

■ A cozy fireplace in the Living Room

■ A Master Suite with a large closet, French doors leading to the patio and a private bath

■ Two additional bedrooms sharing a full bath

MAIN AREA — 1,050 SQ. FT.

TOTAL LIVING AREA:
1,050 SQ. FT.

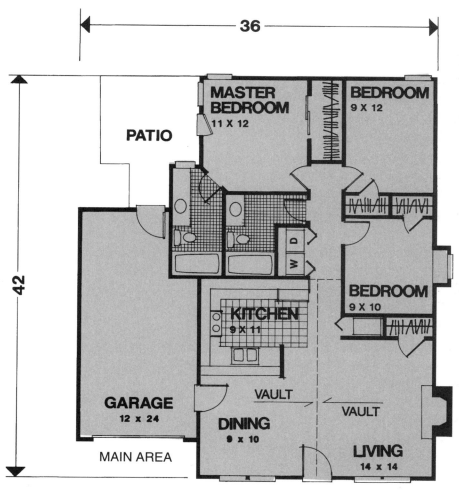

No materials list available

PRICE CODE C

A LONG WRAP-AROUND PORCH TO ENJOY

No. 99765

■ This plan features:

— Three bedrooms

— Two full and one half baths

■ A one story country-style Ranch with a contemporary floor plan

■ A corner fireplace adding warmth to the Living Room

■ A formal Dining Room with sliding glass doors to the deck

■ An eating bar and Nook area in the Kitchen

■ A vaulted ceiling with skylights in the Family Room

■ A Master Suite with private bath and a cedar closet as well as a walk-in closet

■ Two additional bedrooms that share a full bath

MAIN AREA — 1,998 SQ. FT.
BASEMENT — 1,998 SQ. FT.
GARAGE — 635 SQ. FT.
WIDTH — 87'-0"
DEPTH — 48'-0"

TOTAL LIVING AREA:
1,998 SQ. FT.

FLOOR PLAN

An
EXCLUSIVE DESIGN
By Landmark Designs, Inc.

PRICE CODE A

No. 24240

■ This plan features:

— Two bedrooms

— Two full baths

■ A bungalow design that allows breezes to flow from front to back

■ A quaint front porch perfect for a porch swing

■ A cozy Living Room with a fireplace

■ A formal Dining Room, directly accessed from the Living Room and the Kitchen

■ An efficient Kitchen, with a built-in pantry and a cozy booth for informal eating

■ A Laundry Area/Mudroom between the Kitchen and the rear porch

■ A rear Master Bedroom includes a full bath

■ An additional second bedroom

MAIN AREA— 964 SQ. FT.

TOTAL LIVING AREA:
964 SQ. FT.

BE IN TUNE WITH THE ELEMENTS

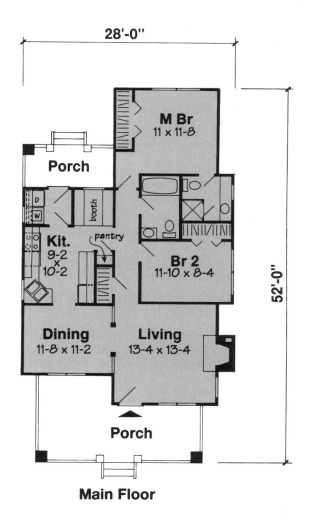

Main Floor

PRICE CODE D

A WIDE WRAP-AROUND RAILED PORCH

No. 99742

■ This plan features:

— Three bedrooms

— Two full and one half bath

■ A country Kitchen with a wide work island, a walk-in pantry, a lazy susan in the corner cupboard and an Eating Nook for informal dining

■ A formal Dining Room with French doors that open onto a small deck

■ A spacious Living Room with a view of the front porch

■ A Family room located at the rear of the house featuring four skylights, a fireplace, a vaulted ceiling and deck access

■ A Master Suite that includes a large walk-in closet and a smaller cedar lined closet, plus a private bath

MAIN AREA — 2,204 SQ. FT.
BASEMENT — 2,148 SQ. FT.
GARAGE — 756 SQ. FT.
WIDTH — 90'-0"
DEPTH — 52'-0"

TOTAL LIVING AREA:
2,204 SQ. FT.

An
EXCLUSIVE DESIGN
By Landmark Designs, Inc.

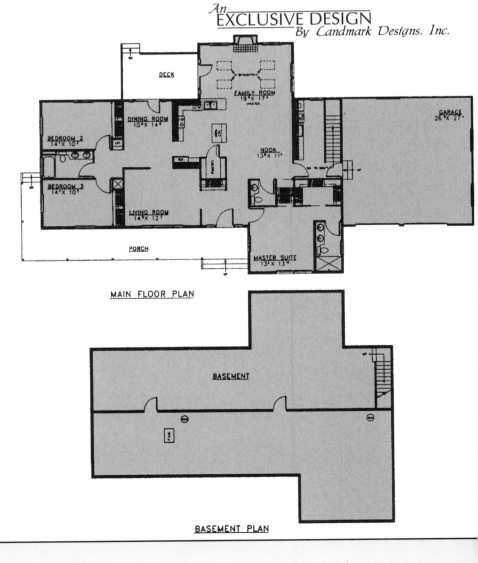

MAIN FLOOR PLAN

BASEMENT PLAN

PRICE CODE D

No. 99355

■ This plan features:

— Four bedrooms

— Two full and one half bath

■ An octagonal porch

■ A vaulted ceiling in the sunken Living Room

■ A lovely formal Dining Room

■ A Kitchen with a cooktop work island/eating bar, a corner double sink and a walk-in pantry

■ An octagon-shaped Breakfast Area, overlaid with a vaulted ceiling

■ An expansive Family Room with a fireplace and a wetbar

■ A skylight illuminating the staircase to the second floor

■ A vaulted ceiling in the Master Suite, with a lavish whirlpool bath and a walk-in closet

■ Three bedrooms using a full bath

MAIN FLOOR — 1,350 SQ. FT.
UPPER FLOOR — 1,163 SQ. FT.
BASEMENT — 1,350 SQ. FT.
GARAGE —433 SQ. FT.

TOTAL LIVING AREA:
2,513 SQ. FT.

UNIQUE PORCH ADDS CHARACTER

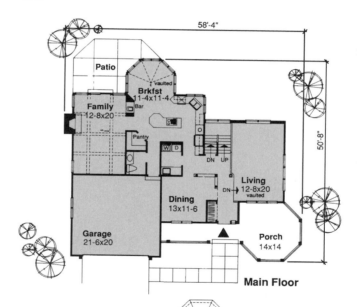

Main Floor

No materials list available

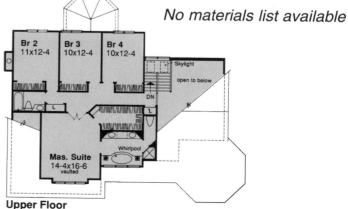

Upper Floor

PRICE CODE C

Country charmer at home anywhere

No. 90237

■ This plan features:

— Three bedrooms

— Two full and one half baths

■ A full length covered porch and peaked gables enhancing curb appeal

■ A roomy Living Room adjoining the bayed Dining Room

■ A Kitchen with ample counter and storage space open to the Dining & Family Rooms

■ Sliding glass doors in the Family Room open to the rear terrace

■ A second floor Master Suite with a walk-in closet and private bath

■ Two additional bedrooms with ample closets

FIRST FLOOR — 1,134 SQ. FT.
SECOND FLOOR — 874 SQ. FT.

TOTAL LIVING AREA:
2,008 SQ. FT.

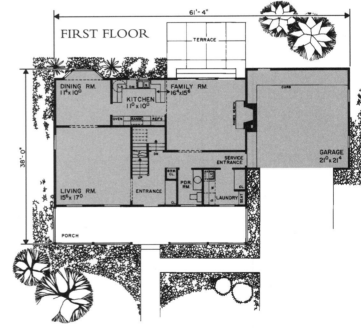

PRICE CODE C

No. 90814

Suited to a Narrow Lot

- This plan features:

— Three bedrooms

— Two full and one half baths

- A large porch providing shelter from the weather and a country flavor to the home

- An eye-catching, open stairway in the Foyer

- A Living/Dining Room combination

- A country Kitchen with a center work island and a bright Breakfast Nook

- A sunken Family Room enhanced by a cozy stone fireplace

- A large Master Suite accented by a beautiful bay window and served by a private bath

- Two additional bedrooms sharing use of a full bath in the hall

FIRST FLOOR — 1,080 SQ. FT.
SECOND FLOOR — 761 SQ. FT.
GARAGE — 420 SQ. FT.
BASEMENT — 1,067 SQ. FT.
WIDTH — 40'-0"
DEPTH — 46'-0"

TOTAL LIVING AREA:
1,841 SQ. FT.

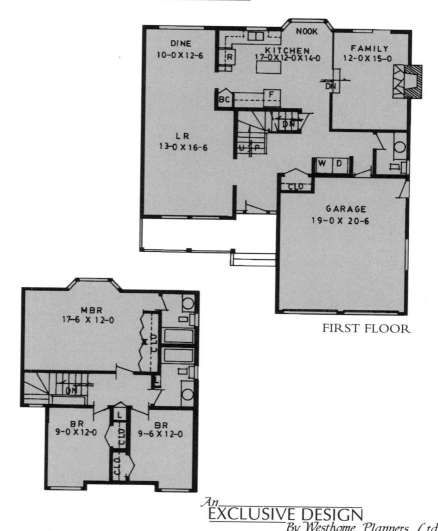

FIRST FLOOR

An
EXCLUSIVE DESIGN
By Westhome Planners, Ltd.

PRICE CODE D

OPEN FLOOR PLAN ADDS SPACIOUSNESS

No materials list available

No. 93303

■ This plan features:

— Three bedrooms

— Two full and one half baths

■ A sheltered entrance leading to an open Foyer area

■ An ample Dining Room graced by the large front window viewing the front yard

■ A formal Living Room

■ An open layout in the rear of the house

■ A Family Room with fireplace

■ Laundry room and garage entry direct to the Kitchen

■ A stepped ceiling in the large Master Suite, served by a compartmented bath and a walk-in closet

■ Two additional bedrooms, one with a walk-in closet, sharing use of a full bath in the hall

FIRST FLOOR — 1,232 SQ. FT.
SECOND FLOOR — 1,050 SQ. FT.
BONUS ROOM — 412 SQ. FT.

TOTAL LIVING AREA:
2,282 SQ. FT.

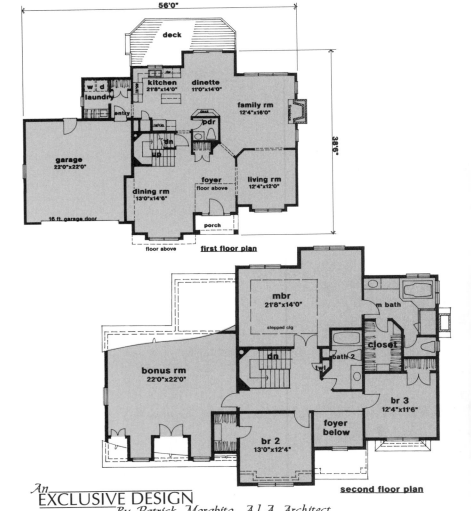

An EXCLUSIVE DESIGN
By Patrick Morabito, A.I.A. Architect

PRICE CODE D

An
EXCLUSIVE DESIGN
By Patrick Morabito, A.I.A. Architect

CLASSICALLY CHARMING

No. 93302

■ This plan features:

— Three bedrooms

— Two full and one half baths

■ An attractive entryway with a transom above leads into a Foyer

■ A spectacular sunken Great Room, equipped with a fireplace and a vaulted ceiling

■ A skylight in the Dinette area

■ A walk-in pantry, angled peninsula counter/eating bar and a corner sink in the Kitchen

■ An elegant formal Dining Room flowing into the Sun Room, topped by two skylights

■ A first floor Master Bedroom Suite features a fireplace, a whirlpool, a walk-in closet and an alternate floor plan

■ A second floor balcony overlooking the Great Room

FIRST FLOOR — 1,689 SQ. FT.
SECOND FLOOR — 537 SQ. FT.

TOTAL LIVING AREA: 2,226 SQ. FT.

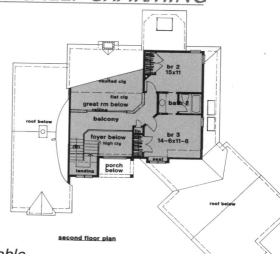

second floor plan

No materials list available

first floor plan

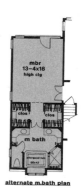

alternate m.bath plan

An
EXCLUSIVE DESIGN
By Patrick Morabito. A.I.A. Architect

PRICE CODE F

No. 93334

■ This plan features:

— Four bedrooms

— Three full and one half baths

■ An unusual Living Room featuring a half-circle of windows topped by a stepped ceiling, and French doors into a Sun Room for elegant entertaining

■ An informal Family Room, with a massive fireplace, convenient built-ins, and a wall of windows, opening to Dinette/Kitchen area

■ An island Kitchen with an abundance of counter space, a double sink, built-in desk and a sky-lit Dinette area leading to the formal Dining Room with a walk-in pantry in between

■ A luxurious Master Suite with a tray ceiling and a private Bath featuring a whirlpool, corner window tub, double vanity and an extra large walk-in closet

■ On the second floor, three additional bedrooms, each with private access to a full bath, and a Bonus Room with many options

FIRST FLOOR — 1,970 SQ. FT.
SECOND FLOOR — 1,638 SQ. FT.
BONUS ROOM — 587 SQ. FT.

ATTRACTIVE ALL AROUND

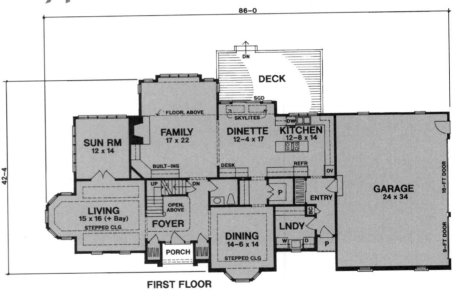

FIRST FLOOR

TOTAL LIVING AREA:
3,608 SQ. FT.

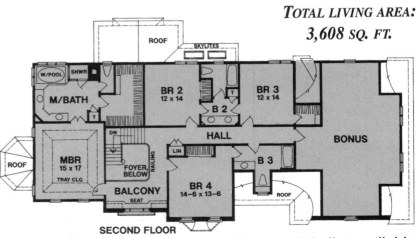

SECOND FLOOR

No materials list available

224

PRICE CODE D

WARM AND INVITING

No. 90827

■ This plan features:

— Three bedrooms

— Three full baths

■ A decorative railing separating the sunken Living Room from the formal Dining Room

■ A Utility/Mudroom at the rear entrance with a laundry center

■ An efficient, country Kitchen with a sunny, pleasant Breakfast Room flowing from it

■ A spacious Master Suite equipped with a private bath and a walk-in closet

■ Two additional roomy bedrooms share the use of the full hall bath

■ A cozy Sitting Area between the bedrooms accesses the second floor balcony

■ A versatile second floor Study can be used as a Den, a Craft Room, or a Children's play area

FIRST FLOOR — 1,349 SQ. FT.
SECOND FLOOR — 1,199 SQ. FT.
WIDTH — 57'-0"
DEPTH — 39'-0"

TOTAL LIVING AREA:
2,548 SQ.FT.

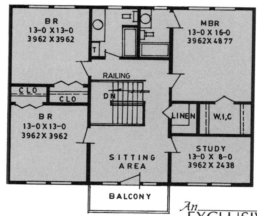

SECOND FLOOR

An EXCLUSIVE DESIGN
By Westhome Planners, Ltd.

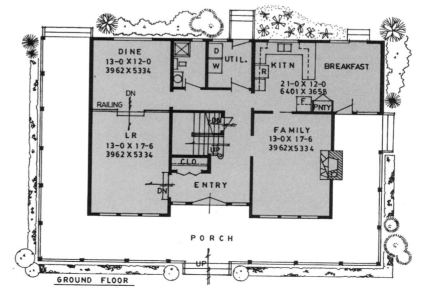

GROUND FLOOR

PRICE CODE C

CONTEMPORARY WITH A COZY FRONT PORCH

No. 20219

- This plan features:

— Four bedrooms

— Two full and one half baths

- A welcoming front porch

- A Foyer that opens to a balcony above, giving a first impression of spaciousness

- A Living Room and Dining Room that flow into each other, allowing for ease in entertaining

- An efficient, well-appointed Kitchen that is equipped with a peninsula counter that doubles as an eating bar

- A Breakfast Area that has easy access to a wood deck and a view of the fireplace in the Family Room

- A Master Suite that includes a pan ceiling, private Master Bath and walk-in closet

- Three additional bedrooms that share a full hall bath

An
EXCLUSIVE DESIGN
By Karl Kreeger

Alternate Foundation Plan

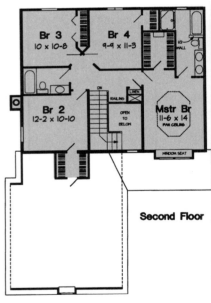

Second Floor

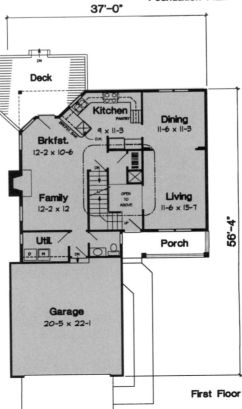

First Floor

FIRST FLOOR — 1,028 SQ. FT.
SECOND FLOOR — 1,013 SQ. FT.
BASEMENT — 1,019 SQ. FT.
GARAGE — 479 SQ. FT.

TOTAL LIVING AREA:
2,041 SQ. FT.

No materials list available

PRICE CODE C

No. 34776

GRACIOUS FAMILY HOME

■ This plan features:

— Three bedrooms

— Two full and one half bath

■ A dramatic, two-story Foyer lit from above by a second floor window

■ A decorative ceiling in the formal Dining and Living Rooms

■ A built-in bar, cozy fireplace and a half-bath in the Family Room

■ A Breakfast Nook with sliding glass doors to the backyard

■ A large Kitchen with a laundry center, built-in pantry, and double sink

■ Entry to the Kitchen from the 2-car garage

■ A decorative ceiling crowns the Master Suite, with a large walk-in closet and a private Master Bath

■ Two additional bedrooms sharing use of the full hall bath

FIRST FLOOR —1,114 SQ. FT.
SECOND FLOOR — 1,067 SQ. FT.
BASEMENT — 1,097 SQ. FT.
GARAGE — 596 SQ. FT.

TOTAL LIVING AREA:
2,181 SQ. FT.

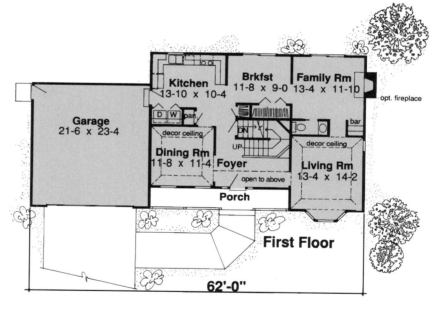

First Floor

62'-0"

No materials list available

PRICE CODE A

QUIET SUMMER HIDE-A-WAY

No. 24241

■ This plan features:

— Three bedrooms

— Two full baths

■ A covered Porch, welcoming visitors

■ A spacious Living Room with a fireplace, adding to the warmth and elegance of the room

■ A formal Dining Room with a convenient, built-in china cabinet

■ Ample cabinets, counters and a built-in pantry in the well-appointed Kitchen

■ A Master Suite with a private bath

■ Two additional bedrooms, one with a walk-in closet, that share a full hall bath

■ A typical bungalow design, allowing the heat to collect in the attic space while keeping the house cool in the summer months

MAIN AREA — 1,174 SQ. FT.

TOTAL LIVING AREA:
1,174 SQ. FT.

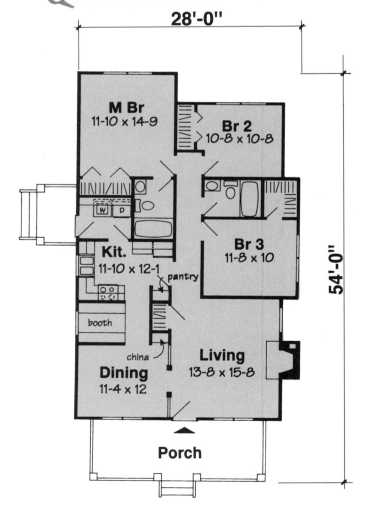

28'-0"

54'-0"

M Br
11-10 x 14-9

Br 2
10-8 x 10-8

Br 3
11-8 x 10

Kit.
11-10 x 12-1

W D

pantry

booth

china

Dining
11-4 x 12

Living
13-8 x 15-8

Porch

Main Floor

PRICE CODE C

ONE-OF-A-KIND

No. 20365

■ This plan features:

— Three bedrooms

— Two and a half baths

■ A porch sheltering the entry

■ A fireplaced Dining Room with warmth and atmosphere

■ A corner fireplace adding a focal point to the Parlor

■ An island Kitchen with a Breakfast area and walk-in pantry

FIRST FLOOR — 955 SQ. FT.
SECOND FLOOR — 864 SQ. FT.
BASEMENT — 942 SQ. FT.

**TOTAL LIVING AREA:
1,819 SQ. FT.**

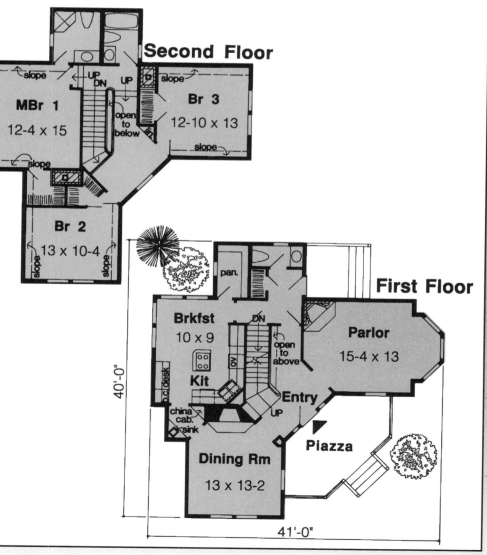

Second Floor

MBr 1
12-4 x 15

Br 3
12-10 x 13

open to below

Br 2
13 x 10-4

First Floor

Brkfst
10 x 9

Kit

Parlor
15-4 x 13

open to above

Entry

Piazza

Dining Rm
13 x 13-2

pan.

china cab.

40'-0"

41'-0"

PRICE CODE F

UPPER DECK AFFORDS ROADSIDE VIEW

No. 10768

■ This plan features:

— Five bedrooms

— Two and one half baths

■ A wetbar in the Family Room, built-in seating in the Breakfast Room, and an island Kitchen with a planning desk and room-sized pantry

■ A magnificent Master Suite including a fireplace, access to a private deck, an abundance of closet space and a tub in a bow window setting

FIRST FLOOR — 2,573 SQ. FT.
SECOND FLOOR — 2,390 SQ. FT.
BASEMENT — 1,844 SQ. FT.
CRAWL SPACE — 793 SQ. FT.
GARAGE — 1,080 SQ. FT.

**TOTAL LIVING AREA:
4,963 SQ. FT.**

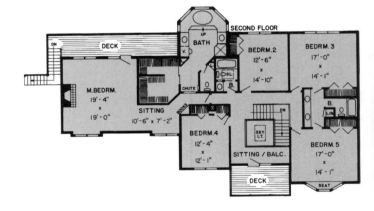

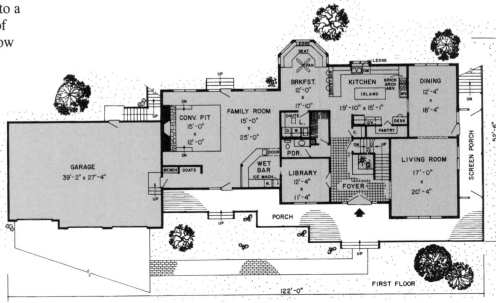

PRICE CODE D

MODERN LIVING WITH A FARMHOUSE FEEL

No. 20222

■ This plan features:

— Four bedrooms

— Two full and one half baths

■ A large Living Room equipped with a fireplace

■ A well-equipped Kitchen that serves both the informal Breakfast Area and the formal Dining Room with equal ease

■ A cooktop island that doubles for a snack bar and a built-in pantry in the efficient Kitchen

■ A large walk-in closet and private Master Bath in the Master Suite

■ Three additional bedrooms, one with a walk-in closet, that share use of a full hall bath

FIRST FLOOR — 1,488 SQ. FT.
SECOND FLOOR — 893 SQ. FT.
BASEMENT — 801 SQ. FT.
GARAGE — 677 SQ. FT.

TOTAL LIVING AREA:
2,381 SQ. FT.

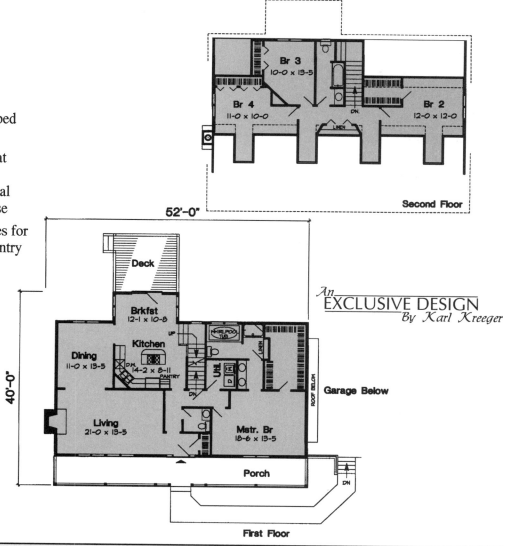

An
EXCLUSIVE DESIGN
By Karl Kreeger

Second Floor

First Floor

PRICE CODE A

BUILD SMALL, THEN ADD ON

No. 92700

- ■ This plan features:
- — Three bedrooms
- — One full bath
- ■ An economical Phase 1 project allowing for all the livability of a much larger home
- ■ A lovely columned front porch adding to curb appeal
- ■ A roomy Living Room that flows into a hexagonal Dining Area
- ■ A efficient U-shaped Kitchen
- ■ A first floor Bedroom with access to the full hall bath
- ■ Two future additional bedrooms with walk-in closets

PHASE 1 — 829 SQ. FT.
FUTURE PHASE 2 — 355 SQ. FT.
WIDTH — 37'-4"
DEPTH — 46'-4"

TOTAL LIVING AREA:
829 SQ. FT.
W/ PHASE 2:
1,184 SQ. FT.

No materials list available

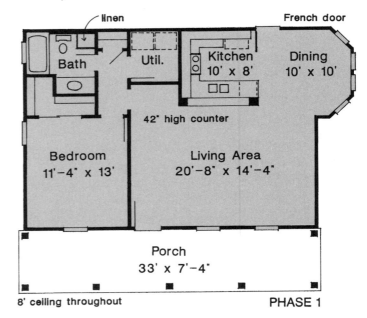

linen

French door

Bath

Util.

Kitchen
10' x 8'

Dining
10' x 10'

42" high counter

Bedroom
11'-4" x 13'

Living Area
20'-8" x 14'-4"

Porch
33' x 7'-4"

8' ceiling throughout

PHASE 1

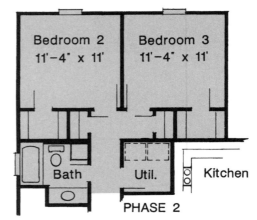

Bedroom 2
11'-4" x 11'

Bedroom 3
11'-4" x 11'

Bath

Util.

Kitchen

PHASE 2

PRICE CODE B

COZY FRONT PORCH

No. 93269

- This plan features:
- — Three bedrooms
- — Two full and one half bath
- A Living Room enhanced by a large fireplace
- A formal Dining Room that is open to the Living Room
- An efficient Kitchen with ample counter and cabinet space, double sinks and a pass-thru window
- A Breakfast Area with vaulted ceiling and a door to the sun deck
- A first floor Master Suite with a separate tub and shower stall and walk-in closet
- A first floor powder room with a hide-away laundry center
- Two additional bedrooms that share a full hall bath

FIRST FLOOR — 1,045 SQ. FT.
SECOND FLOOR — 690 SQ. FT.
BASEMENT — 465 SQ. FT.
GARAGE — 580 SQ. FT.

TOTAL LIVING AREA:
1,735 SQ. FT.

No materials list available

FIRST FLOOR

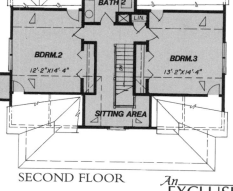

SECOND FLOOR

An
EXCLUSIVE DESIGN
By Jannis Vann & Associates, Inc.

PRICE CODE D

No. 91774

■ This plan features:

— Three bedrooms

— Two and a half baths

■ An attractive wrap-around porch leading to the Entry Hall

■ A lovely bay-windowed formal Living Room with a fireplace

■ A private, first floor Den with built-in bookshelves

■ A country Kitchen with a garden window, a Dining nook and double doors out to the rear deck

■ A classy Master Suite embracing a wide bay window, a romantic fireplace and a skylit bath

■ Two additional bedrooms with private access to a full double vanity bath

■ A Garage with a work area and a Kitchen entry

FIRST FLOOR — 1,315 SQ. FT.
SECOND FLOOR — 1,066 SQ. FT.
GARAGE — 649 SQ. FT.
WIDTH — 72'-0"
DEPTH — 34'-0"

**TOTAL LIVING AREA:
2,381 SQ. FT.**

SPACIOUS, ELEGANT VICTORIAN

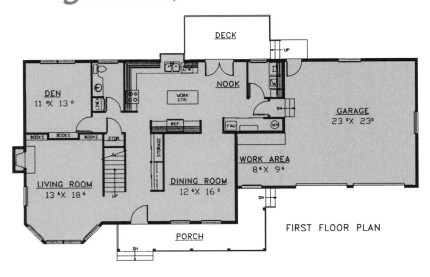

FIRST FLOOR PLAN

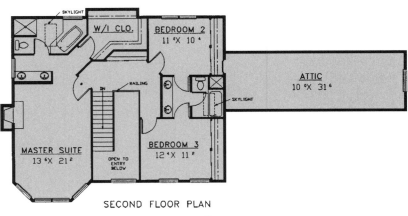

SECOND FLOOR PLAN

An
EXCLUSIVE DESIGN
By Landmark Designs, Inc.

PRICE CODE F

No. 91724

■ This plan features:

— Six bedrooms

— Four full baths

■ A multitude of porches, decks, balconies, and a Captain's Walk

■ L-shaped Kitchen with an angled range/counter and plenty of modern amenities

■ A large, windowed Exercise Room and Wicker Room with a luxurious step-up spa

■ An enormous Living Room with corner window seats, a fireplace, and double doors opening out to a curving porch

■ A Family Room with a wood-stove, two full baths and two large bedrooms complete the expansive first floor

■ A fireplaced Master Suite with corner window seats, a circular sitting room, and access to the Captain's Walk

FIRST FLOOR — 3,031 SQ. FT.
SECOND FLOOR — 1,578 SQ. FT.
OBSERVATORY — 133 SQ. FT.
WORK SHOP/SHOP — 133 SQ. FT.

**TOTAL LIVING AREA:
4,609 SQ. FT.**

SPECTACULAR VICTORIAN

WIDTH 101'-0"
DEPTH 56'-0"

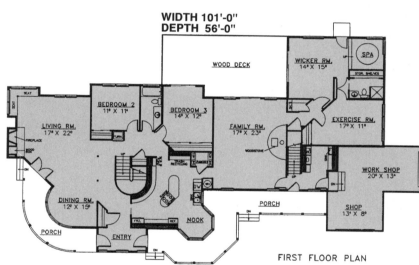

FIRST FLOOR PLAN

An **EXCLUSIVE DESIGN** *By Landmark Designs, Inc.*

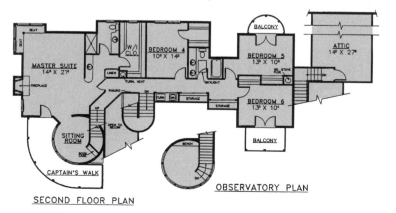

SECOND FLOOR PLAN

OBSERVATORY PLAN

PRICE CODE C

COUNTRY KITCHEN AND GREAT ROOM

No. 90419

- This plan features:
- — Three bedrooms
- — Two full baths
- Front porch, dormers, shutters and multi-paned windows
- An eat-in country Kitchen with an island counter and bay window
- A large utility room which can be entered from the Kitchen or Garage
- A Great Room with an informal Dining Nook and double doors opening to the rear deck
- A Master Suite featuring a walk-in closet and a compartmental-ized bath with a linen closet
- An optional basement, slab or crawl space foundation — please specify when ordering

FIRST FLOOR — 1,318 SQ. FT.
SECOND FLOOR — 718 SQ. FT.
BASEMENT — 1,221 SQ. FT.
GARAGE — 436 SQ. FT.

TOTAL LIVING AREA: 2,036 SQ. FT.

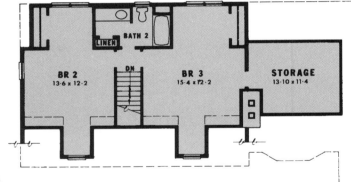

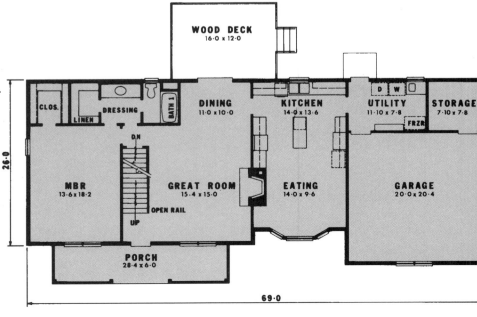

PRICE CODE C

FOCUS ON FAMILY ACTIVITIES

No. 90124

- ■ This plan features:
- — Three bedrooms
- — Two full and one half baths
- ■ A Master Bedroom with a walk-in closet and private full bath
- ■ A Family Room with an exposed beam ceiling and fireplace
- ■ An efficient Kitchen with an eating bar
- ■ A mudroom entrance combined with laundry facilities
- ■ An optional basement or crawl space foundation — please specify when ordering

FIRST FLOOR — 1,080 SQ. FT.
SECOND FLOOR — 868 SQ. FT.

TOTAL LIVING AREA:
1,948 SQ. FT.

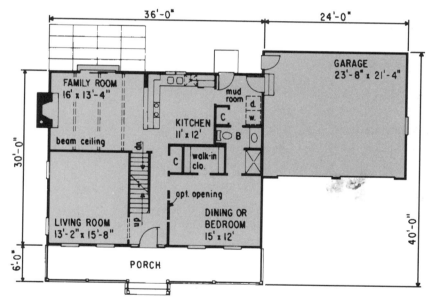

FIRST FLOOR

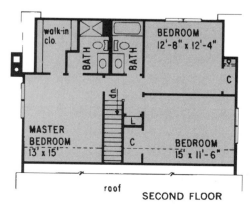

SECOND FLOOR

PRICE CODE E

WHISPERS OF VICTORIAN STYLING

No. 93333

■ This plan features:

— Four bedrooms

— Two full and one half baths

■ A formal Living Room featuring wrap-around windows and direct access to the front Porch and the cozy Den with built-in bookshelves and a window seat

■ An elegant, formal Dining Room accented by a stepped ceiling

■ An efficient Kitchen equipped with a cooktop island/eating bar, a double sink with a boxed window, a huge walk-in pantry and a Dinette with a window seat and an atrium door leading to the Deck

■ A bright, all-purpose Sun Room, with glass on four sides adjoining an expansive Deck

■ A Family Room, with a tray ceiling topping a circle head window and a massive, hearth fireplace, also accessing the Deck

■ A private Master Suite with a decorative ceiling and a luxurious Bath

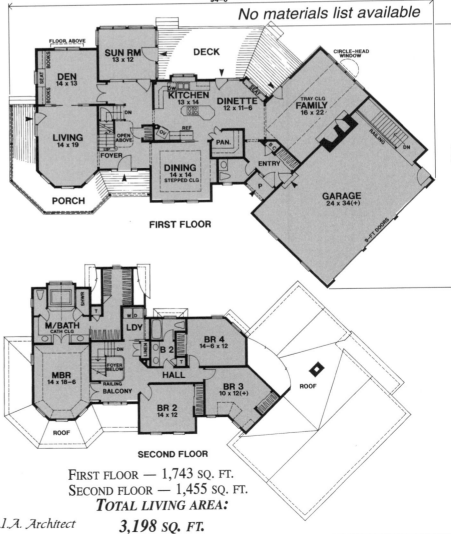

No materials list available

FIRST FLOOR

SECOND FLOOR

FIRST FLOOR — 1,743 SQ. FT.
SECOND FLOOR — 1,455 SQ. FT.
TOTAL LIVING AREA:
3,198 SQ. FT.

An EXCLUSIVE DESIGN
By Patrick Morabito, A.I.A. Architect

238

PRICE CODE B

COMPACT VICTORIAN IDEAL FOR NARROW LOT

No. 90406

- This plan features:
— Three bedrooms
— Two full baths

- A large, front Parlor with a raised hearth fireplace

- A Dining Room with a sunny bay window

- An efficient galley Kitchen serving the formal Dining Room and informal Breakfast Room

- A beautiful Master Suite with two closets, an oversized tub and double vanity, plus a private sitting room with a bayed window and vaulted ceiling

- An optional basement or crawl space foundation — please specify when ordering

FIRST FLOOR — 954 SQ. FT.
SECOND FLOOR — 783 SQ. FT.

TOTAL LIVING AREA:
1,737 SQ. FT.

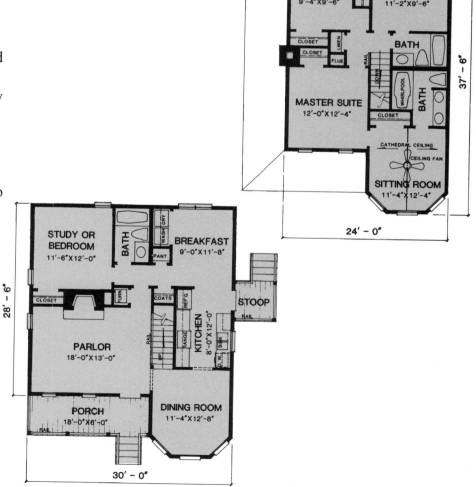

PRICE CODE C

COUNTRY LIVING

No. 90410

■ This plan features:

— Three bedrooms

— Two full and one half baths

■ An eat-in country Kitchen with an island counter and bay window

■ A spacious Great Room with a fireplace flowing easily into the Dining area

■ A first floor Master Suite including a walk-in closet and a private compartmentalized bath

■ Two additional bedrooms sharing a full bath with a double vanity

■ An optional basement or crawl space foundation — please specify when ordering

FIRST FLOOR — 1,277 SQ. FT.
SECOND FLOOR — 720 SQ. FT.

TOTAL LIVING AREA:
1,997 SQ. FT.

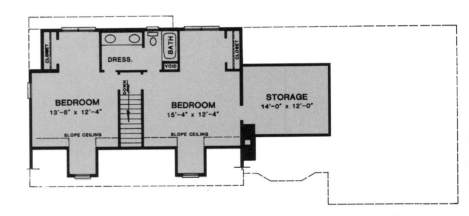

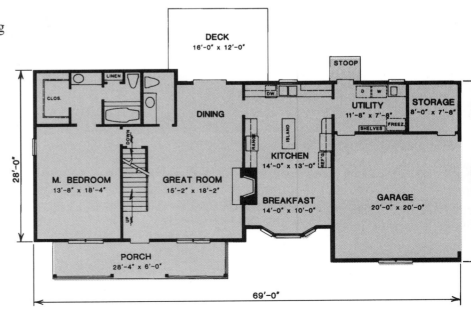

PRICE CODE C

Cape Cod Features Clapboard Siding

No. 90244

■ This plan features:

— Three bedrooms

— Two full and one half baths

■ Clapboard siding, small-paned windows and a transom-lit entrance flanked by carriage lamps

■ A Living Room, removed from the flow of traffic by its location, equipped with a large fireplace

■ A formal Dining Room adjoining the Kitchen

■ A huge country Kitchen boasts a corner fireplace with a raised hearth, a large sunny bay area, and many built-in amenities

■ A second floor Master Suite includes a dressing area and a private bath

■ Two additional bedrooms share a full hall bath

FIRST FLOOR — 1,217 SQ. FT.
SECOND FLOOR — 868 SQ. FT.

**TOTAL LIVING AREA:
2,085 SQ. FT.**

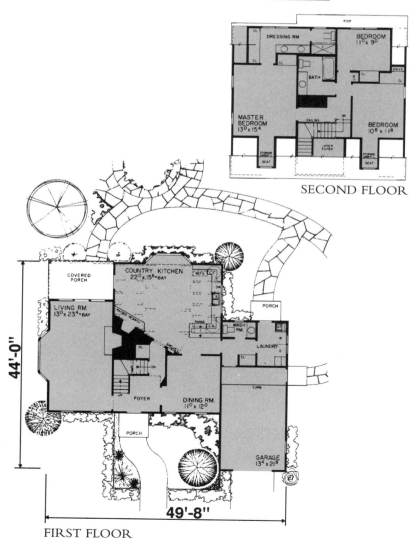

SECOND FLOOR

FIRST FLOOR

PRICE CODE E

PLENTY OF STREETSIDE CHARM

No. 92043

- This plan features:

— Four bedrooms

— Two full and one half baths

- A large wrap-around entry porch, repeating front gables, and half-round transom glass

- Formal Living Room and Dining Room flanking the Entry Hall

- A roomy informal Family Room enhanced by a cozy fireplace

- A spacious island Kitchen open to a Breakfast Room with a vaulted ceiling

- A large Master Suite with a cathedral ceiling, a luxury bath and his-n-her closets

- Three additional bedrooms, with spacious closets, which share a full hall bath

- A second floor Laundry Room

FIRST FLOOR — 1,360 SQ. FT.
SECOND FLOOR — 1,325 SQ. FT.
BASEMENT — 1,360 SQ. FT.
GARAGE — 148 SQ. FT.

TOTAL LIVING AREA:
2,685 SQ. FT.

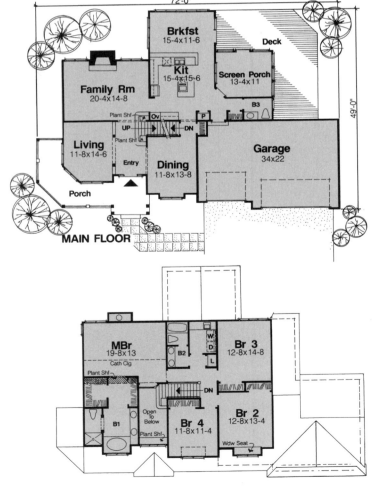

MAIN FLOOR

UPPER FLOOR

PRICE CODE E

No. 93332

ON A GRAND SCALE

FIRST FLOOR — 1,484 SQ. FT.
SECOND FLOOR — 1,223 SQ. FT.

■ This plan features:

— Three bedrooms

— Two full and one half baths

■ An inviting, front Porch wrapping around the unique octagon shape of the Parlor and Master Bedroom above

■ A formal Parlor opening into the Family Room, with a hearth fireplace, for easy entertaining

■ A stepped ceiling accenting a charming bay window in the formal Dining Room

■ A large, island Kitchen with a double sink, a built-in pantry and a peninsula counter/eating bar leading to a large Entry with access to both the Garage and Laundry Room

■ Sliding glass doors in the Dinette leading to the Sun Room, with a cathedral ceiling

■ An elegant Master Suite with a tray ceiling, a room-sized, walk-in closet, and a plush Bath, featuring a raised, corner window tub and two vanities

TOTAL LIVING AREA:
2,707 SQ. FT.

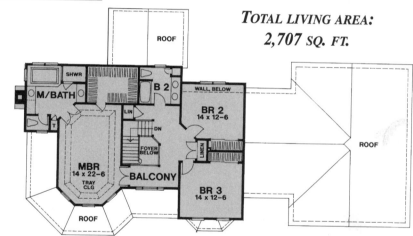

SECOND FLOOR

No materials list available

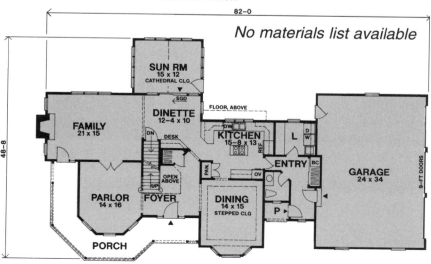

FIRST FLOOR

An
EXCLUSIVE DESIGN
By Patrick Morabito, A.I.A. Architect

PRICE CODE B

CLEVER DESIGN PACKS PLENTY OF LIVING SPACE

No. 24250

- This plan features:
— Three bedrooms
— Two full baths
- Custom, volume ceilings
- A sunken Living Room that includes a vaulted ceiling and a fireplace with oversized windows framing it
- A center island and an eating nook in the Kitchen that has more than ample counter space
- A formal Dining Room that adjoins the Kitchen, allowing for easy entertaining
- A spacious Master Suite that includes a vaulted ceiling and lavish bath
- Secondary bedrooms that have custom ceiling treatments and share a full hall bath

MAIN AREA — 1,700 SQ. FT.

TOTAL LIVING AREA: 1,700 SQ. FT.

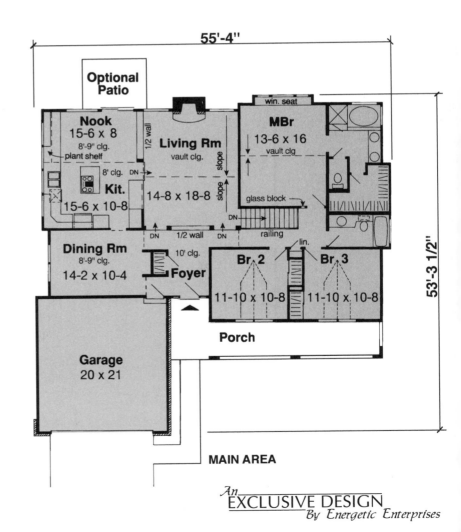

MAIN AREA

An EXCLUSIVE DESIGN
By Energetic Enterprises

PRICE CODE F

No. 93330

■ This plan features:

— Four bedrooms

— Two full and one half baths

■ A gourmet Kitchen with a cook-top island and built-in pantry and planning desk

■ A formal Living Room with a fireplace that can be seen from the Foyer

■ Pocket doors that separate the formal Dining Room from the informal Dinette area

■ A balcony overlooking the Family Room

■ An expansive Family Room with a fireplace and a built-in entertainment center

■ A luxurious Master Bath that highlights the Master Suite

■ Three additional bedrooms that share use of a compartmented full hall bath

FIRST FLOOR — 2,093 SQ. FT.
SECOND FLOOR — 1,527 SQ. FT.
BASEMENT — 2,093 SQ. FT.
GARAGE — 816 SQ. FT.

**TOTAL LIVING AREA:
3,620 SQ. FT.**

A GRAND PRESENCE

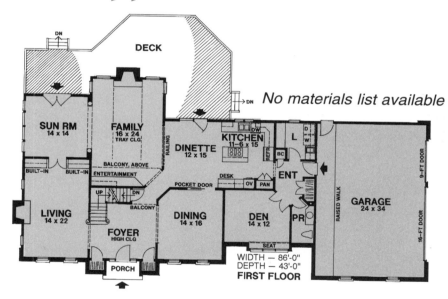

No materials list available

FIRST FLOOR

An EXCLUSIVE DESIGN
By Patrick Morabito, A.I.A. Architect

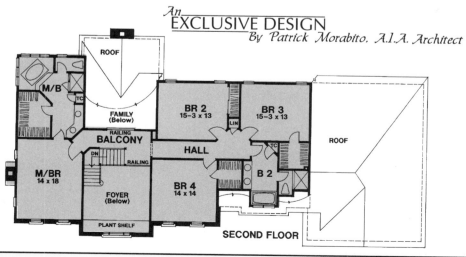

SECOND FLOOR

ENGAGING FRONT PORCH

DESIGN NO. 93245

- This plan features:
— Four bedrooms
— Three full and one half baths
- A beautiful front porch giving a warm first impression
- A stairway graces the 2-story Foyer which is flanked by the Study and Living Room
- A formal Living Room at the heart of the home, crowned by a decorative ceiling
- A spacious Master Suite, crowned by a decorative ceiling, a lavish bath, walk-in closet and direct access to the screened porch
- An efficient Kitchen with ample counter and storage space, including a peninsula counter/-eating bar and an island
- A bayed Breakfast area with access to the sun deck
- A large Family Room enhanced by a fireplace and access to the deck
- Three additional second floor bedrooms, one with a private bath
- Second floor balcony
- A Bonus Room for future needs

An
EXCLUSIVE DESIGN
By Jannis Vann & Associates, In

No materials list available

No. 93245

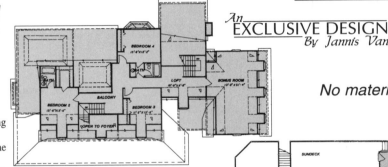

SECOND FLOOR

FIRST FLOOR — 2,708 SQ. FT.
SECOND FLOOR — 1,264 SQ. FT.
BONUS ROOM — 564 SQ. FT.
BASEMENT 2,672 SQ. FT.
GARAGE — 704 SQ. FT.

TOTAL LIVING AREA:
3,972 SQ. FT.

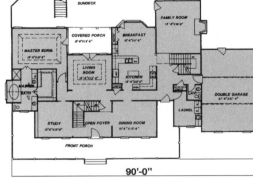

90'-0"

FIRST FLOOR

TRADITIONAL TRENDS

DESIGN NO. 92314

An
EXCLUSIVE DESIGN
By Gary Clayton

- This plan features:
— Four bedrooms
— Three full and one half baths
- A full covered porch and many dormers giving it traditional country style
- An elegant formal Living Room, and Great Room, with massive vaulted ceilings
- A huge wrap-around Deck just off of the Great Room and Sun Room
- A Master Bedroom that is very private and includes a large Master Bath and a walk-in closet
- Window seats in all three bedrooms and two bedrooms with walk-in closets

FIRST FLOOR — 2,825 SQ. FT.
SECOND FLOOR — 1,255 SQ. FT.

TOTAL LIVING AREA:
4,080 SQ. FT.

No. 92314

73'-0"

MAIN AREA

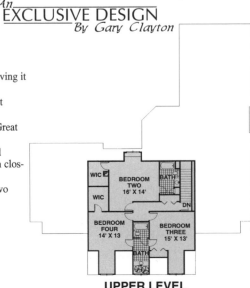

UPPER LEVEL

No materials list available

PATTERNED AFTER A FRENCH COUNTRY HOME

DESIGN NO. 92312

■ This plan features:
— Two/Three bedrooms
— Two full and one half baths

■ A formal main Entry Hall with a striking vista into the formal Dining Room

■ A formal Living Room that is sunken eight inches from the rest of the house to provide a spacious feeling around a large majestic fireplace

■ A large Utility/Laundry Room with many built-ins and a large walk-in closet just off of the garage entrance

■ A Master Suite with many unique features such as his-and-her walk-in closets, a private Sun Room and a Master Bath

■ An optional lower level with an enormous Family Room, second bedroom and a Den/third bedroom

FIRST FLOOR — 1,890 SQ. FT.
SECOND FLOOR — 1,220 SQ. FT.

**TOTAL LIVING AREA:
3,110 SQ. FT.**

LOWER LEVEL

No. 92312

An
EXCLUSIVE DESIGN
By Gary Clayton

No materials list available

PRICE CODE A

COMPACT WITH MANY SPECIAL TOUCHES

DESIGN NO. 93403

■ This plan features:
— Three bedrooms
— Two full baths

■ A vaulted ceiling in the Kitchen/Dining Room

■ An efficient U-shaped Kitchen area that has an attractive bump-out window over a double sink

■ A Family Room that has a wood-burning stove giving the room a certain coziness

■ A Master Suite with a vaulted ceiling over the bedroom, a walk-in closet and a private bath

■ Two additional bedrooms that share a full bath

MAIN FLOOR — 1,304 SQ. FT.
GARAGE — 443 SQ. FT.

TOTAL LIVING AREA:
1,304 SQ. FT.

An
EXCLUSIVE DESIGN
By Greg Marquis

No materials list available

Floor Plan
No. 93403

COUNTRY STYLE FOR A NARROW LOT

DESIGN NO. 92100

■ This plan features:
— Three bedrooms
— Two full and one half bath

■ A country style porch opens into an Entry Hall with a convenient coat closet highlighted by an angled staircase

■ A formal Dining Room flowing from the Living Room convenient to the Kitchen

■ An efficient island Kitchen equipped with ample counter and storage space

■ A sunny Nook area for informal eating

■ A large Family Room enhanced by a fireplace

■ A first floor Den with large corner windows

■ A second floor Master Bedroom with a covered balcony and lavish bath

■ Two additional bedrooms that share a full bath in the hall

FIRST FLOOR — 1,381 SQ. FT.
SECOND FLOOR — 1,125 SQ. FT.

TOTAL LIVING AREA:
2,506 SQ. FT.

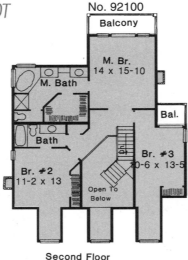

Second Floor

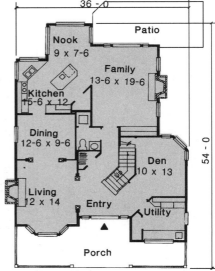

First Floor

PRICE CODE B

SIMPLICITY AND EFFICIENCY

DESIGN NO. 93404

- This plan features:
  — Three bedrooms
  — Two full and one half baths
- A well-appointed Kitchen that serves the formal Dining Room and the informal Breakfast Area with equal ease
- A wood deck, access from the Breakfast Area, that increases the living space in the warmer months
- A garage entrance, flanked by a laundry center and a half bath, which helps to keep the house cleaner
- A wood stove in the Family Room that adds to the cozy feeling
- A Master Suite with a walk-in closet and private bath
- Two additional bedrooms that share a full bath
- A Bonus room for future expansion

No materials list available

An EXCLUSIVE DESIGN
By Greg Marquis

No. 93404

Bonus 20X12

Br.#3 10X10

Br.#2 14X11

Master 14X15

2nd Floor

53'

Deck

Kitchen 13x10

Breakfast 11X10

Family 14X17

Garage 20X20

Dining 14X11

Porch

31'

1st Floor

FIRST FLOOR — 878 SQ. FT.
SECOND FLOOR — 823 SQ. FT.
BASEMENT — 878 SQ. FT.
GARAGE — 427 SQ. FT.
BONUS ROOM — 257 SQ. FT.

TOTAL LIVING AREA:
1,701 SQ. FT.

PRICE CODE D

PRICE CODE E

ROMANTIC PORCH MIRRORS BAY WINDOW

No. 20124

■ This plan features:

— Four bedrooms

— Two and one half baths

■ Bay and bump-out windows, sliders and skylights adding space to every room

■ Formal Living and Dining Rooms flanking the attractive foyer

■ An island Kitchen serving all the active areas with ease

■ A first-floor Master Suite with a garden tub and step-in shower

■ A walk-in closet in every bedroom

FIRST FLOOR — 1,798 SQ. FT.
SECOND FLOOR — 879 SQ. FT.
BASEMENT — 1,789 SQ. FT.
GARAGE — 484 SQ. FT.

TOTAL LIVING AREA:
2,677 SQ. FT.

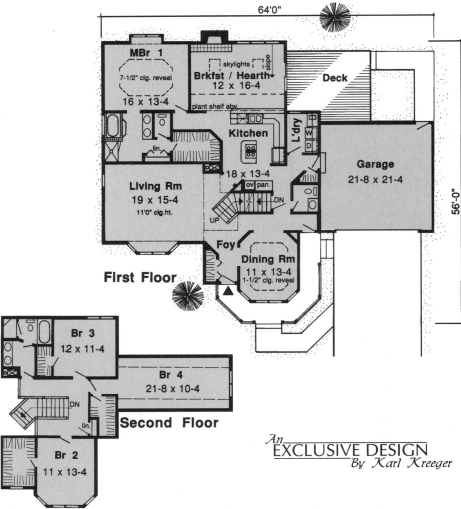

An
EXCLUSIVE DESIGN
By Karl Kreeger

Ignoring Copyright Laws Can Be A $1,000,000 Mistake

Recent changes in the US copyright laws allow for statutory penalties of up to **$100,000** per incident for copyright infringement involving any of the copyrighted plans found in this publication. The law can be confusing. So, for your own protection, take the time to understand what you can and cannot do when it comes to home plans.

—— What You Cannot Do ——

You Cannot Duplicate Home Plans

Purchasing a set of blueprints and making additional sets by reproducing the original is *illegal*. If you need multiple sets of a particular home plan, then you must purchase them.

You Cannot Copy Any Part of a Home Plan to Create Another

Creating your own plan by copying even part of a home design found in this publication is called "creating a derivative work" and is *illegal* unless you have permission to do so.

You Cannot Build a Home Without a License

You must have specific permission or license to build a home from a copyrighted design, even if the finished home has been changed from the original plan. It is *illegal* to build one of the homes found in this publication without a license.

What Garlinghouse Offers

Home Plan Blueprint Package

By purchasing a single or multiple set package of blueprints from Garlinghouse, you not only receive the physical blueprint documents necessary for construction, but you are also granted a license to build one, and only one, home. You can also make any changes to our design that you wish, as long as these changes are made directly on the blueprints purchased from Garlinghouse and no additional copies are made.

Home Plan Vellums

By purchasing vellums for one of our home plans, you receive the same construction drawings found in the blueprints, but printed on vellum paper. Vellums can be erased and are perfect for making design changes. They are also semi-transparent making them easy to duplicate. But most importantly, the purchase of home plan vellums comes with a broader license that allows you to make changes to the design (ie, create a hand drawn or CAD derivative work), to make an unlimited number of copies of the plan, and to build up to three homes from the plan.

License To Build Additional Homes

With the purchase of a blueprint package or vellums you automatically receive a license to build one home or three homes, respectively. If you want to build more homes than you are licensed to build through your purchase of a plan, then additional licenses may be purchased at reasonable costs from Garlinghouse. Inquire for more information.

You've Picked Your Dream Home!

You can already see it standing on your lot... you can see yourselves in your new home... enjoying family, entertaining guests, celebrating holidays. All that remains ahead are the details. That's where we can help. Whether you plan to build-it-yourself, be your own contractor, or hand your plans over to an outside contractor, your Garlinghouse blueprints provide the perfect beginning for putting yourself in your dream home right away.

We even make it simple for you to make professional design modifications. We can also provide a materials list for greater economy.

My grandfather, L.F. Garlinghouse, started a tradition of quality when he founded this company in 1907. For over 85 years, homeowners and builders have relied on us for accurate, complete, professional blueprints. Our plans help you get results fast... and save money, too! These pages will give you all the information you need to order. So get started now... I know you'll love your new Garlinghouse home!

Sincerely,

TYPICAL WALL SECTIONS

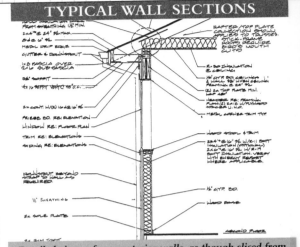

Detailed views of your exterior walls, as though sliced from top to bottom. These drawings clarify exterior wall construction insulation, flooring, and roofing details. Depending on your specific geography and climate, your home will be built with either 2x4 or 2x6 exterior walls. Most professional contractors can easily adapt plans for either requirement.

KITCHEN & BATH CABINET DETAILS

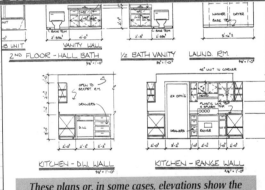

These plans or, in some cases, elevations show the specific details and placement of the cabinets in your kitchen and bathrooms as applicable. Customizing these areas is simpler beginning with these details. Kitchen and bath cabinet details are available for most plans featured in our collection.

EXTERIOR ELEVATIONS

Exact scale views of the front, rear and both sides of your home, showing exterior materials, details, and all necessary measurements.

DETAILED FLOOR PLANS

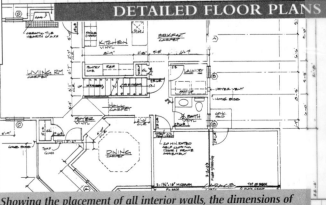

Showing the placement of all interior walls, the dimensions of rooms, doors, windows, stairways, and other details.

ake Your Dream Come True!

for home designs by respected professionals.

FIREPLACE DETAILS

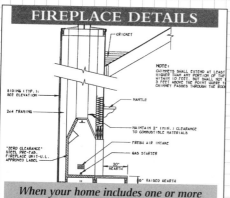

When your home includes one or more fireplaces, these detailed drawings will help your mason with their construction and appearance. It is easy to review details with professionals when you have the plans for reference.

TYPICAL CROSS SECTION

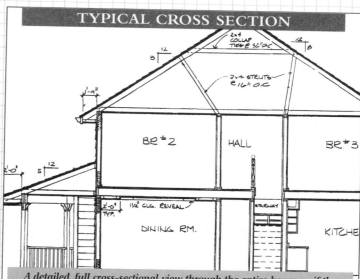

A detailed, full cross-sectional view through the entire house as if the house was cut from top to bottom. This elevation allows a contractor to better understand the interconnections of the construction components.

FOUNDATION PLAN

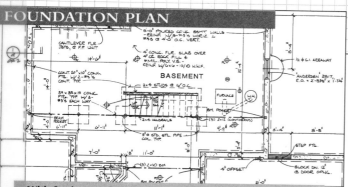

With footings and all load-bearing points applicable to your home, including all necessary notation and dimensions. The type of foundation supplied varies from home to home. Local conditions and practices will determine whether a basement, crawlspace or a slab is best for you. Your professional contractor can easily make the necessary adaption.

SCHEMATIC ELECTRICAL LAYOUTS

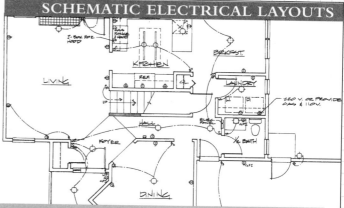

The suggested locations for all of your switches, outlets and fixtures are indicated on these drawings. They are practical as they are, but they are also a solid taking-off point for any personal adaptions.

ROOF PLAN

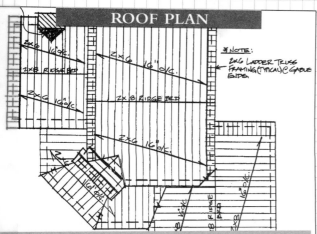

All information necessary to construct the roof for your home is included. Many blueprints contain framing plans showing all of the roof elements, so you'll know how these details look and fit together.

STAIR DETAILS

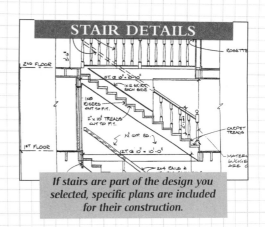

If stairs are part of the design you selected, specific plans are included for their construction.

GARLINGHOUSE OPTIONS & EXTRAS MAKE THE DREAM TRULY YOURS.

Reversed Plans Can Make Your Dream Home Just Right!

"That's our dream home... if only the garage were on the other side!"

You could have exactly the home you want by flipping it end-for-end. Check it out by holding your dream home page of this book up to a mirror. Then simply order your plans "reversed". We'll send you one full set of mirror-image plans (with the writing backwards) as a master guide for you and your builder.

The remaining sets of your order will come as shown in this book so the dimensions and specifications are easily read on the job site... but they will be specially stamped "REVERSED" so there is no construction confusion.

We can only send reversed plans with multiple-set orders. But, there is no extra charge for this service.

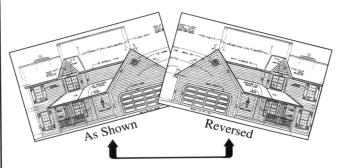

As Shown   Reversed

Modifying Your Garlinghouse Home Plan

Easy modifications to your dream home such as minor non-structural changes and simple material substitutions, can be made between you and your builder and marked directly on your blueprints. However, if you are considering making major changes to your design, we strongly recommend that you purchase our reproducible vellums and use the services of a professional designer or architect. Modifications are not available for plan numbers 90,000 and above. For additional information call us at 1-203-343-5977.

Our Reproducible Vellums Make Modifications Easier

With a vellum copy of our plans, a design professional can alter the drawings just the way you want, then you can print as many copies of the modified plans as you need. And, since you have already started with our complete detailed plans, the cost of those expensive professional services will be significantly less. Refer to the price schedule for vellum costs. Call for vellum availability for plan numbers 90,000 and above.

Reproducible vellum copies of our home plans are only sold under the terms of a license agreement that you will receive with your order. Should you not agree to the terms, then the vellums may be returned unopened for a full refund.

Yours FREE With Your Order

FREE

SPECIFICATIONS AND CONTRACT FORM

provides the perfect way for you and your builder to agree on the exact materials to use in building and finishing your home before you start construction. A must for homeowner's peace of mind.

Remember To Order Your Materials List

It'll help you save money. Available at a modest additional charge, the Materials List gives the quantity, dimensions, and specifications for the major materials needed to build your home. You will get faster, more accurate bids from your contractors and building suppliers — and avoid paying for unused materials and waste. Materials Lists are available for all home plans except as otherwise indicated, but can only be ordered with a set of home plans. Due to differences in regional requirements and homeowner or builder preferences... electrical, plumbing and heating/air conditioning equipment specifications are not designed specifically for each plan. However, detailed typical prints of residential electrical, plumbing and construction guidelines can be provided. Please see next page for additional information.

Questions?

Call our customer service number at 1-203-343-5977.